TRUSTING
Theory and Practice

Carolyn Gratton

CROSSROAD · NEW YORK

1982

The Crossroad Publishing Company
575 Lexington Avenue, New York, NY 10022

Printed in the United States of America

Library of Congress Cataloging in Publication Data

Gratton, Carolyn.
Trusting, a way for human hearts.

1. Trust in God.   2. Trust (Psychology)
I. Title.
BV4637.G68   1982   241'.4   82–9760
ISBN 0–8245–0496–8   0–8245–0548–4 pbk   AACR2

ACKNOWLEDGMENTS

I am grateful to the original six men and women who trusted me with so much of their lived experience, and to the faculty of the Psychology Department at Duquesne University where most of this research was accomplished. I want also to acknowledge a debt of gratitude to my colleagues at the Institute of Formative Spirituality, especially Father Adrian van Kaam, C.S.Sp., to whose inspiration and synthesizing genius this book owes so much. To my students at the Institute and to the Grail Metanoia group at Cornwall, my thanks for being among the first to trust this process. To Fran McLaughlin and Catherine Leahy at Grailville, to the Grail team in South Africa, and to Richard Payne and Caroline Whiting, thanks for generous help in getting the manuscript into print. I also want my family and friends in Toronto and in Pittsburgh to know of my gratitude for their providential presence in my life.

CONTENTS

CHAPTER 1

EVOKING TRUST IN THE PROCESS

A Process for Learning from Experience

Like fish swimming in a sea, we live surrounded by other beings, events, and things. A gracious or seemingly ungracious tide of life experiences ebbs and flows around us, carrying us forward, pushing us back, inviting serene acceptance, evoking angry resistance. At times we go with the flow, allowing ourselves to be carried in trusting confidence that all will be well. At other times we thrash and flail against the tide, against the given—and even the chosen—conditions that make up our lives. As the years go by, we notice changes both in ourselves and in the surrounding environment. Certain experiences that once evoked our heart's affirmation now leave it untouched, cold. We find ourselves drawn in new and unfamiliar directions. Shifts occur in our heartfelt presence to reality. A gradual change of heart has been happening. Like the universe itself, we are in a constant state of becoming. Only now are we beginning to become aware of it; only now are we beginning to understand the power that lies in life itself to form our hearts anew each day; only now are we capable of grasping something not only of where we have been, but also of where we desire to go.

This book is for people who have been "swimming" for some time, who have recognized the foundational truth that in some profound way it is the whole of oneself that gives form to and is formed by the sea of experiences in which one lives, moves, and has one's being. These swimmers have felt changes both in themselves and in the surrounding sea. They find themselves wondering what has been going on not only in the world but also in the depths of their lives. They both need and want to discover how what is happening to them affects that world; how what is changing in that world affects their lives; how all these changes form the basis for their relationship to the deepest dimensions of reality. What has been the effect of yes's and no's already uttered? Is there some way of responding to the constantly shifting flow of life experiences that will be formative rather than deformative for them?[1] For their families? For their community? Can we learn from experience itself how love or lack of love for our everyday world of space and time, people and events, affects not only that world but also the deepest motivations of our hearts?

A process that would attempt to put people in touch with themselves at this level must originate in concrete disclosure of the ongoing dialogue they have with all facets of their experience. It must uncover deformative as well as formative movements and orientations of this dialogue. It must lead toward an appraisal of what Adrian van Kaam terms the feeling, functioning, striving core of their lives,[2] as well as of the multileveled situations and complexities of the society in which they find themselves. It must help them take responsibility for their unique and communal participation as subjects of history.[3] It must, in fact, find its origin precisely in the succession of events, the lived story that in its unfolding constitutes their personal and communal life.

The chapters that follow attempt to take the reader through just such a process. Based on the assumption that life itself is basically formative,[4] and that human beings are capable of guiding themselves and being formatively guided by others, this method of learning about oneself and the structure and meaning of one's life-in-relation is one type of self-direction.[5] When the questions are answered and discussed in a group under the guidance of a well-prepared leader, they partake of the nature of direction-in-common.[6] In either case, the aim is to provide a reliable guide for self-discovery, along with well-documented correctives from the human sciences for the inevitably one-sided perceptions we tend to have of personally significant experiences.

Experience Calls for Integrative Reflection

Everyone wants to be whole, to integrate, to "get it all together" and make sense of life, that seemingly unconnected stream of events making up the human progression from birth to death. It is, however, the ongoing, ever-emerging process of our daily encounters with reality that constitutes the basic dynamic of this life. Jolting us daily out of complacency, life challenges us with the new and unfamiliar just as we have settled into a routine; it forces us to "look again"[7] at what has happened and to be present in response. Adrian van Kaam describes this basic human tendency to go beyond where we already are, to involve ourselves in ever-new aspects of reality, as the human tendency toward "differentiation."[8] He points out that if human beings are not to be torn apart by this tendency, there must be in their lives a corresponding possibility for "integration," for merging the disparate parts of their lives into a whole. He also says that the majority of our experiences are first lived prereflexively, with little or no conscious awareness of their meaning or significance. It is only when we reflect on the spontaneous differentiated flow of our experience that we become conscious of what any one particular event means and of how we have been present to it.

We live first—and reflect later. The questions that introduce the following chapters are designed to guide reflection on events that have first of all been lived. The process begins, not from theory about experience, but from experience itself. The reflective power of the reader's focused consciousness is directed to written descriptions of a segment of his or her spontaneous experience just as it flowed in life. The questions at the beginning of each chapter act as guides for reflecting on the various dimensions of that one limited situation. The content of each chapter is resource material that can be used in interpreting the intent of the question itself or as matter for further study.

What is presented here, then, is a self-directed method of learning—a method that, according to contemporary educators, is best suited for learners who happen also to be adults.[9] From the body of theory and practice known as "andragogy," it has become evident that mature, self-initiated persons can and do make use of their own experience as a rich resource for learning. It is also clear that adults are capable of taking charge of their own education, especially when that means becoming responsible for their unique life emergence in relation to other persons and the communal situations in which that emergence takes place. Most readers of this book will not be looking for another parent-teacher in their lives. I assume that they simply want some guidelines for reflecting on their own life experience or that of the group to which they belong. The resource material presented in each unit is a selective accompaniment to the main thrust of this book, which is to introduce readers to the possibilities for reflective discovery that are hidden in the richness of their everyday experience.

This richness is available to every person who lives and loves in this world. The ways of tapping into it can be modified to suit any life circumstances, even the most hectic. Like any treasure hunt, this search will at times require effortful digging, perseverance and patience, goodwill and a prayerful attitude. This process, though it encourages self-discovery, is not an ego project or an academic exercise whose outcome can be predicted or controlled. In fact, it is meant to lead not only to a deeper self-knowledge but also to a deeper appreciation of the other persons in one's life, and of that very life itself in all its complexity and ambiguity. Finally, the process, if it is allowed to do so, may lead to renewed appreciation of the mysteriously gracious presence at the heart of all reality whom we call God. It might even lead us closer to what Joseph Pieper calls "this experience of existing because of being absolutely, irrevocably willed by the Creator," or, as he earlier expresses it, "the certainty of being so surpassingly, effectively and absolutely loved"[10] that our life is solidly grounded in this as the foundational feeling of our heart.

Traditionally books about trusting God start out from scriptural assurances about the Creator's love for us. This one, on the contrary, begins from where the creations of this Creator live, from the everydayness of human life, from experiences of trust as they occur "between people." It is my conviction that a real understanding of our lived attitudes in relation to other people is the ground from which we understand what we bring to the relationship with God. This in no way equates the Otherness of the transcendent with the otherness of a fellow human being. It simply illumines the attitudes and experience patterns that belong to the human condition—to our side of the dialogue. We start here and move gradually toward the final chapters on trust and the Christian mystery, toward what may be a new and more personal understanding of some scriptural passages to be found there.

Why Explore an Experience of Trusting?

Trusting seems to be a universally recognized human attitude. It is the basis for relations between people on the social and interpersonal level; it grounds much philosophical and scientific thought and research,[11] and it underlies the human impetus for acting according to ethical norms of loving service as well as for living out the ultimate reality of relationship to the triune God. Before it is a suprarational relational attitude, trust is a foundational human attitude. Thus the lived experience of trusting another human being can be, and very often is, foundationally formative. It actually changes the heart[12] of the person who trusts and opens him or her to a new perception of reality. In fact, according to Romano Guardini, the very presence of the person who trusts creates a new environment. He or she "forms as it were a portal of entrance for the creative power of God which is directed toward the world."[13]

Nevertheless, if we look at the history of human thinking from Descartes, with his radical doubt, through the increasing privatization of religious faith; if we look at the process of secularization beginning with Feuerbach and Marx and moving through the nihilism of Nietzsche and the practical atheism of Freud,[14] we find that this fundamental human attitude, in relation both to reality as a whole and to its partial aspects, is a rare commodity indeed. At this moment in contemporary North American society there are tens of thousands of concerned social psychologists, clinicians, parents, educators, religious counselors, employers, and taxpayers talking and writing about the need for trust, extolling its virtues and crying out against its neglect, devising techniques for its encouragement and rules for its development. They want to know where trust between people originates and why people find it so difficult to be trusting of others. They wonder whether the trust experience lends itself to techniques of prediction and control and what its essential constituents might be. Though they sense some confusion in their use of the word "trust," they are nonetheless aware that the blatant inability of most North Americans to live this attitude indicates that something is seriously amiss in contemporary society.

Many, especially social psychologists engaged in laboratory research, write and speak about a kind of trusting that can be produced in planned encounters defined by them and fitting their operational paradigms. Most have never actually grappled with the elements that accompany the unpredictable flaring up of trust in the spontaneous experience of ordinary people. Yet developmental psychologists speak urgently about laying the foundation for whatever they mean by "trust" early in the infant's life; psychotherapists and all manner of counselors insist on the importance of establishing what they call a "trusting" atmosphere between themselves and their clients; social psychologists spend hours in laboratory experiments testing their version of "interpersonal trust" via the Prisoner's Dilemma Game, and applying the results of their experiments to problems of international peace and disarmament. "Trust-oriented" encounter groups for married and single people flourish as the absence of this lived experience and attitude in our culture becomes more and more evident. Our exploration does not directly address the larger questions of trust and peace between groups and nations, but it does show that trust in its interpersonal dimension is clearly a fundamental condition for a full human life. Not surprisingly, it also has something to say to those interested in the spiritual dimensions of that life.

Data from Empirical Research

Some years ago I had the opportunity to do an extensive study of the experience of trust between people.[15] Based as it was on a new paradigm, the qualitative approach and method of the study allowed me as researcher to remain faithful to the phenomenon of trust as it is lived in everyday life.[16] I was able to give primacy to the life-world of the persons who actually experienced trusting rather than to my own or others' preconceived ideas about it. The study uncovered new and exciting data about the person who trusts, about his or her situation, about the trusted other, and about how the experience itself evolves—data that are lacking in more traditional studies. It is on the data from that empirical study that the questions and resource material in this book are based.

At the beginning of the phenomenological movement in Europe, the philosopher Max Scheler described this qualitative approach to the scientific study of specifically human phenomena as follows:

> This new attitude might first of all be characterized vaguely enough from the emotional point of view as a *surrender* of self to the intuitional content of things, as a movement of profound trust in the unshakableness of all that is simply *given,* as a courageous letting-oneself-go in intuition and in the loving movement toward the world in its capacity for being intuited. This philosophy faces the world with the outstretched gesture of the open hand and the wide-eyed gaze of wonder. This is not the squinting, critical gaze that Descartes—beginning with universal doubt—casts upon things, nor the eye of Kant, from which comes a spiritual beam so alien as, in its dominating fashion, it penetrates the world of things. The man who philosophizes with the new attitude has neither the anxiety characteristic of modern calculation and the modern desire to verify things, nor the proud sovereignty of the "thinking reed" which in Descartes and Kant is the original source—the emotional a priori—of all their theories. Instead, the stream of being flows in on him and seeps down to his spiritual roots, as a self-evident benevolent element, simply that, apart from all content . . . it is not the will to dominate, to "organize," to determine unequivocally, to fix, which animates each thought, but rather a movement of sympathy, of not begrudging being, of welcoming an increase in the fullness with which, for a gaze of contemplative recognition, the content of the world is constantly disengaging itself from the invasion of human understanding, excelling as it does the limits of mere concepts.[17]

The reader will notice the connection here between a phenomenologically oriented approach to reality and the foundational trust that characterizes some of the more revolutionary paradigms in contemporary scientific thought.[18] He or she will also recognize the need for a method of self-discovery or direction that proceeds in the first place from a respectful trust in the stream of being that surrounds us and that, for the believer, points to the even deeper mystery of Divine Presence.

At numerous moments during the course of the original empirical research, conclusions emerged that pointed to a flow of divine life and love lying just beneath the surface of everyday experience. As analysis of written protocols proceeded and was followed by hours of taped interviews with the men and women who had agreed to share their personal experiences of trusting someone, I became more and more convinced that this material, even in its primitive state, could be helpful for others. When the opportunity arose, I incorporated the main themes into a three-week summer course that took much the same form as the chapters to follow. The students' response to working through the questions was extremely positive. During the year that followed, several groups of adults studied the material and worked through the exercises, again with much enthusiasm and apparent growth. Because one of the courses was taught at the Institute of Formative Spirituality at Duquesne University, the whole was enriched by the profoundly human and Christian foundational discipline of that institute and its developing science.[19] As the final chapters will attempt to demonstrate, whenever we penetrate deeply into any formative life event—an everyday experience of trusting someone, for example—we find in its very unfolding symbolic pointers for the human heart, directives for the growth and fruitfulness of the life of grace that is the foundation of our Christian existence.

Centrality of the Heart

It is the human heart, what van Kaam calls the "sensible/responsible" symbol of the whole person as actual experiental *presence* to all aspects of reality, that is central to our considerations. It is this core of affective inclinations and responsible decisions that forms the integrating center for all the influences impinging on us from our many "worlds." Besides being the seat of our basic originality,[20] of the unique moodedness coloring our fundamental ability to respond to situations, the heart is also the site of our spiritual conflicts, clashes between our own limitations and the limitations imposed on us by culture and community. Above and beyond our longing for communion with others, the heart is an expressive symbol of the restless aspiration and striving for "more" that has dynamized the life search of every human being since time began. These hidden, often unconscious but nevertheless motivating, dynamics of the heart, this inner drive of love, is always at work:

> Love cannot be idle. What is it that moves absolutely any man, even to do evil, if it is not love? Show me a love that is idle and doing nothing. Scandals, adulteries, crimes, murders, every kind of excess, are they not the work of love? Cleanse your love then. Divert into the garden the water that was running down the drain. Am I telling you not to love anything? Far from it! If you do not love anything, you will be dolts, dead men, despicable creatures. Love by all means, but take care what it is you love.[21]

The questions and resource material are not meant only to give insights into the unfolding of an experience of interpersonal trust. They are also capable of uncovering something of the ways in which we love, of the directedness of hearts toward the dimension of "treasure,"[22] and of the resistances to trusting love discoverable in both human hearts and human situations.

The reader is hereby warned that guided reflection on trusting (or, for that matter, any other significantly formative experience) will probably disclose hints of, if not answers to, some of the following questions:

Where is my heart anchored? What is it in life that I am clinging to? Why am I unwilling to let go? In what direction do I seem to be heading? Why am I so afraid to risk any kind of change? What kind of change of heart would be needed if I let go of some attachments? What are the obstacles in myself, in my culture and society, in my relational attitudes, that are preventing me from growing? Why am I so tense? What do I need to think more about? What are the major sources of directives in my life right now? Where can I find some help in guiding my mind and will in new directions? Why do I hesitate to get in touch with my own experience? How can I become more free to believe in the flow of created and uncreated energy[23] coming into my heart from God? How can I best go out of myself in love and service to others in the power of this divine energy? How do I make decisions in the face of my own limitations and the socioeconomic, political, societal, and sexual limitations that seem to hold me down? Are there ways for me to become more present, not only to the people, events, and things of my day, but also to the flow of energy that constitutes their Source? How can I begin to live in faith that this Source is gracious? How can I stop resisting its flow in my life? Just what are the ultimate desires of my heart?

Beginning the Process with a Group

The first thing that people taking part in this process of self-direction had to do was to write a description of a fairly recent situation from their own life in which they had trusted one other person.[24] They were also asked to describe their feelings just as they remembered them from that moment in time and space. Almost everyone tended to be somewhat theoretical at first, and needed help in becoming concrete about this task. Further on in this section you will find the sample write-ups from which much of the data for the analysis of trusting in this book has been drawn. However, before proceeding, you may be interested in joining this group of three men and two women who contributed write-ups to the project. You can do this simply by writing a description of your own experience of trusting someone. Doing this will give you a feeling of at-homeness in the project, even if you later decide not to answer all thirteen guide questions.

In any case, these are the instructions that were given to the original "group"—Alan, Bill, Carl, Donna, and Ellen (pseudonyms, of course, to protect their privacy):

> Describe a situation in which you experienced that you did trust someone.
> Describe your feelings just as they were when you experienced this situation.

Describe means that you are to tell about this situation of trusting as you would tell a story, with full details of time, place, and so forth, in a conversational way, without trying to analyze or interpret anything. The request for a description of a *situation* points to interest in concrete exterior details of how, when, and where the trusting behavior took place. The reference to *in which you experienced* may prompt recall of what distinguished this from other experiences with differing time, space, and behavioral characteristics. The words *that you did trust* mean only that whatever you choose to call trusting behavior was and is acceptable to the author/researcher, who does not have any particular "correct" type of situation in mind. *Someone* means that the situation must be an interpersonal one. It is preferable to be in face-to-face contact with the other person at least part of the time. In the second instruction, the emphasis on *your feelings*—refers to concrete inner details of your personal experience that could not be known by an observer of the trust encounter. In writing this part of the description, the original group tried to remember how their bodies felt before and during the trust experience, what emotions they experienced, which of their senses were active, what they noticed about how they were perceiving the world around them, what thoughts went through their heads during the experience. The following examples demonstrate how five very average North Americans responded to these instructions.[25]

1. Alan, a young minister, chose to describe his experience of trusting another person who was both a friend and a fellow member of Alan's seminary faculty:

> One morning last summer while I was studying in my room, a friend, a fellow minister, stopped in to see me. He gave me a copy of some notes he had recently transcribed from a tape dealing with the ongoing spiritual training of candidates for the ministry. We had both previously listened to the tapes and were most impressed with the presentation of the material and some of the key ideas that were expressed in the course of the discussion. As I took the notes from him, we began to continue to discuss our common work of training as we often did. In a rather negative way, as I had frequently done that summer, I began to muse over the poor state of the training situation in our seminary. I mentioned that I really didn't see how the situation could improve because of certain closed attitudes and the frequent defensive approach to constructive change that seemed to be in evidence on the part of the majority of the present faculty.
>
> I noticed that he listened to me attentively, even somewhat sympathetically. He let me have my say. When I finished, he began to remark that I was giving him the impression that I was the only one who was concerned and interested in training. He could see from the way my point of view was developing that I was really being the closed one, even the defensive one. If I allowed myself to continue developing this frame of mind, he continued,

I would have very little of positive value to contribute in the training of young men for the ministry. As much as the initial impact of these remarks hurt me, it was during these moments that I experienced that I trusted him both implicitly and explicitly. I experienced at that moment that these words were difficult for him to say but that he cared enough and was concerned enough about me to risk saying them. I really appreciated this and it created within me a deep feeling of trust toward him.

My feelings as they emerged out of this situation of trust can be described first of all as *hurt feelings* when I was confronted with my own negative and critical mode of behavior. It is not pleasant to be told by a friend that you are being negative or critical. At the same time I also realized that what was being said was true and that this truth was being offered to me in a caring and concerned kind of way. This encouraged me to own my negativity as coming from me. In owning my negativity, I began to feel good all over and this lessened the feelings of hurt. This good feeling began to replace or permeate the hurt feelings. This good feeling of being able to accept my negativity as part of me also included a warm feeling that reminded me that I had received someone's genuine care and concern and this evoked a feeling of gratitude.

2. Bill described a job interview in which he felt trusting toward his prospective employer:

I called him on the phone and told him I thought I would be a good man for him to hire. He listened quietly and asked if I would write him my thoughts and meet him later that week in Cincinnati at the Statesman's Club after we both thought about it. I drove in from my home town. I walked into the club and was told Mr. M. was expecting me. He was sitting in a stuffed high-backed chair, with a friend of his in a large elegant room. I walked up to him and he stood, put out his hand, smiled, looked me in the eye, and shook my hand very sincerely, saying, "Bill, that was an interesting letter you wrote and I've thought a lot about it. Have you?" He introduced me to his friend, Mr. S., and said he had asked him to sit with us since many times in conversations like this, a third party can attest to what was actually said or promised or assumed, and later on perhaps clarify what might have been misunderstood. We talked and asked questions of each other and generally discussed what responsibilities were involved and what the opportunities were in the job. He was very serious, sincere, thoughtful of me and my position. He looked and acted like a lean, well-dressed, clean, 50-to-55-year-old successful man. His manner was quiet and self-assured—not nervous, but still a hardness in knowing what he expected or wanted.

The feeling I had first could be described as nervous, anxious to do and say the right thing, hoping I could get the job and glad I had a chance at it. As soon as we started talking, he put me at ease since he knew I was "on the spot" and guarded in what I might say. The feeling soon turned into full confidence after he explained very carefully why Mr. S. was present. I relaxed and we talked about me, my wanting the job, moving to Cincinnati, and also my personal happiness, my girl. I felt that he felt genuinely concerned about if I would be happy and satisfied if I joined him. I knew he had the problem of hiring someone, but he didn't have to, and I couldn't feel confident that it would be me. But the more we visited that day, the more I felt that this guy was really interested in me, and I had great respect for him.

He made me feel more confident as time went on. I felt I wanted to be like him, and I felt I could really trust this guy—say anything to him—look forward to see him again and again—sort of a hero—"this son of a bitch is the greatest" feeling. Even if I didn't get the job, I felt privileged to be so close to it and have all the questions answered. No doubts that I had done the best I could to get it. I felt relieved when the visit was over—open, confident, trusting him and what he said.

3. Carl described an unexpected experience of trusting his attorney, who had helped him carry out a litigation against a rival business firm:

The company of which I was president was trying to settle a dispute with a customer. I had made numerous attempts to settle the dispute by mail or telephone, and we were finally consulting our attorney in preparation for settlement through arbitration or court action. My attorney, ten years my senior and rich in human and legal experience, was exerting continuing and strong pressure on me to think critically and act effectively. I was annoyed and sick of the matter and pressing him to take over and seek a solution through litigation. In the course of the morning's discussion I found that I was able to trust him and be led into a more critical and practical appraisal of the status of the case as well as the events which shaped it.

My initial feelings were frustration and annoyance. In Mr. B's examination I was asked to explain and justify the actions of subordinates as well as my own. In each detail I was painfully aware of the vulnerability of our position but clung to a one-sided idealistic defense. Areas of compromise and practical considerations of viable solutions were repugnant. A relative righteousness blinded me to all courses of practical action. Things that awaited my doing at the office passed through my mind.

But in spite of my torment I was unable to see Mr. B. as a tormentor, and at some point I began to appreciate his patience and kindness in the resolute way he was stalking me. His offensive became less threatening and my attitude changed so that I was able to join him in an investigation that was critical of myself and my associates. I dropped my bias, or some of it, and trusted him with a more factual presentation. I was able to search my memory and the history for the arguments which our customer would likely present. In doing so, he trusted me and prepared to put the case to arbitration.

4. Twenty-four-year-old Donna described how her husband-to-be proposed to her and evoked a deep experience of trust that remained with her after four years of marriage:

It was a beautiful warm spring night when John and I walked up a large hill and viewed the valley below. John (my husband) and I were not married then. We sat down on the hilltop and talked at length, first about our views on life. We had known each other only three months but our friendship had grown so much in such a short time.

Towards the end of our conversation, he asked me to marry him (even surprising himself, I think!). We spoke at length again and then I accepted. This moment was not just merely an emotional one, but many reasonable thoughts went through my mind and my feeling of complete trust in another person was the most prominent feeling at this time. To be able to commit my whole life to someone I had known for such a short time, I had to feel this trust.

The trust I felt was overpowering and still is. At that time, I felt a sense of security with John, and his honesty with me about many things helped my sense of trust in him to grow even stronger. It was not an unrealistic trust, for I knew that I could never know John completely and this is when my trust in God came in. In between the time he asked me to marry him and the time I answered him, I remember saying a silent prayer in hopes that my sense of trust and love was very *real.* I felt happy and somewhat content and also pleased that he expressed his trust in me. This mutual trust seemed even more meaningful. The feeling that someone actually loved me for just being me and I loved him for the same—with this mutual trust, this gave me a definite feeling for once in my life of peace, inner peace with myself and the world.

5. Ellen, a Catholic nurse, wrote about what was for her a crucial life decision involving trust in God:

I am a Catholic nurse working full time in a hospice for patients with terminal cancer. Several years ago I moved to a large city and was living alone, with few friends except for the people at the hospice. I loved my work and found it an enriching and fulfilling way to spend my time and energy every day. I think this kind of work expresses a sort of religious commitment in my life, even though my friends and family never did see why I was not content to work at a less demanding type of nursing back home. Anyway, in the midst of this very satisfying time of my life, I had an affair with a married man.

Naturally I felt very guilty because I felt this was a betrayal of my whole Catholic upbringing and life dedication. Then one day I discovered that I was pregnant. This was a terrible shock and I really panicked. I spent long hours tensely discussing it with my friend who, in view of the total inappropriateness of the situation from all points of view, suggested I have an abortion. I must admit I was tempted in view of the terrible mess having a baby would make of my career, my reputation, my relations with everyone at the hospice, my family, friends, and all the people back home who had trusted me to manage on my own, to say nothing of how separated I felt from God. I spent a lot of time going over in my mind the various people I might trust to help me, the various places I might go. But each person or situation lacked something.

Then one day while trying to pray about it, I was reading the Bible, feeling at the end of my rope, and another way of seeing the whole thing just opened up for me. I was able to trust God at the very moment of my whole life when I had felt most weak and helpless and unrespectable, the least deserving of his love and care. I found myself feeling loved and cared for and certain that all would be well. I felt encouraged to go ahead and have the baby and go on from there. I felt relieved, relaxed, open for a new adventure and hopeful about the future in spite of the difficulties I knew this decision would inevitably bring.[26]

Each of these five descriptions of an experience of trust contains four recognizable structural elements. First, there is the *subject* of the experience: Alan, Bill, Carl, Donna, or Ellen—the person who chose to write about this event as one in which he or she trusted someone. Then there is the *other* (Alan's friend, Bill's Mr. M., Carl's Mr. B., Donna's fiancé, John, and for Ellen, the Holy) who was trusted, who symbolized the larger community of other persons in the life of the one who trusts. A third element is the *situation* in which both find themselves at this particular moment in time. Actually, the situation has several layers, one of which we would characterize as the space and time that makes up the immediately relevant environment of each: Alan's task of seminary training, Bill's and Carl's world of business, Donna's vocation of marriage, and Ellen's work as a nurse. Finally there is the overarching larger meaning situation embodied in the culture and society that constitutes the *outer world* of each separate person and situation. For some, this world is permeated by ultimate divine meaning; for others, it is not. The chapters of this book follow the structural elements of these five typical human experiences. We begin by examining the outer situations in which trust happens. Then we look at the inner life of the persons who did the trusting. Then we see how they describe the other whom they trusted, and the kind of pattern their experience follows when they find themselves living through an event they call "trusting." However, there is still another way of understanding the overall purpose and plan of this book.

Plan of This Book

The main aim is to demonstrate how reflection on the human experience of trusting another person can light up our understanding of the trust that God asks of us. Thus the first three parts, while dealing primarily with data from empirical research and theoretical material from the human sciences, point in the direction of that final aim. Part One, "Data from a Study of Trust," lets life speak in order to analyze and interpret the essential conditions involved in the trust experience. Situations like those described by the five people—a chat with a friend, a job interview, a meeting of lawyer and client, a marriage proposal, and a significant decision, are clearly defined, down-to-earth encounters. They embody definite limitations of time, of physical circumstance, of social custom and expectation, of human possibility and probability. The trusting that took place within these five people little resembles the vague and unworlded phenomena that come to mind when we hear global commands to "become a trusting person" (what does that really mean?), to "be more trusting of others" (of what others, and why should I?), or even to "trust in God" (how can I do that?).

Part One also contains a number of quotations from taped interviews in which the five freely described their families' attitudes toward others, the roles their families and, later, society laid on them as they grew up, and their thoughts about their own identity, the meaning of their relationships, their present understanding of themselves and their society, and their future hopes and dreams. They were willing to share these concrete details, not only in terms of external meanings, but also in terms of inner meanings—meanings perceptible in depth only to themselves. Part One introduces the essential dimensions of any interpersonal experience and lays out guidelines for further reflection.

Part Two, "A Mixture of Theory and Practice," brings together the thinking of phenomenologists like Merleau-Ponty, Heidegger, Husserl, and Schutz, with further insights from the Science of Foundational Human Formation.[27] The reader is encouraged in this section to listen to the possibilities for growth and change, for shifting one's life stance, that inhere in human freedom as it dialogues with horizons that beckon beyond stages already reached.

Then, in Part Three, "Three Approaches to the Human Condition," we turn to psychoanalysts, sociologists, and developmental psychologists for a view of what prevents the unfolding of these possibilities. Obstacles that obstruct change or newness, that block the flow of growth energy, are examined in the realistic context of the lives of these quite ordinary people who continue to share their personal stories with us.

Part Four, "Trust and the Christian Mystery," takes its departure from the parallel pointed out by theoretical physicists between the world views of modern scientists and those of Eastern mystics.[28] The scientists indicate that although both a mechanistic and an organic view of the universe are valid and useful, the latter seems to be more fundamental, pointing as it does to a reality concealed beneath the appearances of everyday life.[29] The scientists' knowledge is derived from empirical analysis of experience; that of the mystic from meditative insights into it. Readers who have absorbed the exhaustive and finely tuned conclusions of the empirical study of the human experience of trusting another person from

Part One, and have followed its unfolding in relation to various theoretical and scientific insights in Part Two, and in relation to psychological and sociological views of it in Part Three, will at this point have a new awareness regarding the phenomenon of trusting. They will recognize at least some of the essential conditions belonging to the lived event of trusting another person; they will be aware of the actuation pattern of interpersonal trust and of the risks and consequences for human action and decision involved in its unfolding.

Especially if they have worked through their own description of a personal experience of trusting someone, they will be ready to look again at that foundational human experience, this time from a more meditative stance. They will look at the parallel between the empirically founded conditions for and obstacles to interpersonal trust on the one hand, and the presence of trusting as a foundational theme in Christian scriptural revelation on the other. It is for the sake of leading the reader to this "meditative readiness" that the questions at the beginning of each chapter and the corresponding resource material have been written.

A practical suggestion may be in order before you get caught up in reflecting on the questions. Most people who took this course found it helpful to keep their descriptions of a situation where they trusted someone in a loose-leaf notebook. They wrote each question at the top of a separate page and then, before reading the resource material, jotted down their own spontaneous response. As they read the resource material, many more thoughts emerged and were added to the original response. Sometimes reading what others had experienced evoked more than a page of reflection, and they were happy to be able to slip in an extra loose-leaf sheet for additional notes. A loose-leaf notebook was also helpful for those discussing their reflections with others in a small group or with the group leader because they could remove certain sections of their response from the notebook. There was general agreement that having a personal experience of trusting to work with made the questions and resource material come alive in a way that simply reading about the experience of other people does not provide.

A new appreciation of the meditative or dwelling mode of reflective presence was also engendered by the process. Preoccupied people seldom take time to look twice (much less thirteen times!) at the same personal experience. The process of dwelling with a moment of interpersonal trust, of exploring it again and again from different angles and approaches, of going deeply into one particular segment of experience, is contrary to our usual mode of perceiving and dealing with the ebb and flow of life's events. Because of its repetitive nature, you will at times be tempted to drop the process, to turn to something new and different, to resist its gradualness as maddeningly slow. Yet those who stayed with it were amazed to discover the "gold beneath their feet," the till now unrealized richness that inheres in any one lived event. Usually it was only after working through at least Part Two that they saw clearly how this process of dwelling on the same event can be a means of digging deep into the gold mine that is concealed in our everyday experience.

Part One

———— · ————

DATA FROM
A STUDY OF
TRUST

CHAPTER 2

A PRELIMINARY LOOK
AT TRUST SITUATIONS

Examine your description in terms of
1. what you said about your lived space and the flow of time;
2. what you found to be the immediate context of your focus of attention;
3. what seems to have been the quality of lived life between the two persons;
4. which directives from the culture seem to have been relevant at the time;
5. how you saw the possibility of an ultimate horizon;
6. what the personal significance of the situation was for you.

Space/Time as Basis of Situation

Any significant event or situation, any interpersonal encounter with reality experienced by a human being, is bound to be multidimensional. At the very least it involves four of the six elements listed above as they come together or gestalt in a moment of space and time. When we look, for example, at the descriptions of trusting situations from Chapter 1, we notice that each writer mentions concrete details about the physical space in which his or her meeting with the other took place. Although none makes much comment on the change experienced in his or her lived space during the interaction, everyone except Bill has something specific to say about time as it flowed by during the trust experience.

Alan remarks that "during those moments I experienced that I trusted him." Carl also discovers himself trusting "in the course of the morning's discussion." Donna speaks of the time span "in between the time he asked me to marry him and the time I answered him," and Ellen "spent a lot of time" worrying before "the very moment of her whole life" when, feeling most weak and undeserving, she was able to see everything "another way." For each one, the quality of lived time prior to trusting is somehow different from that during and after. It is Donna who points to the fact that the standard in interpersonal trust is lived, rather than clock, time. She says "we had known each other only three months but our friendship had grown so much in such a short time." Each writer seems to have been aware of the exact moment when interpersonal trust emerged—which is hardly surprising since they were specifically asked to pinpoint such a moment.

Nevertheless it is interesting to note how awareness of any one experience is always part of a larger ongoing life stream. As Alan put it in a taped interview,[1] "I had been kind of reflecting on the negative feelings previously and the idea had been kind of with me. Therefore I was a little more open to the criticism when it came." Carl commented, "I had gone to work that day with the idea of getting a lot of backed-up work done, and this was one of the things that was supposed to be taken care of that morning so that I could play tennis in the afternoon." Ellen's consciousness of time is reflected in her reference to her work as a fruitful way of "spending time and energy," to the "very satisfying time of her life" when this incident took place, and to her overall feeling about the consequences of this decision for her future time.

When you examine your description of trusting someone, try to look at it structurally and discover how it was a small segment in the much larger ongoing flow of your life. Probably you will find that it drew a good deal of its meaning for you from this more extended ground. In fact, its inner meaning for you is a product not only of your immediate space/time situation such as a period of self-questioning, being in the job market, needing to accomplish a multitude of backed-up chores, but also of your future life intentions (like hoping to settle into a career, seeing marriage as a calling, expressing commitment in dedicated service to others). The meaning of any experience is never found simply in itself, but always also originates in both the past and future "temporality" of its subject and his or her lived worlds of activity. No mere observer can ever totally decipher these layers of inner meaning for us. In fact, even for the one who experiences, the life-world in its spontaneous emerging is overlaid almost immediately by all kinds of conceptions, expectations, idealizations, and thought habits absorbed from the given cultural time and space in which the experiencer was born and presently finds him or herself.

The Immediate Context of Trusting

In somewhat the same way as the overall directedness of one's lifetime gives unique meaning to individual events that occur, so, too, one's involvement in immediate situations (such as conversations with other people, personally embarrassing predicaments, challenges to one's self-image) takes on a certain coloration from the here-and-now concrete circumstance in which it occurs. For example, Bill and Carl, both businessmen, chose to describe an interpersonal encounter in which the trusted other person was a business acquaintance rather than an intimate friend. They were involved with the other person primarily because of their respective business roles. Bill, a salesman, was seeking a job, and Carl, as president of a company, was consulting his lawyer. Alan, a teacher, described a situation bearing on his work (also his business, in one sense), but he looked on the other person as an intimate friend. Although involved with him in his role as seminary professor, Alan also wanted to share his more personal thoughts and concerns with his friend. Both Ellen and Donna chose to focus on situations that were primarily personal, and their involvement with the other was considerable since it touched on the total possibility of commitment in their lives.

In turning to your own description, you will begin to notice how, on a continuum from the personal to the impersonal, the different relevancies of a situation (a business meeting compared to a marriage proposal, for example) tend to almost automatically open up or close off certain meanings. In daily life, every experience is potentially a bearer of directives for living. Yet by their very nature, some situations are more likely than others to offer directives for truly interpersonal behavior toward others. Moreover, the other person tends to be seen differently according to the place or situation in which she or he is encountered. Thus Bill, with his attention focused on customs of the world of business (such as a handshake, the presence of a third party, exchanges peculiar to a business deal), tends to see his prospective employer primarily as a means toward the end that interests him. In contrast, Donna, concentrated as she is on the world of persons in love (with its romance, shared values, possibility of permanent commitment), tends to see the other no longer merely as a means, but as a to-be-cherished end in himself. The culture, too, imposes rather clearly defined modes of behavior on certain types of situations. In twentieth-century North America, the common ways proper to getting a job or settling a legal matter differ widely from those proper to encountering a member of one's immediate family or even a prospective member. It is differences like these that you will discover when you examine your written description for the nature of its immediate context.

In the process of discovering the immediate context of an interpersonal situation of trusting, not only will you see how hidden directives are present and at work in various types of situations, implicitly governing the kind and intensity of the trust that is allowed to unfold. You will also grow in your understanding of how the very presence of these smaller segments of life within a larger culture or society (which inevitably suggests customary ways of dealing with certain socioeconomically, ethnically, and sexually oppressed classes) influences the possibility that trust will grow or deteriorate between yourself and another human being. In this process you may perhaps become more alert to how any immediate work, family, recreative, social, or professional situation helps or hinders the efforts of the persons involved in it to trust one another.

Quality of the Lived Life "Between"

Since all the writers were asked to describe a concrete situation in which they experienced a face-to-face moment of trust with another person, dyadic space and time was built into all the write-ups. Yet, as mentioned in the previous section, the quality, intensity, and possibility of lived intimacy differed widely in each situation. This possibility has something to do with the quality of interpersonal perception that is present. For instance, it is apparent from their remarks that both Alan (whose description includes the words "during these moments . . . I experienced that I trusted *him*") and Donna (who wrote of her "feeling" of complete trust in another person) perceived and respected the other as a person, as a relatively free subject of his own actions. At the beginning of his description, Carl is obviously perceiving the other in a semiobjectivistic manner, as a more or less expert dumping ground for his legal problems.

However, Carl does allow the lawyer to remain subject, the "other," in the sense of respecting him as an independent source of meaning, even though the other continues to make him uncomfortable because of the "resolute way he was stalking me." Nor does Carl finally see this person merely in the confines of his role as lawyer. In a taped interview he protested, "Well, this man is more my friend and that predominates in our relationship. See, you really don't get close to an employer or to an attorney. There have to be more complete persons involved than that." Alan also appreciated the "otherness" of his friend, as can be seen from the following remark: "I was glad he could remain free to criticize me, even though it meant he could also let me down." Both he and Donna seemed able to rely on some deeper level of mutuality existing beneath the apparent differences between themselves and the other person.

On the other hand, Bill's description, when analyzed structurally, revealed that he never stopped regarding the other primarily as a useful means or object for himself.[2] Mr. M. is not allowed to unfold for Bill as

other-opposed-to-me. Rather, Bill keeps trying to min
ences between them, to keep the other under some kir.
stead of allowing him to be free.[3] In spite of the fact that
Mr. M. "felt genuinely concerned" about whether or n
happy, Bill's immersion in the technicalities of the busines
its behavioral norms and expectations only serves to empnasize the narrow focus of his own ambitious project. Unable to respond on other
levels, he succeeds in canceling out almost entirely the personal "subjectness" of his prospective employer. What has happened? Very simply
Bill's behavior illustrates the fact that, aside from any depersonalizing
outer circumstances that may be operative, all of us, by our manner of
perceiving others, have the inner capacity to prevent the other person
from emerging as free subject even in what appears to be an interpersonal
encounter. Each one of us can, by the quality of our presence to a situation, turn the other involved into object for us.

Why, since he began with an obviously objectivistic frame of mind
toward his attorney, did Carl not fall into the same trap? After all, Carl's
was also a business situation, and he admits that in the beginning he was
only interested in getting his lawyer to function efficiently for him. However, during our interviews it became apparent that he and Mr. B. had
a prior personal relationship of long standing. Carl had grown to appreciate this man, not only as an expert lawyer, but also as a "very wise, human
individual, for whom I had a lot of respect. I enjoyed him. He was humor-
ous and had deep insights. He was a good storyteller, with a very rich
experience in political and human situations." (Compare this with Bill's
situation: he had never before met Mr. M., and they had had only one
brief phone conversation.) Moreover, although Carl's trust situation does
center around his concern for his business, its horizon is wider than that:
it includes the more intimate level of Carl's questions about why his
attorney refused to stop short at a mere lawyer-client relationship. According to Carl, it was Mr. B's decision to widen the horizon of their
mutual concerns that "made possible a much closer feeling between us."

In Alan's case, the other is in an even more intimate relationship with
him. Besides sharing a common work of "spiritual training of candidates
for the ministry," the two are also friends whose long-standing sharing
of central concerns ranges from their work to their personal lives. As Alan
expressed it in an interview, "We agreed about a lot of things, not only
about our attitudes toward our work, but also about the choice [of the
ministry] we had made for our lives." This situational mixture of the
social and the personal levels lends an air of authentic intimacy to Alan's
experience of trusting. When asked to comment on the intimacy of the
interpersonal trust situation she described, Donna replied that she saw

marriage proposal as more intimate than either of these other situations because it would lead to a permanent relationship, and demanded from both partners a sharing of outlook and values far in excess of what a business relationship or a friendship could ask.

There was general agreement among the five that interpersonal trust does not depend on an intense sharing of central concerns similar to that found between lovers or prospective marriage partners. However, in dyadic situations, there seems to be a cutoff point where the term *intimate* ceases to be operative, and where, as a consequence, the level of trust can no longer be termed *interpersonal*. In this light, it may be interesting to reflect on how you usually tend to structure dyadic interactions. Do they often become interpersonal situations? In the one you are examining, does the other person tend to emerge as subject or object? How would you rate the general quality of shared central concerns between the two of you?

Directives from the Wider Situation

The interviews raised one or two questions about how the five saw themselves as products of twentieth-century North American culture, and about how this affected their ability to trust other persons in that culture. Alan explained his difficulty in trusting another person in terms of society's discouragement of that attitude, partly because of "the technical functional orientation most of us get from the beginning of our education. We're told that we have to compete, to be self-sufficient, to watch out for ourselves first, that we should never risk our precious selves unless we have some guarantee of getting something in exchange. But with its violence and threat of war, our culture never lets us forget the weakness and insecurity of the human condition. The paradox makes trust hard." Carl found trusting hard, not only because of the increasing homogenization and predictableness of modern man ("you don't even have to talk to the person or have an interpersonal relationship . . . you can look him up in a book"), but also because of his (our) constant need to unmask others, to see through them lest we get taken in by them or harmed in some way. He characterized our culture as one in which "dupes are losers, so you should never trust anybody." He claimed that it is very difficult for the individual to affirm an attitude that is not acceptable in the culture. But he also wondered whether the "great explosion in modern communications had made trust more possible on a worldwide scale."

It was just this wide-ranging possibility, with its accompanying anonymous masses, automation, and lack of community, that makes trust less possible for someone like Donna, who sees herself situated in the century of the "Third Wave" and "Future Shock."[4] She blames some of her confessedly "paranoid" attitudes on frightening "big city" incidents (being mugged, having her apartment broken into, witnessing several thruway crashes) that she experienced recently. She compared urban tension today with the comparative peacefulness of her small-town childhood. Ellen, who chose urban life precisely because of the stimulation it offered, spoke about the "technological takeover" in her own profession of nursing. She had personal questions about the predominance of the objectivistic "medical model," particularly as it relates to the care of dying patients, and about the life-and-death nature of the ethical decisions being forced on hospital personnel by the overwhelming progress in medical techniques. Both she and Donna also commented on issues raised by the women's movement and the increasing array of life choices open to women after marriage.

Clearly none of the five was deluded into thinking that he or she was an island. All acknowledged being formed in some way by society. As members of adult, white, middle-class culture in northeastern urban America, each one admitted to being radically affected by a common socioeconomic meaning system. One might say that their remarks reflect problems experienced by all members of a society that has failed to move from prepersonal collectivity to community, and from post-Renaissance individuality to true personality. Regardless of personal choice, they share to some extent in the egoism of a consumer society; in its social and racial divisions; in the injustice brought about by the maldistribution of the earth's resources; in the ever-present threat of nuclear annihilation and all the other evils, as well as possibilities, inherent in our present culture. The conflict apparent in their descriptions also reflects the tension that accompanies twentieth-century preoccupation with absolutizing pragmatism and efficiency, with living the myth of "objective consciousness" in both cooperative and competitive situations. In such a society the institutions that shape experience, perceptions, actions, and values are constructed from—and, in turn, construct—their makers primarily on the basis of functionally oriented assumptions about reality. These assumptions become the focus of a high degree of confidence for everyone. The majority of twentieth-century people scarcely question the mythical proofs and guarantees provided by the tools and techniques that occupy such a central place in their consciousness. They are embedded in the "natural attitude"[5] espoused by their contemporaries. The subjects of this study were no exception.

Nevertheless they took a critical stance toward the attitudes that naturally prevail in contemporary Western society. By reflecting on their own experience, they recognized the contradiction that exists between a functional society where relationships tend to have only the external character of "purposes to be reached," and a personal community where relationships are disinterested, witnessing to a solidarity of interests. They were able to see how a consciousness engendered by orientations that favor socioeconomic and functional reliability resting on merely rational and technical proofs is less able to adopt a trusting attitude than one that arises from the more personal ground of living out the implications of human coexistence.[6] This foundational fact of coexistence that underlies the entire human situation is described by Martin Plattel and others as the "sphere of intersubjectivity."[7] In the quotation that follows, Plattel illustrates how this sphere is to be preferred as the horizon of a trust that, forgoing technical proofs, is truly human:

> If through an integrally human attitude I know the other as trustworthy in intersubjectivity, I would destroy the certainty of his trustworthiness by wanting to verify and test it. Moreover, in this sphere of intersubjectivity I feel no need to verify the point, for I am quite certain of it. In this way, I evaluate all signs of trustworthiness, not as proofs for an as yet undemonstrated certainty but as manifestations of an existing trustworthiness.
>
> If, on the other hand, I want to discover and base the other's trustworthiness merely upon proofs, I will never be able to go beyond a certainty that in his socio-economic relations and his functional contacts he will probably show himself trustworthy. On "rational" grounds I am certain of his reliability. This socio-economic and functional reliability, moreover, is not yet the certainty of being able to trust someone in all the conditions of life. Yet it is of this trust that I possess a supra-rational certainty in my mutual intersubjective surrender to my fellow man. This form of certainty on the spiritual level is not verifiable; besides I have no desire at all to seek any verification.[8]

This distinction between socioeconomic or functional reliability grounded in a technical-functional society, and trustworthiness that rests on the sphere of intersubjectivity, is being dwelt on in some detail here because it is important for understanding the wider situatedness and universal solidarity proper to the kind of trust we are interested in exploring. As you reexamine your description in terms of the directives from the culture, you may begin to recognize the roots of the cultural and societal assumptions that in all probability underlie your own attitudes. You will begin to see who these two persons are in terms of their situatedness in the larger culture and society. You will perhaps also see more clearly how the larger society affects the ability of individuals to trust one another.

Reference to an Ultimate Horizon

In all descriptions except Ellen's there is little or no explicit reference to a transcendent horizon, a faith view of the universe. So far in this chapter, we have been able to trace certain influences stemming from the subject's lived inner time consciousness, from his or her immediate contextual situation, from the relatedness that exists "between" the two persons, and from the larger societal dimensions of this particular trust situation. We have acknowledged the difference in experienced environment provided by a personal community as compared to that provided by a merely functional society. But we have not yet asked specifically how the persons involved in the trust situation perceive the flow of time and events in their global or cosmic proportions. Was any type of belief system operative, was there any faith view of the world and its history underlying the more mediated "worlds" of the persons involved in this study? If so, how did this faith view actually coform what happened in their experience?

Of the five, Donna and Ellen were most consciously tuned in to the "beyond in the midst of everyday life." They held a view of salvation history derived from their situatedness within the Catholic faith community. Ellen was the more articulate about her sense of an encompassing faith horizon against which the events that made up her life were unfolding. In the interviews she referred more than once to her upbringing in the beliefs of the Catholic "tribe." Both she and Donna were aware of belonging to a particular tradition that centered its view of history on the Mystery of Creation, Incarnation, and Redemption. For Ellen especially, the flow of daily time was highlighted by its relation to the cosmic time of salvation. Like Donna, she had at least heard about the eschaton as fulfillment of earthly time and had some idea of directing the concrete details of her earthly life toward that destiny. Thus her life situation was potentially open to a meaning horizon that was ultimate, that could relate her experience in a formative way to what van Kaam calls the "Eternal Trinitarian Formation Event."[9]

Alan and Donna were both intent on relating to this same ultimate horizon in terms of life commitment. Donna mentioned more than once that she saw marriage as a way to live her life in relation to God, who has called her to that life. Alan had also experienced a calling or vocation from the Divine Being and confided that he rested his trust in his friend ultimately on the fact that his friend had responded to a similar call.

For Bill and Carl, questions about an ultimate faith horizon were more or less irrelevant. The world of meaning in which Bill lived out his days was very much confined to the visible scene of his and others' practical interactions. He admitted that there might be "more," but at this point in his life journey he did not experience the need or desire to seek after it. Carl, on the other hand, was a total skeptic when it came to notions of an ultimate horizon. For him, "there is nothing beyond death, no transcendent meaning to any of life's events and religious people are simply seeking comfort in a cold, cold, world." Carl did, however, recognize and respect the dimension of "more" in others when he felt it to be an authentic expression of a lived faith. Even if you haven't directly mentioned this dimension in your written description, can you trace its possibility or actuality in your own situation? Does it play a part in giving meaning to the events of your life? To the people you encounter and the situations in which you find yourself? How was an ultimate horizon present or absent in your trust experience?

Personal Significance of the Situation

From an external point of view, it would seem that Donna's marriage, Ellen's decision, and Bill's new job were most personally crucial. Yet Alan's experience of the challenge presented to his taken-for-granted pattern of not appearing negative is far more of a personal crisis than Bill's situation. As Alan expressed this point, "It is not pleasant to be told by a friend that you are being negative or critical." Each person had something at stake. For Alan, it was his image; for Bill, it was a job; Carl and Ellen both, in different ways, saw their reputations at stake, with the additional trial for Ellen of uncertainty regarding her relationship with God; while Donna experienced her whole life project hanging in the balance during those few moments on the hill. However, it is not just the seriousness of the situation but also what the person brings to it in terms of biography that makes it significant for the one who trusts.

For example, even though the situation is significant for Bill, he merely "hopes" he will get the job, and if he doesn't, he will still be "glad he had a chance at it." Carl finds himself in an unusual and somewhat distasteful business situation, having to "settle a dispute with a customer" that involves his immediate responsibility as president of the company. He explained in the interviews that it was a situation where he "really found out something about trust in and through its problematic nature." The possibility of learning to trust by actually having a problem with trusting came as a revelation to him. Alan also commented that exploring his own moment of confronting another rather than resorting to fusion or "blind trust" made it possible for him to see trust in a new way, "as arising from a moment of conflict rather than agreement." He compared this problematic or personally significant aspect to "the image of a baby at the breast who may not trust the mother till the breast is withdrawn. In the moment of having to wait rather than in the moment of being satiated, that's maybe where trusting really appears."

It was in his sense of the problematic—of appearing negative and critical despite his "nice guy" reputation—that Alan came to a new realization about himself. He found that if he went on being "closed and defensive," taking it for granted that he was "the only one who was really interested in and concerned about training," then "I would have very little of positive value to contribute to the training of young men in the ministry." In other words, his whole life project was as tied to this particular moment in time as were Donna's or Bill's to their particular experiences.

Bill does not seem to have experienced any significant break in his usual life-style. Carl, however, undergoes an "examination" that breaks into his taken-for-granted view of himself and his world. On tape, Alan mentions being jolted out of long held but never really examined ideas about himself, "when even my self-trust became questionable, to say nothing of the breakup of my taken-for-granted expectation of my friend's behavior." Donna says that her fiancé also experienced a break in the usual pattern when he proposed, "even surprising himself, I think." The external significance of the marriage proposal clearly called for "talking at length about our views on life"; its internal significance was that her life project was momentarily thrown into question. Later she pointed out that the experience of love and trust had broken up the usual pattern of her life-style in a positive way, giving her a "definite feeling for once in my life of peace."

Ellen had the most to say about the personal biography she brought to the situation. She spoke of having belonged in high school to a youth group whose members were highly idealistic, of having been inspired to live a "life of service and loyalty and devotion." She spoke of seeing nursing as a way of "dedicating her life to God" and of how others knew about her view and therefore counted on her to "be a good sort of person who witnessed certain values to them." The event she described had the effect of shattering the "sort of integrity I saw in my life," jolting her into the realization that she had let everyone down, "including God and myself."

As this preliminary look at the situated aspect of trusting events makes clear, no experience can be explored in depth without some understanding of the concrete life situation of the person who experiences it. There can be no event unless there is a situated human being who lives it. The next chapter focuses on the situated persons who did the trusting. The emphasis there will be on neither their social nature, their relatedness to others, nor their response to the pulsations of our history and culture.

Rather, we will attempt to understand the inner self, the interior dynamism, the heart of the person who trusts, and how the orientation of that heart influences how the person experiences reality. We have already focused on the centrality of this heart with its life-giving capacity, or its ability to integrate all other aspects of a person's life. As a symbol of the whole concrete human being, the vulnerable heart is the locus of inner orientation, of felt movement toward, against, away from, or simply being with reality as it touches us—as it pushes, pulls, moves us or stops us in our tracks.

Emphasizing this mysterious inner motivating core of the person in no way contradicts the fact that he or she is also always social in nature. But many people in our culture are so embedded in the natural attitudes of the social self that they live in almost total unawareness of the more foundational form of their life symbolized by the heart.[10] They do not always perceive clearly the overall direction of their lives. They cannot even imagine themselves as different, as changed, transformed, as more fully their truest selves. Perception of self and reality tends to be clouded by illusions and by disordered memories, imaginings, and anticipations. These are times when we need to concentrate on what van Kaam calls the "intra" dimension, recognizing as we do so that true formation can never be confined to one's isolated interiority. It is always communal in nature, a dialogue between oneself and one's community or intersubjective situation, a fruitful interaction that points to and affirms the basic truth of the "inter" or social nature of human life.[11]

CHAPTER 3

THE PERSONS WHO TRUSTED

Describe the subject of this event (yourself) in terms of what you know about

1. yourself as context of your own experience;
2. your own embodied presence as basic mood, feeling about the world in general, yourself as temporal synthesis (the influence on you, for example, of your family's style and the feeling tone it engendered);
3. yourself as movement of transcendence, or going beyond in terms of your limited freedom, foundational life form, your desires and wants for the immediate future in terms of life goals, career intentions, ideals, and projects;
4. your growing awareness of where the "treasure" of your heart might really lie;
5. the self you are at this moment in terms of how you currently appear to others and feel about yourself particularly in regard to your societal role, your class, ethnic roots, socioeconomic reality, and current lifestyle.

Self as Context of Experience

One of the most illuminating insights human beings can arrive at about themselves is the recognition of the effect their emerging, ever-changing presence has on the reality they experience. You are never merely the passive victim of any situation. Always by virtue of the inner openness or closedness, the lived yes or no that you are in relation to that situation, you are at the same time the active co-producer of it. Realization of this fact can be a direct path to discovering the central mode of presence that underlies and integrates your entire life. In the taped interviews with Ellen, for example, the external event of being faced with a crucial decision became the catalyst for a whole series of disclosures about how she herself had coproduced her relation to others and to God. Without this insight, these disclosures might have remained completely outside her consciousness for the whole of her life.

She confided that before that event, her rather complacent self-image had been one of "good Catholic nurse from a respectable family living an exemplary life of service to others." Her encounters with people, things, and events had been subtly contextualized by her rather superficial sense of herself as "exemplary presence." Her various responsibilities had taken on the self-satisfied aura of living up to this lawful mode of existence in which one kept the rules and expected others to acknowledge it. The sudden shift from self-satisfaction to self-disgust, from respectability to feeling very "unrespectable," from unquestioned trust in herself as "good Catholic nurse" to serious doubt about the validity of her entire service-oriented existence, moved her to new and hitherto unexpected insights about her real self.

From the midst of her tangle of self-doubt, she recognized how illusory and one-dimensional her former consciousness of herself as presence to reality had been. Gradually she realized that there was more to her than merely being a respectable nurse, just as there was more to life than what she had so far experienced within the narrow confines of how others had convinced her it was. She recognized for the first time in her life that she owed her existence and that of her unborn child, not to other people, but to their Creator. She came to a new awareness of herself as a presence to reality "ultimately destined for God." This new way of perceiving herself and her life gave a new context and thus new meaning to the everyday responsibilities of nursing. No longer was she content with a merely well-functioning, efficient response to the day's demands. The experience of "feeling loved and certain that all would be well" had deepened the presence she could be to all that might happen, had made less narrow the limited openness she was, had transformed the quality of her yes to her situated world. The next crucial decision that came her way would be experienced differently because the experiencer herself, as living combination of consciousness, affect, and willing, would be changed and be differently present to it.

At every stage of our lives we tend to live one central mode of presence that founds the current forms our life is taking at that period. We are not usually aware of this powerful integrating focus until an event happens that upsets our usual stance, jolting us out of a superficial orientation and focusing our attention on what life really means to us, on where the love of our hearts is truly anchored. At such moments, the others in our life may seem to have undergone some mysterious change, until we realize that it is we ourselves who have changed. We are experiencing the others differently because of our own transformed heart. Thus human beings are free throughout their lives to be constantly liberated in the direction of new depths in their perception of persons, events, and things. As new directives emerge in our lives, we notice gradual shifts in our experience. From time to time, it is good to become conscious of the quality of the embodied contextualization you impose on your own experience. The following section should help with this task.

Embodied Aliveness and Temporality[1]

In the write-up of her experience of trusting someone, Donna spoke of a difference she recognized between the predominantly vital level of "feeling complete trust" and the more rational level of "reasonable thoughts about it." For her, trusting someone could never have been merely a reflective, rational enterprise. From her own account, it had to be primarily a sensed or felt reality—"an emotional feeling, a vibration you have with a person, a feeling of warmth," which on this occasion provided the atmosphere for reflection on the shared project of marriage with her husband-to-be. The trust experience unfolded for her contextualized by her own embodied, lived perception of another person she could "have this feeling about." The whole of Donna's subjectivity, rational and irrational, head, heart, and willing, was bound up in her perception of the other. Yet this perception was not simply a given natural confidence about which she had nothing to say.

Granted, in the interviews with me, Donna described herself as naturally trusting toward others. She acknowledged that she and John were both naturally confident people and that her "feeling of complete trust toward another person predominated in this situation." However, prior to this experience of trusting one particular man, she had also experienced a lived pattern of lack of trust ("never trusting an awful lot, getting hurt . . . I had had experience of men, including my father, walking out on me at different times in my life—I'm a little paranoid even about John"). These incidents from the past had obviously tempered her basic feeling of at-homeness with others, especially male others, and challenged the trusting yes she was naturally inclined to give in life encounters. Alan also, although he described himself in interviews as "basically optimistic and generally very trusting about life and about myself," as "more affectively than cognitively present," and as "very at home with others," admitted that prior to this situation he had been feeling quite negative toward the others with whom he worked. He, too, had had to decide in favor of a fundamental yes in the face of what could easily have called forth a more immediate no.

Thus for both Alan and Donna, trust seemed to move gradually from the level of ideas into the realm of contact with their more fundamental disposition or "feeling" way of being in the world. This partly given, partly chosen fundamental mood comprises our basic reaction to the preformed[2] aspects of our inherited organic and vital embodiment. Each human being finds him or herself permanently involved from birth in a biologically rooted structure of brain and nervous system, glands, blood pressure, and other factors of genetic makeup inherited from generations of ancestors. This inheritance partly determines each person's general emotional predisposition or temperament. For example, with his energetic body and exuberant health, Bill emerges as an almost overly optimistic character, the ideal salesman with lots of confidence in himself ("I would be a good man for him to hire") whose pragmatic orientation and functional approach guide his behavior and directly influence his style of openness to his world.

Carl, on the other hand, told me enough about his father to make me recognize the source of his self-confessed "negative moods and pessimistic outlook." Phrases from his description come to mind ("I was annoyed and sick of the matter," "frustration and annoyance were my initial feelings"). I remember during the interviews how his inability to get in touch with his deeper feelings ("undoubtedly there was a whole life there of personal feelings, but I don't remember them") was combined with a natural skepticism and need to be in control that suggested a basic tendency toward alienation or mistrust. Here was a person in whom the reasonable or ideological seemed to predominate over the vital, who seemed to have opted very early in life for a stance of isolation from, rather than participation in, the dimension of vital feeling. His rather cool, distanced style contrasted sharply with Ellen's passionate empathic sensibility and the mixture of optimistic idealism and efficient at-home-ness in the world that she brought to her trust experience.

Each person's innate propensity toward or away from trusting behavior is traceable also to the stream of community or "tribal" life into which each newborn child is inserted. The particular time in history, the nation and class and parents, the entire extended family into which we are born, plays a part in forming our basic attitude toward reality. Before we have any choice in the matter, we are inserted into a uniquely limited perception—our family's inevitably one-sided world view, for which in later life we must either assume responsibility or have the courage to reject. Part of Ellen's guilt feelings undoubtedly owed their origin to just such an embodied perception of "how things ought to be." Rules of conduct and precepts absorbed from the community that surrounded her as a child were still very much alive in the conscience and heart of Ellen, the sensible/responsible adult.

To the temporally oriented question of whether their families had given them the idea that other people are trustable, Alan, Donna, Bill, and Carl all claimed that the implicit image of the human person handed on by their families had tended to be positive. Even strangers were basically to be trusted. Alan mentioned that his "capacity to trust came from my mother rather than from my father, who was a very cautious businessman who feared being cheated." Carl said that as children, "we were made aware of trust in a kind of blind-faith way," and Donna characterized her family's trustfulness as "being sort of gullible" with those outside, while within the family itself "trust was not focal." Bill related that he and his brothers and sisters were brought up to view others as more or less "the competition." Ellen was frank in her remembrance that "no one really felt comfortable trusting other people in our family. I guess we were more or less expected to make it through life on our own."

When asked about the patterns of interpersonal encounter common in their respective families, all described relations as being distant rather than close. Alan commented that even though some of his family's relations could be called intimate, he seldom revealed himself to anybody, "even my parents." From remarks of the others, it became evident that the past encounter history of these men and women was not marked by frequently experienced intimacy with others. They seemed to take it for granted that a more or less generalized distrust of intimacy predominates in most contemporary American homes. Since all tended to describe the trust situation as being one of experienced intimacy, this intimacy itself, along with trusting, would seem to have been a significant exception to their usual mode. How do you see this point as, in the light of the material from this section, you question the embodied aliveness that you are and attempt to probe the fundamental option or choice you have made with regard to that aliveness?

Temporality and Dynamic Tending

There is in the phenomenological approach to the person a presupposition that the meaning of human subjectivity rests on its deeper relationship with temporality—on the person's actually "being" time, a temporal synthesis of past, present, and future.[3] Persons who trust, then, are not simply a sum of vital aliveness acquired from the past. They are also, and perhaps even more importantly, a dynamic tending toward the future, a transcending movement beyond the "already" of the now toward the "not yet" of the future. It is precisely within this dialogue, not only with the situated limitations of their own characteristic impulses, needs, and strivings, but also with evocative and resisting situations of their present and future world, that restless human hearts find the freedom to reach beyond where they already are and to grow. Thus it was important to question these restless human hearts about where their lives were going just before the trust experience. What were they wanting out of life at that moment? What was moving them, either by attraction or repulsion, to behave as they did? Had they been aware of any personal life projects on which they were embarked when the trust situation happened?

On a somewhat different level the question might have been phrased: Do you see yourself as embodied spirit, as situated yet free spiritual presence, as natural or even supernatural desire for "more"? Or it could have been simply: How do you understand the structure of your human life as being different from that of an animal? In other words, we need to draw attention to the reality that is human freedom, to the limited yet real capacity that is ours to break out of the vital-functional closed circuit of determined reactions to stimuli, and to structure our lives in terms of aspirations and inspirations for the future. This kind of questioning can help people appreciate the actual, if limited, free choice they possess in relation to their own growth and development. It helps them also to become aware of what van Kaam calls the foundational life form,[4] the embodied soul or life principle that is the dynamic inspirer, director, and mover of the ongoing formation of human life.[5] Source also of the human capacity to "image" God, this divinely created soul is the foundation of our aspiration for abundant life in the Mystery of the Word made Flesh.[6]

Most people in our society are not aware of the Divine Mystery that is the invisible surrounding atmosphere of our lives and of the whole of human history. Thus it was not surprising that in the interviews the five were not very articulate about the transcendent dynamic that attracts and moves their daily decisions and actions. The question of the quality of the love "that moves absolutely any man, even to do evil,"[7] was certainly not in the forefront of anyone's consciousness. Ellen perhaps came closest to articulating something of her life striving for ultimate happiness and fulfillment when she spoke of the desire for God that had motivated her choice of career and life-style. Donna was also moved by wanting, in "the commitment of her whole life to someone," to "do something beautiful for God."[8] She envisioned her marriage in that light: "When I met John we started getting back into the religious thing together and we wanted to grow closer to God." However, no one made much of a connection between these somewhat obscure desires for ultimate peace and joy and the immediate life plans each one was involved in at the time of the trust encounter. In the interviews Alan did make a connection between his personal questioning of his "nice guy" self project, the ideals of seminary formation that were popular at the time, and his own concrete life commitment to teaching there. Carl saw his will to master a difficult litigation and Bill saw his desire for the job as directly related to the larger project of succeeding in the world of business that represents fulfillment for many people in our society.

Typically, however, there was a curious lack of conscious integration of life goals, specific career intentions, and concrete projects for the future among these men and women. Absent for the most part was a conscious grasp of the underlying thread of their lives; their active projects of transcending themselves to enter the world of everyday immediacy failed to derive meaning from the deeper dimension. Even those who mentioned a vague sense of the wider, more spiritual meaning of what they did, the decisions they made, and the activities they engaged in were hard put to understand how the dynamic energy for those very projects could reside in a source that infinitely transcended both themselves and the "worlds" of their projects.[9] They were all in a state of ignorance[10] about the transcendent nature of their own dynamic tending. They had little or no realization of a spiritual push within them toward not only the visible but also the invisible world of value, light, and life. They were for the most part ignorant of the true nature of the hope that can energize and inspire every person who lives and moves and has being in this world. They could not rest their confidence on a life-giving dynamism of whose existence in themselves they were so little aware.

The Awakening Heart[11]

Even those unfamiliar with Scripture know that in both the Old and New Testaments the "heart" symbolizes our human selves, in particular the part of us capable of existing in direct relationship to God. It is the heart that yearns for God, that is open to examination by God, that is the source of thoughts, sins, good and bad inclinations: envy and malice, joy, peace, and pity. The heart is an expression of the whole person. Never merely thought or feeling or sentimental emotion, the heart represents what lies deepest within us, the innermost core of our being, the root of our existence. In our everyday life the heart hardly reaches the surface of our consciousness. We prefer to stay put in our outward senses, in our impressions and feelings, in all that outwardly attracts and repels us. And should we opt to live at a deeper level of our personal being, we usually end up in abstraction: we reflect, combine, compare, and draw logical conclusions. But all the time our heart will be asleep.

Our main enterprise, according to André Louf, is over the course of a lifetime to find our way back to our heart and gradually wake it up. For it is in the heart that God meets us, and it is from there that we in our turn can encounter other people. It is from the heart that mind and will, senses, memory, imagination, and anticipation give their qualified yes or no to what the world presents. It is the overall orienting love or lack of love in this heart that defines our impulsive, ambitious, or aspiring relationships to ourselves, other people, our life situation, and the world of nature and culture. It is this integrating center of our being that is the object of the New Testament process of transformation known as *metanoia*.[12] Capable of being touched primarily by preconcious means, this relatively permanent symbol of the primary affective self is also the pointer to each person's deepest originality, to what is called the *real me*. Unless I become aware of this unique self, it is difficult indeed to identify what is not me, what is contrary to the heart's proper direction. Ignorance of the unique desire of my loving, striving, destined heart can make for either a false and illusory life pattern or for a willful and rationalistic stance, as the restless heart searches blindly for it knows not what.

Nourished by the earthy vitality of embodied aliveness and kept in the right direction by the insights of a healthy spirit, the responsible/sensible heart grows, expands, and is modified by all the encounters of life. As we mature, we should become increasingly aware of the continuity of our unique life direction—a continuity of faith, hope, and love for the goodness of that self created for delight in God and for functioning in the world. Buoyed up by trust in the overall meaning of that life direction in relation to the Mysterious Love that permeates and carries it, ideally the dispositions of human hearts should center more and more firmly around the heart's treasure, whatever that may be. Life, however, is hardly ever ideal on this earth. The human heart often experiences crises,[13] when, in the midst of change, trials and difficulties, failure, meaninglessness, and loss of direction come to the fore, the undergirding Mystery seems to disappear, and, with it, confidence within the heart.

One of the greatest challenges that faces us at such times is to continue to trust in the basic goodness that upholds the unique directedness of our own life; to keep on believing in the worth of the continuing heartfelt interest that is the axis of our life story and in the personal providential care of God for that life, for that embodied heart. It is only on recognition of the basic trustworthiness of one's own life and of life itself that lasting commitments motivated by love can be made. It is only in the reality of God's faithfulness in the midst of ambiguity that these commitments can be kept. The task of becoming aware of where the treasure of your heart really lies might be greatly helped if you adopted the reflective steps indicated by contemporary explorers of autobiographies of faith.[14] The first step consists in remembering events that gave you new life in the past, the second in grounding these past events in your present situation, and the third in locating the event in a horizon of hope for the future. Here we find ourselves again immersed in issues of temporality, in the ways in which our heart is motivated not only by what happened in the past or seems to be happening in the present, but also by how the future appears to us. If only chaos and evil can be perceived, the response of our heart will be a movement away from or against such a reality. If, however, the future invites with a promise of value and fulfillment of our hopes, we instinctively trust and move toward what is promised. Potency becomes act as human mind and will appraise and move into action. Ask yourself: What do my most recent acts have to say about the values to which my heart is inclined to respond? How you spend the greater part of your time and energy can tell you quite a lot about where the treasure of your heart lies.

Present Identity or Social Self

Not much has been said up to this point about the present or current self of the five. In talking with them, I did attempt to find out how each one regarded him or herself in terms of what psychologists call the typical ego constellation and of what foundational theory calls the current and apparent empirical life form.[15] How did their family and friends typically see them—from the outside, as it were? Alan was of the opinion that everyone perceived first of all his "nice guy" image, and he admitted to having a real stake in keeping up this appearance, since "it seemed to win approval from others and this was important" to him. For Donna, the outsiders' view coincided with her role of being the baby in the family, the littlest one who was always called upon to referee fights and to be the peacemaker. Now, as an adult, she saw herself as still making efforts to organize everyone, to "make things good," while at the same time never expressing her own anger, never allowing herself to cause any trouble for anyone.

Carl confessed that he was seen by his family as the "black sheep," but when asked to comment further, he demurred. He did say, however, that while the role others cast him in did not coincide with his self view, it somewhat negatively affected his adult role in the community. Ellen's preoccupation with what others thought about her came out quite strongly at this point in our conversation. She recalled how her life was very much lived out "under the eyes of the others" and that this pressure of "what people might think" about her was a deformative factor her whole life long. She was rueful as she traced its powerful influence in her history and its shattering effect when she "stepped out of line and became pregnant." Until that moment, she had not realized how strongly she had identified with the desire to appear "respectable as well as good" in the eyes of others.

When asked about the effect of specific societal roles on their consciousness of ego identity (as opposed to their deepest identity) and about how these roles might have structured their encounters with others, each thought some time before answering. Probably this was a new way of looking at themselves. Alan as "member of the clergy," Carl as "president of the company," Bill as "supersalesman," Donna as "mother and housewife," and Ellen as "perfect nurse" all found that these present societal identities structured their meeting with other people in certain ways that were outside their control. In general, Alan seemed to feel most pressured by the role itself and its consequences for his life-style. Ellen admitted that most of the pressures on her probably came more from inside herself than from the expectations of other people. Donna seemed most capable of hanging loose and not becoming hemmed in by what others thought of her, while Carl oscillated between rigidity and a "to hell with them all" attitude.

It was Bill who, in spite of his professional attentiveness to the likes and dislikes of other people, seemed most free of the fear of what others might be thinking and confident of his own personal ego project. Was this because he encountered the other in his role as salesman most of the time? In any case, his style of encountering others was noticeably functional even off the job. Carl also tended to see others, at least at first, from a more or less functionally oriented stance, and only after some acquaintanceship did he move to an interest in the persons themselves. Ellen saw the danger of her role as nurse encouraging her to view others primarily as recipients of her care rather than as sources of meaning in themselves, and Alan complained rather bitterly that people often saw him as merely a dispenser of consolation and advice rather than as "a person in my own right." Although Donna might have been momentarily tempted to see John in his role as necessary partner in her life project, her loving heart did not allow her to remain in that stance for long. But she, too, realized how in living a certain role, you could functionally contextualize the other by means of that role.

These examples demonstrate the power of societal roles and the opinions of others in the community to give shape to our encounters with them. The current identity that is yours by virtue of your role in society or family, the social you that exists because of personal choices you made in the past, self-projects you are presently engaged in, or responses you feel impelled to make to real or illusory expectations in the future are powerful shapers of your interpersonal behavior and attitudes. We suspect that a person's class, ethnic, or socioeconomic identity will be equally powerful in structuring the interpersonal presence he or she brings to a trust encounter. This is why it is suggested that you look more concretely at the role expectations, strivings, ambitions, and vital-functional impulses belonging to your role in your immediate community at the time of your trust experience. As we will see, particularly in Chapter 11, those who live in a society that emphasizes the vital-functional at the expense of the transcendent dimension are more likely to be trapped in the requirements of what is actually only a provisional identity. Though experientally available, this identity is only temporary and will be replaced by another as one's life moves on. Even one's operational orientation changes with time and experience. To shape one's attitude and encounters from anything less than one's unique identity given by God and nourished by the life of the Spirit is to run the risk of deformation, of becoming identified with one's counterfeit self. Thus even when you have come to some conclusions about the influence of class, ethnic origin, role, and socioeconomic reality, you still have not reached the deepest roots of either your own self or its transcendent meaning in the Mystery of God's divine plan.

CHAPTER 4

THE TO-BE-TRUSTED OTHERS

Try to put into words what it was that made the other
person appear to be trustworthy in your eyes. What ap-
pealed to you in the way that the other person
   1. represents the common world in which you both dwell
      and which contains directives that you usually identify
      with;
   2. exists in the world in a manner or style that is affirma-
      ble by you;
   3. emerges from value horizons (transcendent as well as
      vital-functional) that you accept as valid for your own
      life;
   4. initiated this experience of trust?

Community as Influential "Other"
From the first moments of your life you were coexistent with others,
a member of a certain group or family that represented for you the
evident goodness or the problematic questionableness of all that is. Your
developing presence was formed and directed by the surrounding otherness of your parents, who in their turn had been formed by the larger
cultural and social community. As an infant, you could only hope that the
community mediated by your parents would be kind, would nourish and
shape your development along the right path. Yet the surrounding others
who mediated the community's directives to you did not always appear
to nourish and foster you. At times, in its vast otherness, your originating
world awakened anxiety and a feeling of helplessness and vulnerability
from which you needed protection. In the face of its infinite variation, you
developed certain defenses, certain stylistic patterns that were not conge-
nial to your spontaneous self but coincided more with expectations and
directives from that original community.
   No one manages to grow up in this world, in whatever early communal
situation was theirs, without developing certain feelings about them-

selves as being either acceptable or unacceptable. This felt knowledge about oneself as having been approved or disapproved of is bone deep and more or less permanent. It witnesses to the power of the dialogue we are with "otherness," whether this otherness takes the form of significant persons, the atmosphere they generate, or the ideology they profess. Whether we grow up rejoicing in the customary ways of our group or experiencing the bondage in which it places our hearts, as van Kaam insists, interformation by immediate and mediated others is basic to all human life.[1] Thus the social dimension of our existence, the radical character of our presence as also always "participative,"[2] underlies the meanings the to-be-trusted other can have for us. He or she is an inevitably unique representative for us of solidarity with the values of a world that is also and at the same time necessarily "other."

It should not surprise us, then, to find ourselves at times in conflict with that community or that person simply because it/he/she is not me and cannot possibly correspond exactly to the gestalt of desires, prejudices, and dreams that makes up my own uniqueness. Thus, some personal ways of being in the world, some core dispositions of your heart, may have been from the beginning in conflict with the directives coming to you as significant behavioral signals from the surrounding sea in which you originally learned to swim. For example, your heart may have been naturally inclined to trust others and take a "laid-back" attitude. The message from your family, influenced in its turn by the larger culture, may have been "Don't trust anyone, be efficient and make it to the top." That message represents for you a ground of values, traditions, and horizonal meanings that has had a part in forming the sensible/responsible presence you are in the world. It is a mixed ground on which your being rests, a collection of persons whose sensibility corresponds or conflicts in some very important ways with your own.

Others may well be bearers of value around which you have been inspired to shape your life. This certainly was the case with Ellen, whose understanding of what life is all about emerged directly from her participation in the world view of the Christian Catholic faith, and whose desires for becoming her most true self coincided with what she had absorbed from the church community in terms of its directives and founding myth.[3] The gap between what she actually was (her current empirical self) and what she desired to be (the revealed ideal of human capacity to image forth its Creator) was filled not only by her own efforts and striving but also by the helpful and unhelpful guidance and example available from others around her. Evidently Ellen found more support for her aspirations in the group's tradition than in any particular members of the group, all of whom in the final analysis appeared to "lack something" she could really trust. Carl, on the other hand, had spent a lifetime carefully avoiding allegiance to group cultural life directives or personality theories, especially as these were sedimented in institutionalized religion.[4] He lived in what Ellen would have called the illusion of being autonomous, not only as regards historical-cultural pulsations, but also as regards the Divine Otherness addressing him through a human community.[5]

The capacity for self-transcendence in both these individuals was modified by their respective orientation toward others who were formative in their lives.[6] Whether they acknowledged it or not, the groups and communities to which they either adhered and were committed or regarded as theoretically or practically deformative for them in some way influenced them for good or for ill. Try to become aware of the world of meanings and values that the other person in the trust experience you described represented for you. In what way did this person bear with him or her values that appeal to your heart and with which you identify? Your answer may come as a surprise to you.

The Other's Trustworthiness

In answer to my interview question, "What was it about the other person that made it possible for you to trust him?", all five were alike in the inadequacy of their attempts to describe the "something about the other" that made that person emerge for them as to-be-trusted. Alan mentioned his friend's "genuineness and friendliness, the fact that he doesn't come on so strong that you feel overpowered, that he let me be myself, but is always there if I need him . . . he has a certain gentleness and kindness, we share common goals and values, I had a sense of confidence in him." Bill wrote about the other's goodwill toward him, noting that "he was very serious, sincere, thoughtful of me and my position." Carl spoke appreciatively of the other's attempts to "pressure me to think critically and act effectively." Donna tried to explain what she perceived as the other's "honest look. I saw it as being very sensitive and gentle. You don't find many people like that." Ellen was finally able to say only, "Well, I felt even though I had botched things badly, that somehow he [God] still trusted me."

Alan seems to have rather effectively summed up this something about the other person when he commented simply, "It was his concern and love for me that made the real difference. He just accepted me . . . you know, he likes and respects me." Here we have an echo of Ellen's observation that what she finds trustworthy about the other is basically his trust in and love for her. Each one, then, expressed this rather circular pattern involved in trusting the other by stressing that "he cared enough and was genuinely concerned about me" (Alan), "I felt that he felt genuinely concerned about if I would be happy" (Bill), "I was unable to see Mr. B. as a tormentor" (Carl), "he loved me just for being me" (Donna), and "I found myself feeling loved" (Ellen). The aura of trustworthiness seems to surround others with whom, because of their love for me, I can identify; others who like and trust me, who appear to be in the world in the way I would like to be in the world; the Other who is greater than the world and the merely human others who can at best be only partially helpful to me. The other's claim on my trust, then, stems from his or her affirmation of love (liking, respect for) the person who trusts. He, in turn, is affirmed (loved, liked, respected) by that person. But there is more.

Equally difficult to grasp and put into words were aspects of the style of the other who is worthy of trust. For Alan, the other was a "fellow minister" with whom he shared not only life vocation, values, and immediate work but also a past history of intellectual exchange on topics of common concern. This person had always evidenced goodwill toward Alan and seemed to confirm his attitudes toward the rest of the faculty. Alan had a basic or natural confidence in him even before the event described in the written experience. Thus when the other person explicitly criticized him, Alan was still able to perceive his implicit good intentions, his respect for and acceptance of Alan ("he listened to me attentively, even somewhat sympathetically, he let me have my say"). He sensed the horizon of loving concern from which criticism emerges: "I experienced at that moment that these words were difficult for him to say, but that he cared enough about me to risk saying them."

For Bill, the to-be-trusted person was a very successful businessman whose style embodied Bill's ideal. He described him as "a sort of hero," "a lean well-dressed, clean, fifty-to-fifty-five-year-old successful man"; "his manner was quiet and self-assured, not nervous"; "I felt I wanted to be like him." Unlike Alan, Bill had only a slight history of immediate shared basic confidence and had to build[7] trust himself by his actions and awareness of this person's reactions. He, too, perceived the other's goodwill toward him and appreciated his visible appearance and behavior. He rested his growing trust of Mr. M. on certain predictable elements of the job's responsibilities and opportunities that proved to him that he was not mistaken in his judgment of this other person with whom he planned to cast his lot and who could be for him the means of attaining his ideal and accomplishing his life project.

For Carl, the to-be-trusted person emerged from a context "rich in legal and human experience" that inspired Carl's basic confidence in both his expertise and his personal qualities. Prior to this moment of trusting him, Carl perceived the other as someone "to take over the problem of the litigation." But he was also vitally aware of this person's genuine goodwill toward him despite the fact that they had not been particularly close, since Carl's pattern of interpersonal relations was one of isolation rather than closeness to others.

From Donna's point of view, her to-be-trusted future husband shared not only her life project but also an intensive friendship, "which had grown so much in such a short time." There was also appreciation of each other's past-present-future views on life, about which they "talked at length." This sharing of underlying value horizons was most significant for Donna, whose own sense of trust in the other was founded on a transcendent value horizon. She expressed this ultimate horizon in her write-up when, after a moment of realistic indecision, she made up her mind "and that was when my trust of God came in." Two visible aspects of John's behavior that substantiated her basic confidence in him were his "honest" style and her sense that "he loved me just for being me." This sense of being loved that revealed to her the invisible horizons of his care and concern for her was expressed in her description: "I felt a sense of security with John, [I had] the feeling that someone actually loved me."

Like Donna, Ellen gave little indication that she was expecting the other to *do* a great deal for her. She just expressed gratitude that he probably would not let her down, even though she felt "like a sinner who had let him down." In fact, all five strongly agreed that another person who could function perhaps even more reliably would not have been equally acceptable to them in the particular situations they described. Somehow there was a good "fit" between themselves, the other, and the particular situation of interpersonal trust they recorded. A certain style of trustworthiness seemed to be emerging. The trusted style of the other "who loves me for just being me," and who "lets me be, yet is always there when I need him," "who accepts me as I am" (implying "without trying to control, manipulate, or change me by force"), who respects me and continues to have good intentions toward me, who shares my central concerns and value horizons, who as other always respects our "mutual subjectness," all imply a certain level of nonegological living, what Gabriel Marcel calls the level of *being* as opposed to the level of *having*.[8]

During the interviews an attempt was made to explore this distinction further by asking Alan, Carl, and Donna what would have happened if, on the level not of *being* but of *having* or *doing*, the other had somehow failed to function well for them while still assuring them of love and concern. All three accepted the distinction and were sure they could go on trusting and tolerating fumbles on the level of *doing* if they were assured of the other on the level of *being*. Alan volunteered that he tries in a moment like that to see and know the other with "heart knowledge" rather than "head knowledge," because reason alone would not be sufficient for the survival of his trust if the other really messed things up. He added that he finds it impossible to trust egoistic people who are "only interested in promoting themselves, by competing against you, putting you in a box," people whose intentions toward him he perceives as not open-ended and who may thus easily betray him.

In considering the possibility of continuing to trust his attorney if he, while demonstrating his care and concern, had turned out not to know as much as was needed about the particular point of law under discussion, Carl reflected, "Well, as a matter of fact, he probably did say something like that, because you know how legal situations can be. He didn't pretend he had it all sewed up or that he could predict the outcome; those who give great assurances are the ones to be suspected. From the little experience I've had in this field, I'd say it's absolutely unpredictable, so I wasn't trusting his functional knowledge: it was something deeper in him—his willingness and ability to cope with me and not be put off by what I was trying to put him off with." When asked to consider the same mixed bag of self-level trust combined with ego-level fumbling, Donna said she thought that "trust definitely overrides that—the love mainly overrides it. You can have functional downfalls and uphills as long as love is still there, but without trust it just doesn't work out."

Enough, maybe too much, has been said about how the five perceived the other as a whole prior to his functional parts, as a physiognomy or style of being that awakened a response in them of trusting. Now it is time for you to reflect on the modes of being in the world that are in your description, that correspond to your favored style, that are affirmable by you, that you can trust. What does your response to the style of the other trusted by you reveal about your own lived world and the way you inhabit it? Can you put a name on the lived world of meaning that the trusted other represents for you? How does the style of the other make it possible for you to maintain your own subjectivity—to be other, to be unique, to be free?

The Other's Value Horizons[9]

An incident from my own life world raised the question around which this section revolves. At the stage of graduate studies when I was beginning to think of centering my research on the topic of trust between people, the class happened to be learning via practicing the various modes of doing therapy. For several weeks at a time, students alternated in the roles of "therapist" and "client" in hour-long practice interviews that were structured in the light of one particular school (Freudian, Jungian, Rogerian, or whatever). Each student therapist was instructed to adhere strictly to whatever technique was being stressed that particular week. I found myself in one of these interviews in the "client-centered mode" with a very talkative student who brought to the session a problem he was having in trusting a certain member of the department faculty. As he went on about his difficulties, my interest not only in the problematics of current student-faculty relations but also in what he had to say about trust became intense. At a certain moment, forgetting completely all instructions about mirroring the client's responses, I burst out, "Honestly, George, you can't be serious! I don't agree at all!" Although these tape-recorded exclamations were proof of my inability to maintain the detached Rogerian "cool" we were supposed to be learning at the time, they serve to remind me of a moment of real insight: What is trustable for someone else is not necessarily trustable *for me.*

Until this point in my life, I had taken it for granted that if something or someone was trustable, that meant it/he/she was equally trustable for everyone. Yet here was an intelligent fellow student calmly giving me all the reasons that he could not trust one of the faculty members whom I found most trustable. I could not believe my ears. "Well, who do you trust?" I asked. He named the faculty member I considered to be least trustworthy of the group. Again I was astounded. Couldn't he see how wrong he was? What kind of values did he have, anyway? Values—could that be the clue? As I thought further, I realized that although we temporarily shared a situation as graduate students feeling oppressed by faculty, George and I lived our lives out of totally different value systems. What he admired in the faculty member he found trustable I considered to be of questionable worth, and what I saw as worthwhile motivations in my trusted faculty member, he obviously felt were of little or no value in the real world.

This recognition of the way in which I coproduce my experience of other persons as trustable-for-me led to a further examination, not only of the lived context I bring to any encounter with another, but also of the lived context that the other brings. How much would these value contexts or horizons have to say about the quality of the experienced encounter itself? How much would certain differences in the kinds of trust that seemed to be emerging in the pilot studies have to do with these life horizons or contexts? Could the style or overall manner of being in the world of either or both persons in the trust encounter influence the quality of the trust itself? Later on, these same questions emerged in the research itself, when the components derived from Bill's description differed radically from the rest, causing a real problem in analysis.

Gradually it became evident that for Bill, the example of trust emerged in his life mainly on the functional, pragmatic ground of his own project-to-be-accomplished. Beginning with a basic confidence in himself and his ability to win the confidence of the other, and relying on the predictableness of the formalized social intercourse of the business world, Bill "trusts" that Mr. M. will indeed function well for him in the sense of fulfilling his project—that is, hiring him. This is basically a fairly unambiguous level of trust in what the other can do, in how well he can be predicted to function in the truster's best interest. As initiator of the trusting situation, Bill in a certain sense "controls" the other, who remains almost entirely locked into his role as ideal businessman and proven success for Bill. As Bill gains in his capacity to inspire "trust" in the other, he relaxes but feels no need to shift from the original confidence with which he began the project. He wrote, "I had no doubt that I had done the best that I could to get [the job]," and had nothing to lose and everything to gain from the meeting.

In describing the other as he does, Bill reveals that in this instance at least he perceives the other in a horizon focused around the more pragmatic, calculative values of control and ego-functional accomplishment, on the level of *doing* rather than *being*. This may reveal a lot about Bill himself. Or it may simply point to the fact that there are at least two distinctive levels on which people in our society speak of trust. One, "social trust," is exemplified by the description of trusting written by Bill. The other, "interpersonal trust," depends for its quality on horizonal or contextual considerations, as is clear in the other examples.

Alan began to sketch in the value horizon from which his friend emerged by speaking first of their "ability to dialogue," their "common intellectual approach to things," their identification with shared values. Finally, when asked to describe the horizon in which he perceived his friend, he said, "I understand the religious belief common to both of us to be a source of a lot of his everyday actions, and this helps me to trust him. I would be more inclined to trust someone who shares these religious values with me over someone who can't or won't do so, even though I can sympathize with and trust people who don't. But it makes a positive difference to me when I can feel in touch with the *origins* of a person's behavior, with where he is living from, comes from. It is the same source where ultimately I place my own trust. It's linked to trust in an ultimate Other, and is connected with my recognition of my own finiteness and the ambiguity that sometimes goes with it."

Carl also began with references to the similarity between his life-style and that of his attorney, between the hierarchy of values espoused by himself and the other, explaining, "I would say that in a certain very basic fundamental way, I identify with him." Carl also mentioned that, on another level, you trust everyone according to his function, pointing out that "in the area of mechanics, you trust an automobile expert; in the area of law, you trust a lawyer." When asked what was the good in trusting above and beyond the level of mere function, he replied, "Well, maybe the good is a reflection of yourself, at least the part that you understand as good. The other is like me, so I trust him, and maybe he can bring something to the situation that I can't." As a nonbeliever, Carl, although he felt the "religious dimension was a big part of his attorney's stance and situation," declined to separate that particular horizon from others that he saw as equally valuable.

The first to mention an ultimate (in the sense of transcendent) horizon in her description, Donna explained that it was enough for her if people were willing to admit that "life is a mystery," but that in her relation with John, it was important that they establish a common value horizon regarding belief in God, orientation of their life, having children, not taking each other for granted, being faithful, being sensitive to life, and so forth. She felt that "thinking alike about life would be one of the most important things in judging who she was going to marry," that is, going to trust. On the other hand, she also valued the capacity to "grow from each other's different points." At a certain point she spoke of her difficulty in trusting other people who did not live in the horizon of values that "belief in God" implied for her.

Ellen was the most explicit with regard to the horizon or ground that her own belief in God implies. She spoke of her understanding of the Father as being the one who sent Jesus Christ, and "that is why I believe in Christ, because I'm not believing only in a man, even a great human person, but I believe in the person Jesus Christ who came out of the Trinity." For Ellen, the Christ whom she trusts is God. At one critical moment in her life she found herself living toward this person and toward the God who sent him in a mode of presence that does not want to use or control. This mode of living toward God is what she calls "trust." The value horizon of the trusted other in many important ways coincided with the ground or lived horizons out of which emerged the attitudes not only of Ellen but of Donna and Alan as well. It is also evident that these lived attitudes profoundly influence the quality of the to-be-trusted other who can emerge for you in any situation where trust is a possibility. It is important, then, that you at least glimpse the value horizons of your own life, whether these be from science and technology, human nature, instinctive drives, aesthetic beauty, pragmatism or spirituality. An ability to view the other person as emerging from a loving God who creates and keeps him or her in existence adds enormously to the meaningfulness of that created reality. But no matter what its nature, the horizon you affirm as valuable for you is what influences the kind of interpersonal trust that can appear in your life. It reveals the qualities you trust in yourself. It may also conceal some values both in yourself and in the other.

Initiative from the Other

Another naïve notion that I brought with me to the trust research was that the people who did the trusting were themselves the ones who took the initiative in the encounter. However, when I questioned the five about whether they themselves could· have planned or decided to trust, their answers dispelled this notion. Alan replied, "No way . . . I simply found myself trusting. If I had had to plan for that meeting, I would not have been open to what happened because I would have felt so strongly about the points I had in mind. It was important that I hang loose at the moment so that trust could come out like it did, without previous plans. I could not have set up the situation, at least not so that trust would happen. Trust is kind of like a gift that happens in the midst of a situation . . . really unplanned."

Carl's answer was essentially the same. He said, "It was a unique combination of individuals, time, and place. I was quite trusting of this man in almost any situation; we conversed and we communicated freely. I didn't feel any great reserve with him, and this time he showed unusual persistence in tracking me down. He really ran the show, not me."

Donna said in response to my question, "No, I found myself doing it. . . . It just sort of came. I don't think I could have said ahead of time, 'Oh, yes, of course I will trust.' It's just a question of everything working together . . . the way things were said right down to the very words we used, I'm sure. The total experience with everything that was involved in it. Trust flowed from that. Could have been the same time and the same place and the wrong words or the wrong person, that kind of thing, and it wouldn't have worked out."

Ellen observed that although she had been reading Scripture and trying to pray at the time, it was in despair rather than in faith that she was praying. Then, somehow, without her doing anything, God was just there, and her whole predicament shifted from catastrophic mess to tremendous opportunity and challenge. "I felt peaceful and held together even though I didn't know any more practically how things would work out. I was really surprised to find myself suddenly so calm and somehow together."

Now look again at your own description. Where does the initiative come from—from you or from outside yourself, or perhaps from a combination of the two? Are you able to detect anything of the "gift" aspect of the experience that Alan talks about, or the fortuitous gestalting of time, place, and persons mentioned by Carl and Donna? Does your experience involve any invitation from beyond yourself, any evocation that calls you forth in a new way? Or is this moment you described more in the nature of the experience Bill wrote about, in which the initiative was entirely his own? If you find that this interaction between yourself and another person was simply the result of your own willful project, then perhaps you should look further to determine whether the interaction was confined to the merely functional level. In such a case, the other could easily have been a mere means for you to attain your project. Now you begin to become aware of how the meaning of your future project, of what you really want, not only with your head, but also with your heart, can and does influence whether the other emerges as object or freely initiating fellow subject *for you.*

CHAPTER 5

EVENTS AS OPENNESS MOMENTS

Return to your description to find out what made the event
of personal significance to you. Did it stay with you because
1. although you worked your way through it, the event
   brought with it some of the stressfulness that accompanies moments of differentiation;
2. it made figural a conflict of directives bringing tension,
   risk, and the demand quality of life into the fore-
   ground;
3. it was accompanied by a detachment or distancing of
   some sort;
4. after the event you realized that you had matured, you
   were different, you had experienced a change of heart?

Dynamics of the Ongoing Life Flow
The world gives itself to us in an ongoing stream or flow of life experiences. Seemingly unconnected, this differentiated flow of people, ideas,
directives, insights, interests, situations, ambitions, motivations, and varied spontaneous impulses calls for some kind of ordering, of integration.
We have observed how the presence of the person who trusts is evoked
as situated openness or closedness to the other person who is there. Each
time that a differentiating event or person finds a receptive subject, actuation[1] ensues and the newness is integrated into an already ongoing structured life. When the five were asked whether they were able to recall any
change in the flow of their experience, the question referred directly to
the shifts each one had indicated from "before" the moment of trusting
to "after."
Alan pinpointed the change in himself by remarking that although
there had been a gradual growth in their friendship over the years, after
this moment of trust his appreciation of his friend deepened considerably
because "I realized how much courage this took for him to do, knowing
him the way I do and knowing how much he doesn't want to hurt any-

body." In speaking of "after," Carl answered, "Yes, I recall there was a shift in my attitude, an acceptance of the situation, a going with it. There was a difference within myself, as I remember, a relief and a relaxation. Whereas before I had been wondering and thinking other things, not being focused on the situation really, afterward I was able to do my part and stop trying to dump it all on him." Donna began by speaking of the "gradual flow of getting to like each other more and more," but eventually picked out a quite definite moment of transformation in the quality of her trust for John, when "it became a deeper and more intimate relation, we shared more things, we became much closer and I was able to say 'Yes.' " Ellen, too, reported that she moved much closer to the object of her trust "after" this critical event in her life history.

This is the way the normal flow of daily life transcendence moves people toward new growth and fulfillment. Inevitably there will be some lack of balance as the spontaneous unfolding of life with its attendant crises, large and small, calls forth an integrating response. Because they involve detachment from the old in order to make way for the new, growth and maturation periods are always somewhat stressful. In fact, in describing what he calls "transcendence crises,"[2] van Kaam points out that such differentiating moments almost always involve "uncertainty about appropriate directives for the new current life form," and as a consequence are not lived through without anxiety.[3] Nevertheless, in spite of the temptation to cling to what has become familiar, most people manage to work through the temporary uncertainty and detachment these everyday openness moments involve and integrate whatever newness they offer into the central mode of presence that is theirs.

In the events under discussion we see, for example, how a new awareness of the trustableness of the other person was integrated into the ongoing perception of all five. This trustworthiness, acknowledged by Alan as having been "already there" in his friend, had first to emerge from the "obviousness" that veiled his perception of him. It took a mini-crisis in their relationship for Alan to finally allow his friend, no longer simply part of the environment, to emerge as a to-be-trusted other. Carl, too, admitted that "I needed to be led into that critical and practical appraisal of myself and my methods. The situation really did change between us once I felt the heat." Both Donna and Ellen were vaguely aware that after events had forced them out of their comfortable complacency, they were more able to flow into a new awareness of and relationship to the other. Ellen, commenting on her former lack of awareness, said, "I didn't consciously realize any need for trusting God. I thought I was quite capable of being a good person on my own." Like the others, she founded her new trust on an already existing but until now unaware confidence in the other. Gradually it dawned on the four of them, as it never did on Bill, that there was something more to be perceived than what had hitherto been perfectly obvious to them about the other.

It is time to return to your own description and see once more how the experience was personally significant for you. Do you detect even a little of the new awareness toward which it was drawing you? Was there resistance as well as resonance[4] in your response? How would you describe the change in you from "before" to "after" the experience of trusting someone? How did you integrate your new perception of the other as you moved from your embeddedness in former ways of seeing him or her? If your description had been of an event of mistrust, unreflective embeddedness in the familiar might have predominated to such an extent that the normal flow of change from former ways of perceiving to a new possibility would have been blocked. There would not have been a pattern of openness, actuation, integration, that in an event like trusting allows life energy to flow.

Conflict Moments That Bring Openness

Actually the situations described in four write-ups (a talk with a friend, a discussion with one's lawyer, even receiving a proposal of marriage or becoming pregnant) were not overwhelming crises in themselves. However, they took on crisis proportions because of what each person brought to them. Carl, for instance, after having tried for almost a year to solve a messy business relationship, was in what has been called a situation of "ego desperation."[5] Alan, confronted with his negativity, found that his "nice guy" image, carefully cultivated over a lifetime, was being threatened. Donna and Ellen, because of the former's lifelong desire for home and family and the latter's concern for the opinions of other people and of her God, felt that their whole life project was at stake. They were unable to remain in their former state of complacency, and were rather forcibly awakened to reflective awareness. In this new openness they were no longer able to control things; confidence in their ongoing ability to manage was disrupted and they experienced anxiety over this new state of affairs. Just before the actual moment of trusting, each one underwent what could be described as an internal marginal situation, an awareness of human limitedness that made them stop and think.

Not all marginal moments are internal. There are many external life situations of significant loss and breakdown of taken-for-granted ways of doing and being that bring about a comparable openness to the new conflicting directives for the person undergoing them. But whether the marginal moment originates within or outside the person, it is a jolt that tends to set up a conflict either between the person and the directives coming from the exterior environment, or between the actual self the person currently is and the ideal self the person desires to be. We can see both conflicts being activated for Ellen. When she found herself in a personally crucial "openness moment," she experienced a death to her ego identity as "exemplary Christian." Her actual self, unfaithful and pregnant, was in conflict with the community's expectations of a "good Catholic girl" or a "faithful nurse." Moreover, she had forfeited the harmony between her own feelings of being good and in control of her life, and her confidence in her previously held, somewhat rigid notions of where God's presence in one's life is actually to be found. Her former complacency was shattered by her heartfelt insight that she was less important, more ordinary, than she could previously have imagined.

Daily, people in our culture are disturbed out of their complacency by differentiations that, whether they are perceived in a positive or in a negative light, open them up to new horizons of meaning and questioning. Events as personal as the realization of having sinned, of having reached the turning point of middle or old age, or of having given oneself in a supposedly permanent situation that has deteriorated out of all recognition can serve as the catalyst for this necessary breaking open of the self to what is still to come. But there are events on a less immediately personal scale that can open people just as surely to new options for living and for trusting. The contemporary breakdown of certitude in the entire culture, the changing and often morally suspect possibilities of human fulfillment and self-actualization available for all, the upheaval of taken-for-granted structures in the Church, in one's community, group, or family, are examples of this type of event. In addition, the self can now be broken open, by media exposure and travel never before possible, to human anguish on a worldwide scale. The conflict induced by these and other contemporary life situations centers on the choice we must make between the directives they bring with them, choices that lie in a transcendent or less transcendent direction. The very term *transcendence crisis* implies stress and uncertainty, a locus for the presence or absence of trust.[6]

Yet it is these very situational crises that are the raw material of human spiritual growth and development. Without them, and the conflict and choices they bring, there would be no opportunities for opening up to one's fellow humans or to the Divine. Without the creative tension belonging to the differentiation-integration dynamic, there would be no changes in self or world, no possibilities of deepening and redirection. Without a built-in conflictual element of transcendence/immanence, human life would atrophy and the spiritual hope for the future of both individuals and groups would die. This truth is brought home daily to therapists and spiritual directors who know from experience that it is the client or directee who has been jarred out of complacency, who has been opened up by his or her lived conflict with self, others, or God, who is most likely to benefit from psychotherapy or spiritual direction. Helping such persons to pay intelligent attention to the messages for them embodied in each changing and thus conflictual moment of their history is a great service to be offered by such guides.[7]

It would be good to look once more at your event, keeping in mind this element of conflict that may be hidden in it. What did you yourself bring to the situation that contributed to its internal marginality? Can you trace the roots of your tension to the various warring directives present in the situation? Does the conflict have anything to do with changes in the community or group or culture? If you were to bring this incident into a therapy or spiritual direction session, how would you present it?

The Breakthrough Potential of Ambiguity and Death

Because of the ambiguity that pervades all human situations, all five admitted in the interviews that it would also have been possible—even easy—to distrust the other in the situation they described in their write-ups. Alan mentioned how paradoxical the situation was for him: "You know, I could also have challenged everything he said and proved he was wrong and I was right because in a sense a lot of what I was saying about the seminary training and faculty attitudes was true. But it was my interpretation and self-involvement that was falsifying it, and he helped me to see that. If I hadn't seen his care for me, or if he had been playing a role (which he sometimes does), it certainly would have been tempting and easier to lash out at him and defend myself and my precious image." Alan was confronted unexpectedly with the "otherness" of a friend by whom he was accustomed to being confirmed. He had a lot at stake in the situation; he was anxious and had, in a sense, to make an effort to risk believing in the other in the face of such incertitude.

Carl also experienced a strong and effective "otherness" in his attorney, who "was exerting a continuing and strong pressure on me." In his interview he commented on the ambiguity inherent in making oneself vulnerable, in trusting another human being, as follows: "I would say I experience more than ambiguity. That's just one name for it. You go on doing and living in a relationship on the basis of the trust that's established, but the trust is never complete, because you are separate individuals, and you never share completely. Even in agreement, there is a very limited area of identity in common. Agreement is usually on certain small areas. The other is always 'other.' " In his write-up is the phrase: "I was unable to see Mr. B. as a tormentor." We have the impression that although he was unable to distrust this particular other in these particular circumstances, he might actually have found it easier to do so.

Ellen readily agreed that her "mess" lost none of its ambiguity once she began to trust, but then, she "hadn't expected it would." Donna denied that her trust was unreflectively naïve or blind ("it was not an unrealistic trust"). She knew that she had to risk confronting the "otherness" of John, the invisible horizon of the other person as always subject who is beyond control or predictability ("for I knew that I could never know John completely"). Her "reasonable thoughts" told her that there is inevitable incertitude in human relationships, especially in one that had been going on for "such a short time." Also, she was planning to trust him with what was of ultimate value to her—her whole life—and this raised the level of risk and tension, turning the situation into one that would draw forth from her an unlimited type of trust. As she said, "My feeling of complete trust in another person was the most prominent feeling at this time." Still, she was aware of ambiguity, of other possibilities, when she commented, "I think you could go too far in trusting."

Thus trusting appears to be an ambiguous rather than a clear-cut project, one that demands reflectiveness and the ability to endure the tension of not knowing, of not being sure. It also asks for a certain willingness to accept the relative ambiguity of other persons and of life itself. Actually the event that brings life to a close, death, is the major crisis of ambiguity that must be faced by all human beings. Yet most of us do everything in our power to avoid the tension aroused by its confrontation. In our attempts to maintain the illusion of security, to put off or deny the insecurity and contingency of human existence, we blunt the edges of death's intrusion into our lives. We tend to speak of it as an impersonal something that happens to others every day:

> In the publicness with which we are with one another in an everyday manner, death is "known" as a mishap which is constantly occurring . . . as a "case of death." "Someone or other dies," be he neighbor or stranger. . . . People who are no acquaintances of ours are "dying" daily, hourly. "Death" is encountered as a well-known event occurring within the world. As such it remains in the unconsciousness characteristic of what is encountered in an everyday fashion.[8]

We are unwilling to face the anxiety this major change from the familiarity of the known to the unfamiliarity of the unknown brings with it. So we pretend as long as possible that this powerfully ambiguous transcendence crisis will not happen to us. We ignore its paradoxical inherence in the very fabric of everyday possibilities. We deny its foundational reality as the one ultimate that can underline the meaningfulness or absurdity of existing at all as a human being.[9]

Yet even as it heightens our sense of the unknown and unpredictable, death sets a priority on the experience of trust. As our everyday life unfolds, it presents us with all manner of ambiguous situations. Simply to risk getting out of bed in the morning demands a certain trust in Being. As we go about our daily interactions, we meet a mixture of the affirmable and the nonaffirmable for us. A series of detachments is required, as well as an acceptance of contingency and limitation. Life in its maturation process asks for the same kind of trustful letting go throughout as it does in the end. There is no way to avoid the suffering and limitation involved in the human condition. Up to the moment of death, however, we remain free to risk a trusting response or to refuse the possibility of meaning. Believers are those who are able to regard the detachments or little deaths demanded by authentic living as preparation for the final break-through moment of death, when spontaneous confidence will have passed through final ambiguity and doubt to a new birth of full participation in a communion with God and others. As one writer puts it, death is the great ambiguity present with us as a fact of human existence, like birth and growth and sex, and no way of living is possible that does not demand from us some kind of attitude, some way of shaping our values and decisions, in relation to these basic facts of our existence.[10] He adds that the basic choice we make in view of this ambiguity reflects our overall view of human life and its meaning in terms of trust, hope, and confidence.

The Shifts That Signal Growth

The changed awareness of the other that the five reported in connection with an experience of trusting was accompanied by a change in the whole structure of the way each truster usually lived toward the other person. Alan's perceptual shift took place when he found that his taken-for-granted pattern of being together with his friend ("In a rather negative way, as I had frequently done that summer, I began to muse over the poor state of the training situation in our seminary") was shattered by the realization that his friend was capable of becoming his critic. This new way of seeing his friend created within Alan a qualitatively new level of trust. Alan tried to describe this change by saying that his friend's facial expression and manner of behaving underwent a shift from "enthusiasm" over the tapes to "caution and serious concern" for Alan, "a difference in his eyes and manner and voice tone; I just saw him in a new way, that's all."

Donna also specified that the particular "overpowering" moment allowed her to perceive John differently and thus trust him more strongly. She contended that this overpowering trust was distinguishable from her natural everyday confidence in him, and continued to have a "powerful transforming influence on her present life and perception." Ellen also noticed a break in her former way of seeing and thus dealing with her God. She had been doggedly trying to save the situation by all kinds of plans and schemes, including the possibility of abortion. Then she *saw* in a new way the futility of all her schemes in the face of who God really was and could be for her. She no longer viewed herself as the only one capable of saving the situation.

Carl described his rigid style of perception prior to the shift as a kind of blindness: "I was unable to see clearly." He added, "The fact that Mr. B. precipitated a break in my rigid setup with his insistence and persistence is perhaps the most important element." After Carl "dropped his bias," his perception of the situation changed. "The other's offensive became less threatening," and "I began to appreciate his patience and kindness, and prepared to put the case to arbitration." Carl could now perceive the parallel intentions of himself and the other. He could no longer see Mr. B. as a mere causal factor in his distress, a mere functionary. Bill, on the other hand, did not seem significantly changed by his encounter, but simply became strengthened in the natural self-confidence with which he had entered the meeting. This lack of change was a clue that the phenomenon described by Bill was not necessarily interpersonal trust.

Reflective examination of such a moment reveals that the entire relationship between the two people undergoes a shift. When asked about the experienced change in the other's behavior toward him, Carl commented that at first "there was this distance between us, him trying to get something and me being unwilling to go into it. When the barrier broke and I relaxed and trusted him with the information, then we did become closer. At that moment we reestablished a situation of trust that had been broken." As his attorney grew in trust of his "more factual presentation," Carl in turn was able to trust him, thus creating a sort of circular sharing of trust between them. Ellen also experienced something of this circularity, recalling that a lot of her earlier confidence in God came from "things she had read and been told about his trusting goodness toward people." It was finally the memory of this goodness coming directly from him that helped her see his saving action in her life.

Donna was also transformed in her ability to trust another by her pleasure "that he expressed his trust in me." This mutual trust transformed her prior relations with herself and her world, moving her from resistance to openness to "a definite feeling of inner peace with myself and the world." Alan "really appreciated" being trusted by the other person, and this generated in him a reciprocal feeling, which he expressed as follows: "This good feeling also included a warm feeling that reminded me that I had received someone's genuine care and this evoked a feeling of gratitude." On his part, Bill certainly experienced a growth in respect and familiarity toward the other, but he did not seem to discover a mutuality of central concerns nor did he come to a recognition of the other as subject and therefore ambiguous for him. Interpersonal trust seems to call for both this recognition of "mutual subjectness" and a crossing-over of mutual trust "between" the two persons. Also, the truster's feeling of relatedness shifts from relative isolation to a closer mutual sharing between self and other as subjects of their experience.

The shift to a more relaxed way of being stands out for everyone. In answer to the second question, "Describe your feelings just as they were when you experienced this situation of trust," Alan wrote that he went from a fairly calm mood to "hurt feelings" at being jolted out of his everyday stance ("these remarks hurt me"), to "feeling good all over" as "this good feeling began to replace or permeate the hurt feeling." Evidently the shift for him consisted in moving from positive to negative and back to positive bodily and emotional well-being, as "I felt more comfortable and even glad to be where I was. My body felt softer, and a little more relaxed, lighter. I guess you'd say the direction was from relaxed to tense and back to relaxed. I had a moment of wanting to control and be vigilant, then there was relaxation into vulnerability and openness to what my friend was up to—an attitude of acceptance, of letting go, of letting myself be seen as I really was." Bill simply commented, "I relaxed." Ellen described how very tight the upper part of her body had been during the days that she wrestled with her decision and how she had felt an overall stiffness grow in her whole body until the moment of trusting made her "relieved, relaxed, open for a new adventure."

Carl termed his initial feelings "frustration and annoyance," a rigid clinging to a "one-sided idealistic defense." Then he shifted from a rigid to a more relaxed stance. "Up until that point I was fidgeting, looking for a way to break off and be gone, my mind was back in the office. But after the turning point, I relaxed and came back into the chair, sort of letting him take the show." In losing his tenseness and relaxing, he found that he had less to be defensive about ("the other's offensive became less threatening"). Donna also spoke about the affirmable perceptions and affects ("I felt happy and somewhat content and also pleased") that resulted from the change in her self/world relation. In the interview she explained further: "When you're trusting a person, you're closer, and so we could just feel each other more. We could feel each other's bodies more really, we were like magnets. You surrender your body, you surrender everything in love, I think, and we didn't want to be apart. There was a definite change in our experience of our bodies."

Certainly all experienced a shift in the general direction of bodily relaxation, which they variously described as "surrendering everything," "letting the other take the show," and relaxation into vulnerability and openness, "acceptance . . . letting myself be seen as I really was." This relaxation on the bodily level points in the direction of risk. It points to a letting go of defenses, a certain lack of protection, a vulnerability, a not-being-in-control, an experience of being "poor."[11] Ellen, for example, had to let go of her "perfect record" and risk being "just a sinner" before God. Alan had to abandon his defenses and risk acknowledging his negativity, becoming vulnerable to being hurt by his friend's remarks and feeling inferior and in need of help from another ("I felt I was trusting my friend with myself in terms of my self-image"), which was not his usual way of being. In fact, in the interview he admitted that anxiety over his lack of control of his self-image made him "feel a certain poverty and neediness, a kind of defenselessness—a dependence on the other."

Carl also found himself necessarily shifting from a more independent stance because of his failure to settle the dispute on his own. In having "to explain and justify the actions of subordinates as well as my own," Carl risked becoming open and vulnerable to the other "in an investigation that was critical of myself and associates." Later Carl added, "I guess there was risk from the standpoint that he was stripping away the hard defenses I had built up, and this involved the risk of making my involvement a lot deeper than I had hoped to make it. I suppose there was a risk, too, in admitting and really taking another viewpoint toward some of the aspects of the case."

Donna experienced the risk of vulnerability as in direct correlation with the degree of what she was being asked to trust the other with—her "whole life," as she saw it. She had a sense of having to protect what was of central concern to her, and at the same time, in the horizon of vulnerability, she risked not protecting, not being in control, but letting go in a trustful surrender to the other. "You're not positively certain when you surrender yourself to a person in a situation like this, and that's where the trust comes in. You have no answers, you have no certainty, but that's where the risk comes in. You just have to take the risk."

All indicated that they were somehow able to act differently after their respective experiences of trusting another. Ellen, once she had slowed down long enough to acknowledge her rigidly self-sufficient attitude and ask for help, was able to stop trying to control everything and go with the flow. Alan could now "own my own negativity as coming from me," a new attitude for him. "I saw that perhaps there might be another point of view to what I was saying, that I had been narrowly caught up in my own point of view, as my friend pointed out. It was his presence that helped shift my perspective. I felt there was a kind of new space between us for me to move in, and I was able to reevaluate my own attitude without feeling threatened."

Carl, whose "relative righteousness" had blinded him to "all courses of practical action," could, after his internal shift to trusting the other, begin exteriorly to relax his paralyzed mental capacities. "I was able to search my memory and the history for the arguments which our customer would likely present and undertake a less isolated, more critical and practical appraisal of the status of the case." In the interviews he added, "My trust of him allowed me to be freer with him and with myself in questioning and doubting any particular idea or fixation. I had become hardened to a sort of fixed attitude and defense and one-sided view of the thing, and I was able to get rid of some of the boxes I had built, find freedom, be open, find solutions instead of building up defenses." In interpersonal trust, Carl could risk what for him was a new and more effective way of being. In order to act in what for her was an ambiguous situation, Donna also had to "feel this trust" before she was able to take the significant step of committing "my whole life to a person." In the interviews she elaborated on the effect of this newfound trust in herself: "Yes, because I was more loved, I was more self-confident. It wouldn't be there if I didn't have that sense of trust. The person who gave me the trust helped me develop that confidence." For Donna, too, the other person was the decisive factor in opening her to the possibility of new action.

With regard to the process of exercising freedom in deciding to act, we have already observed that in interpersonal trust the initiative seems to come both from within and from beyond the person who is doing the trusting. Alan, Carl, Ellen, and Donna expressed the moment as one of a decision taken by themselves as subjects. Alan said, "This encouraged me to own my negativity as coming from me"; Carl remarked, "at some point I began to appreciate his patience and kindness"; Donna commented, "I accepted . . . and I loved him"; and Ellen wrote, "I felt encouraged to go ahead and have the baby." Yet at the same time each discovered that the initiative actually came from the presence or action of the other, like a gift. For Alan, "a friend . . . stopped in"; in Carl's case, "he persisted in stalking me"; in Donna's, "he asked me to marry him"; and Ellen notes, "I found myself feeling loved."

Alan discovered himself appreciating and affirming the good intentions of a friend who risked offering him the gift of a painful truth "in a caring

and concerned kind of way." He could have negated or at least questioned his friend's intentions, "but I didn't in this situation. I wasn't
compelled to trust him. I could make a decision to trust or not, and in
other situations I have decided not to trust him." Thus Alan was free to
affirm or deny the goodwill of the other toward him. Carl also pointed
to this kind of receptive decision when he said, "You can't exactly decide
to trust, but you could go into the situation to promote trust. In that
sense, we can plan for it to happen. We can plan to make something out
of the situation, we can prepare, like Mr. B. did, to facilitate trust. I would
hope that from that experience of changing my own attitude, I can make
incidents like it in the future more trust-producing." Thus Carl found
that "my attitude changed," but this change was neither totally determined from the outside nor totally willed by himself.

Ellen reported that the decision to have the baby "just made itself,"
while Donna, in a mixed moment of freedom ("John and I were not
married then") and ambiguity ("for I knew that I could never know John
completely"), also decided to affirm and accept rather than negate the
good intentions of the other person toward her, even though she believed
that "you can't plan (or decide beforehand) to trust someone." Thus, for
at least four of the five, trusting was almost a question of deciding to allow
trust to happen to them. They could have decided not to allow the other
to emerge as to-be-trusted, in order, perhaps, to avoid risking the consequences that accompany most decision making. Evidently trusting requires a change of heart in the direction of risk.

As you look again at yourself, the subject of the experience you described, ask yourself how do you tend to act in a risk situation—is your
pattern fight, flight, or what? Can you detect even a slight change in your
awareness of the other, in the way you tended to see and relate to him
or her, in the feeling aspect of your relationship? Did you experience any
bodily relaxation and consequent vulnerability? Was risk an issue for you
in this experience? Was there an evolution in your ability to decide and
act on your decision? If, as you look back on your experience of trusting
someone, you discover none of these changes; if, as in Bill's experience,
there was little feeling of risk and no shift in your awareness of or relationship to the other person, chances are the incident you described was not
one of interpersonal trust. It may have been instead an occasion where
you lived out attitudes proper to a situation of social reliability with
regard to the other person. You may have been involved with this person
as socially reliable other or simply as an object to be depended on.[12] In
that case, you may want to turn right now to Part Three, which explores
why people in our society find trusting so difficult, why they are so afraid
to trust one another, and the favorite coping mechanisms they substitute

for trust. Or you may prefer to move forward with a more philosophical[13] approach to what happens when one person trusts another. Answers to the questions about your own trust situation, the person who trusts, the other who is trusted, and events as openness moments are the working basis for Part Two. In Chapters 6 to 10 we will look at what happens when the conflict of directives does not become so strong that it produces paralysis; when the inevitable stress due to being jolted out of one's complacency is gracefully accepted; when inner freedom overcomes outer determinism and the flow of new life and attitudes is allowed.

Part Two

·

A MIXTURE
OF THEORY AND
PRACTICE

CHAPTER 6

FACILITATING FREEDOM
TO TRUST

Can you put your finger on what had actually changed in
you from "before" the event to "after" that
1. allowed trust and the shift to happen;
2. indicated a relaxation in the lived striving body;
3. pointed toward the confidence you have in yourself;
4. induced you to "let go" in some way;
5. allowed the preconscious self to surface?

Allowing for an Integrative Shift

Empirical data from the study have shown clearly that when you really
do trust someone, there is an unmistakable restructuring or shift from
"before" to "after" in the way you experience the coming together or
gestalt of space and time. In fact, often the only way to identify and name
an experience (like interpersonal trust) and distinguish it from what it is
not (e.g., mere social reliability) is to look carefully at how it changes,
even slightly, the trusting person in relation to what is "other" in the lived
space and time of his or her world. Part One ended with an account of
how the trust dynamic operates. A person's life flows on in the creative
tension between its spontaneous vital/functional unfolding and the transcending freedom with which the person responds to it. In the midst of
this complexity—which, by the way, could never be described as mere
"absence of trust"[1]—all the elements of a personally meaningful space/
time event come together or gestalt into an "openness" moment, and the
stage is set for a trusting (or nontrusting) response to another person.

In Chapter 5, in the section titled "The Shifts That Signal Growth,"
you read descriptions, in the trusters' own words, of the evolution they
experienced in their bodily, perceptual, sensible, interpersonal, and volitional relationship with the trusted other. What we want to do now is to
look at these five experiential areas from a more theoretical point of view.

But first we will recall the Sufi legend[2] that tells of a group of fish who, having heard about the sea, are very eager to reach it and drink from it themselves. So they spend all their time busily swimming about, thrashing their tails and wearing themselves out looking for the sea. Not finding it, in desperation they finally ask a wise fish what they should do next. He advises them to stay still and pay attention, to notice for the first time that they are *already in* the sea, surrounded by the water. With all their effortful swimming they had not even noticed where they were. Like humans whose busy striving keeps them too preoccupied to notice where they are, the fish in their willful pursuit of the sea missed it entirely.

This legend points up something the data have shown us about the way trust between people happens. In the midst of the trusters' original attempts to cope with the stress of conflicting directives and anxiety-causing impasses, they learned a first lesson about the to-be-trustedness of the other. This quality of the other is not "obvious," nor does it emerge as a result of a willful effort. Like the fish, humans may have to learn to be still, to cease their busy doing in order to notice what is "already there" in the sea of life around them. Growing in the freedom to trust, finding any new direction for your heart or your life, can never be a matter of willpower alone. It is, in fact, the willful heart, which puts obstacles in the way of trusting, that can be labeled "hard." Such hardheartedness may indicate a rigid, compulsive need to manage everything, to control all thoughts and actions so that nothing unpredictable can touch and move the heart from outside the defended boundary of its stronghold. Like the sea surrounding the fish, the to-be-trusted that surrounds a hard, willful heart is scarcely noticed. The water of divine energy is not allowed to flow, the other is permitted no initiative, and the movement of actuation cannot occur. Yet there are also moments, as the descriptions verify, when the heart opens toward the other, when defending barriers drop away, and what is there to be trusted can emerge and flow back toward hearts thirsty for love. Such movements are rarely noticed, yet they are available all the time and constitute the quality dimension of our existence.

This ability of the human spirit to dialogue with, accept, integrate, and thereby transcend the limiting nature of so-called openness moments is illustrated by Ellen's response. Like the others, she experiences a negative moment. Torn by conflicting directives, she feels frustration, fear, and the crunch of immediate circumstances. Resisting the temptation to willfully ignore reality and to try handling the whole thing by herself, she allows her heart to be touched by this differentiating experience. In trusting openness to the "other," she tunes in to her own reality as limited partaker in a life she did not create. She lets go of her illusory ideal of being perfect, and accepts this failure of her ideal self. Instead of blocking the flow, Ellen freely responds to reality as it is. She lets go of her present ego identity. In so doing, she goes beyond the paralyzed, rigid, compulsive person she has been, and moves into a new, flexible, and creative acceptance of what seemed at first to be an impossible situation.

In speaking of such moments, when experience is restructured and when there seems to be a discontinuity or break that eliminates the previously experienced self, Merleau-Ponty notes not only that a new region of phenomena is opened up, but also that this new constitutive layer of meaning is conserved and integrated into layers of meaning already established.[3] Ellen, though she undergoes a deep change or conversion here from her former rigid and fearful self, never experiences a complete break with the "old Ellen." The underlying temporal synthesis[4] of the Ellen who remembers past experiences of both trust and lack of trust remains, as does the learning she retains from the experience that now becomes the origin of new trusting by her in the future. Thus we see that as the trusting attitude evolves, there is a movement from openness to actuation and integration. Like human beings everywhere, Ellen with her yes facilitates an integrative shift to what van Kaam calls a new current life form.[5]

The Trusting Body

Two notions from phenomenological thinking, that of the person as *presence* and as *body subject,* can be helpful in understanding what happens to the human body in the action of trusting. This action, like all other actions, receives its meaning from the whole movement of the trusting person's life. Every act of trust must be seen in relation to that total living self—that dynamic, continually emerging whole person. This was the reason for attempting in Part One to look at each person in the study as a temporal synthesis of vital, psychological, and spiritual meanings embodied in the various modes of feeling, behaving, knowing, perceiving, valuing, imagining, remembering, and so on that he or she tended to adopt in relation to others in the world. In speaking of this dialectical unity of subject and the world that human existence most basically is, Merleau-Ponty calls it *presence*—an openness to the world of persons, events, and things that is not conceivable without, first, something in the way of meaningful reality to which the subject is present, and second, a world or "field of presence" that does not make sense without the perceiving subject.[6]

Thus every human being who relates to any aspect, or even to the whole, of reality relates in a way that is not an immanent activity self-enclosed in either the body or consciousness. Humans are always in self-transcending intentional relation or *presence* to what is other than themselves. All persons who trust are first of all "present," going beyond themselves toward the world or the other. Interpersonal trust is one way of transcending self that is never a mere feeling or inner condition independent of its object (the other person). It depends both on what is "already there" in the situated concrete world to-be-trusted and on what the lived intentionality of the truster's perceiving embodied self allows to emerge for him or her. Thus there is no way in which the perceiving body can be ignored in a study of the experience of interpersonal trust.

Merleau-Ponty sees the body as preconscious intentional *subject,* rather than simply as object separate from intentional consciousness. He sees this lived body (which for him includes the person, the situation, and the other) as the fundamental ground for every interpersonal relationship. He contends that when we as lived body subjects perceive the other, we perceive him *in* our own bodily experience of his gestures, his physiognomy, his intentional bodily behavior. Moreover, as we have mentioned, built into the embodied being of the person who trusts is a prereflexive vital predisposition, a unique interrelation of glands, temperament, fundamental mood, prehistory, drives, feelings, biological interaction with the environment, and so on that inclines him or her to certain situated ways of relating to others.[7] There are, in other words, certain embodied perceptual possibilities and limitations already built into each truster's lived capacity for trust. In pointing to this incarnated quality of human consciousness, to this anonymous transcending body subject beneath conscious, volitional life, Merleau-Ponty contributes much to our understanding of why willful striving and conscious effort alone are incapable of producing a moment of trust.[8] His remarks encourage us to look again at how the five people described what happened to their bodies in the trust experience.

Alan speaks of being jolted out of a positive, relaxed, at-home confidence into a more or less negatively colored awareness of what was problematic for him. This awareness was succeeded by relaxation into a new confidence that he calls trust. He uses phrases like "a calm mood," "hurt feelings," "my body felt alert and hurt," "I stiffened and got tense," "my body felt softer, more relaxed, lighter," "I felt good all over." Carl also speaks of bodily relaxation and loss of tenseness succeeding his decision to trust. He says, "My body came back in the chair." Donna also experienced a "surrender" of her body's defensive stance, a relaxation of control, and a new openness and vulnerability toward the other. Ellen told me that for a few minutes before "the whole thing opened up" for her and she was able to trust, her mind had been "sort of blank." She had not been consciously worrying or going over things in her mind. In fact, the bodily relaxation she mentions in her description was actually preceded by a relaxation of the mind. In each experience there seems to have been a similar movement. Apparently the person who trusts begins from a sort of generalized confidence in the other. Then he or she experiences a reflective moment of withdrawal or detachment from that generalized confidence. The restoration of relaxed presence is detectable not only in the embodied perception of the trusting person but on the level of reflective consciousness as well.

Before further exploring the nature of the above-mentioned generalized confidence, you may want to take time to recall any bodily changes that you noticed in yourself as *presence* or *body subject* in relation to the other person in your own experience. Was there any shift to a more relaxed attitude in body or mind or both? Are you aware of how you as body subject react with sympathy or antipathy to objects in the world before your conscious mind has made any personal decision for or against? Have you ever tried to *will* trusting someone? Do you suspect that there are elements in your bodily makeup that constitute obstacles to being a relaxed presence to others?

The Body and "Doxic Confidence"[9]

How does it happen that the person who trusts comes to perceive or intend the other as to be trusted by him or her? The question itself points to a level of meaning below or beyond that of consciousness, a level that has to do first with the lived body. In speaking of this level, thinkers like William James and Edmund Husserl refer to *doxa*, the vague everyday knowledge we have of the world as we live it prior to thinking and reasoning about it. The former in its daily givenness, in the obviousness of its appearing, is the taken-for-granted foundation of all human life and science. It is the basis of our generalized confidence that what we perceive and take for granted as being there for us is really there. The appearing world, as we perceive it and live toward it with our bodies, is the basis of our generalized or doxic confidence in its existence. Conversely, the term *doxic confidence* implies a feeling of confidence in the self-evident reality of that world (and others) as we participate in it (or them) through our body. We can, as Alfred Schutz does, equate this doxic confidence in the unquestionableness of the world "just as it appears" with what he and others call the natural attitude[10]—a level of perceiving reality that betrays an essentially practical interest in, a pragmatic attitude toward, the world as field of our embodied functioning.

It is with this vital or physical level of meaning having to do mainly with the functioning lived body (from which, of course, consciousness is not excluded) that we must begin if we are to understand the origins of an experience of interpersonal trust. It is on this level of what Merleau-Ponty calls bodily synthesis that the truster has his or her most direct access to the other; that the truster, along with conscious knowledge of the other, has a lived prepersonal experience of the other as embodied. In fact, it is from this level, where both the person who trusts and the one trusted are inserted via their vital dimension, that they find themselves sharing an even deeper kind of embodied "trust" in the world itself. Merleau-Ponty points to this crossing or "chiasm"[11] that makes for a certain preestablished kinship or harmony between truster and person trusted. It parallels in a sense the chiasm he speaks of as existing between the seer and the seen, or between that which touches and that which is capable of being touched.[12] It reminds us of what Carl was referring to when he said, "You trust in the other what you trust in yourself."

This notion of chiasm raises for the person who trusts the whole issue of confidence in him or herself as trustable. Just as the one who sees must at the same time be one of those who are visible to be seen, so, too, it would seem that the one who trusts must also be one of those who are trusted. He or she must be available for others to trust, not foreign to the lived world of being trusted. We see how confidence in herself as belonging to this world grows in someone like Donna, whose trusted other, like the object that is seen, offers back to her an image of herself as one who can be trusted because of the fact that she trusts. Referring to her written claim that "he expressed his trust in me," she explained how this mutual trust gave her a new experience of confidence in herself as one who can be trusted.

Returning to the notion of doxic confidence, it may be helpful to look at some of the characteristics of this attitude as it is lived by most people every day. On the one hand, doxic confidence is rooted in the person's bodily being in the lived world. It denotes a certain security, a familiarity or at-homeness, a natural bond with the world and with others in that world. It carries with it a natural confidence in others and in the everyday world of commonsense meanings we share with them. It also connotes a rather opaque, preconscious or prereflective presence to this everyday-ness, a sort of basic ability to operate in practical affairs because of one's bodily "pact" with the world.[13] It recalls what Emmanual Levinas terms the life of enjoyment, of being happy in the world that nourishes, of having a certain confidence in one's own history of retentions and possible protentions with others in the world.[14] People who have doxic confidence in their world are naturally able to enjoy life. When the opportunity offers, they can rather easily relax into playful attitudes. They dance and sleep and cook and play with children. They are able to eat and digest their food well. They find pleasure in breathing, in sexual activity, in laughter, and in sports. In the interviews Alan, Donna, Ellen, and Carl spoke about these aspects of their lives.

On the other hand, even in the process of asking questions about it, you realize that life lived on the level of mere doxic confidence, in the natural attitude, can be an alienating experience. Such an existence, embedding the person within the finite horizon of the natural world, might well block him or her off from the transcendent flow that is already there. He or she might be deprived of the human capacity for transcending these two less integrated structures of behavior.[15] In addition, overimmersion in this level of experience interferes with the possibility of pneumatic presence[16] to which human beings are also called. Gradually we see that mere doxicality, with its limited pragmatic horizon, does not partake in the lived structure of what finally emerged in the research as interpersonal trust. It remains confined to a level that can falsify perception of the other, reducing him to the visibility of flat, unchanging categories of the natural attitude, to "dime-a-dozen" typifications that characterize perception in a taken-for-granted world. Interpersonal trust undeniably originates and is anchored in the lived bodies of both the one who trusts and the one who is trusted. It seems, in fact, to be one of the necessary conditions for this dialogue between two persons. Nevertheless, we conclude that it is not identical with what we are coming to recognize as the lived experience of interpersonal trust.

Have you become aware of a basic layer of doxic confidence in yourself that not only grounds you in the world as nourishing and enjoyable but is also a basis for your own self-confidence and the confidence of others in you? Do you find yourself, in other words, at home in your body, able to more or less gracefully gear into the world of practicalities and sensual pleasure without too much awkwardness or feeling of alienation? Do you see any problems that might arise if you began to totalize this dimension, if its actualization were to become your main aim in life? Have you ever met anyone whom your body trusted or distrusted before you (consciously) did? Do you sense the necessity of doxic confidence as the underlying earthy base for your trust in others who share with you the human condition of being embodied?

"Letting Go" as Needed Element

With a new understanding of the implications of embeddedness in the natural attitude, we can return to our analysis of the movement that characterizes an experience of trust between people. As noted earlier, the person who trusts seems to begin from a sort of generalized confidence in the other that has built up over the years and can be defined as "doxic."

This confidence toward the other person perceives him mainly in terms of spontaneous feelings of antipathy or sympathy. Tending toward a pragmatic interest in the other, this attitude also brings about a certain at-homeness and familiarity with regard to others who share the world with us. It can also falsify or reduce perception of them to the limits of their vital, functional possibilities. In fact, seeing the other primarily from the vantage point of the natural attitude may well evoke a certain degree of exaggerated striving in the one who so perceives the other. Tendencies toward domination and control, toward a partial rather than a holistic view of the other, may accompany this merely natural perception.

A predominance of mere doxic confidence in the person who trusts may simply blind his or her eyes to the "more than" that inheres in the invisible mystery underlying the existence of the other person. Fixation in such a stance would surely cripple his or her ability to go beyond a somewhat rigid and false sense of what is there to be relied on in the other person. Moreover, interior fixations in striving on the vital/functional level, especially if for some reason they are unduly exaggerated, will be mirrored in bodily expressions. There are persons, for example, who have only a vitalistic perception of the other as object of sexual impulses, or who can only approach others in terms of their "usefulness" or their "victim" potential. The bodies of these persons reflect their inner attitudes. They are usually somewhat fleshy and undisciplined, or they seem rigid, intent on achieving their ends. There is little grace or freedom; much restlessness and pent-up tension.

Carl's stiff body, for instance, mirrored his inner pragmatic striving to get the litigation over with in the shortest possible time. His initial perception of his lawyer as "dumping ground with power to ask embarrassing questions" signaled a defensive message to his muscles and nerves. Trust cannot flow in a situation where the other is perceived merely in terms of his or her usefulness, where there is no room for a reflective second look. Nor can the body be abandoned, as Carl would have liked. He admitted to an attempt at one point to withdraw into his thinking self as "things that awaited my doing at the office passed through my mind." When he abandoned this project of isolating himself from the situation, his body relaxed and he "came back into his chair." He was no longer in flight from his lawyer, nor was he aggressively manipulating him to back off from the needed interrogation. He simply decided to be with him, sharing as well as he could in an "investigation critical of himself and his associates." What happened here that made possible this shift, this new flow of energy between people who can act together in trust, is that Carl loosened the frantic clutch of his functional ego. He let go of his vital impulse to master the situation. He let go of his exaggerated striving for control. He surrendered something of his impatient sense of urgency and expectation of immediate results. He returned to a more relaxed bodily engagement in the world.

It is interesting to note that the direction of Carl's shift from doxic confidence through the "letting go" proper to reflective distancing did not move him back to the prereflexive opaqueness of a natural attitude rooted in vital/functional modes. Rather, he as well as all the other trusters, once they had let go of whatever was blocking the flow of energy between themselves and the other, found themselves beyond the point where they had started. They found themselves in a new stance, partaking of what might be called the "leisurely attitude."[17] Much current literature on leisure points out that as a fundamental mode of being, the leisurely attitude not only involves the vital, bodily stance but also requires a "letting go" on the part of the controlling, managing ego. The shift toward a more relaxed, leisurely attitude in interpersonal trust, then, is not in the direction of restoring mere doxicality. Rather, the body's project orientation recedes into the background while receptivity and openness become figural.[18]

A shift from the pragmatic attitudes natural to products of twentieth-century North American culture does not come easily. Contemporary persons whose membership in the harried leisure class, with its penchant for keeping busy rather than taking it easy, for keeping things under control rather than allowing things to happen,[19] have difficulty attaining the kind of relaxed presence that seems to be an essential part of the experience of interpersonal trust. The prevalence in our society of coronary heart disease, hypertension, and "burnout" witnesses to our inability to slow down and relax.[20] Yet this society, this culture, is our "second body."[21]

Typical of "urban Americans of virtually every class and occupation"[22] in this country is the well-known Type A pattern of behavior, with its "excessive competitive drive, impatience and harrying sense of time urgency."[23] This profile will fit a majority of the people reading this book. In Part Three we will look more closely at Type A behavior, as well as at other lived cultural, developmental, and relational patterns that tend to prevent trusting encounters from happening. However, at this point, where the focus is on what facilitates freedom to trust, it may be more helpful to contemplate the quest for stillness and relaxation being pursued by many North Americans today.

Stilling the Focused Consciousness

According to contemporary medical opinion, one of the ways in which we block the flow of healing power between ourselves and others in the world is by expending energy needlessly via the sympathetic nervous system.[24] This aggressive alarm system of the body, with its addiction to producing adrenalin, keeps our bodies in a state of arousal, perpetually ready for fight or flight. In those who need to be always in control and to dominate every situation, this bodily system produces neurotic tension. Contemporary overachievers wear the "character armor" that results from this buildup of unused serotonin in the muscles.

Fortunately we possess as well a parasympathetic system, the energy-gaining receptive side of ourselves that is also rooted in our biological being. When aggressive tension builds, this system keeps us in touch with the nurturing aspects of our being by allowing relaxation to happen. The healing that it promotes through deep breathing, for example, allows us to "let go" of muscle tension and the fatigue and psychological tension that accompany it. Without this nurturing system and the healing effect it has on our hypertension, aggression, and hostility, and on the restlessness that seems to invade most contemporary lives, there would be even more barriers to be overcome before we could hope to attain a relaxed state of mind and body.

For centuries, meditators in many different belief systems have known that when the body is relaxed, the mind will follow. They have also been aware that when the mind is relaxed, the body will follow. Today millions of men and women are learning from ancient and modern wise men the stilling techniques of yoga, massage, acupuncture, muscle relaxation, Tai-chi, deep breathing, aerobic dance, and jogging in order to calm the tensions in their bodies. Similarly, they follow the techniques of biofeedback, mantra repetition, transcendental meditation, guided imagination, and contemplative prayer to relax and quiet the accumulated tensions in their minds. They know from experience that when tension in an area like the focused consciousness is alleviated, the body also undergoes a change. That is, when the fully aware, concentrated attentiveness that guides and controls conscious presence is somewhat stilled, one's preconscious presence, the bridge between one's consciousness, one's infra-conscious drives, and transconscious aspirations can emerge.[25] Mystics also witness to the fact that when the preconscious is stilled, the barrier between the transconscious and the preconscious can break open so that the preconscious, and ultimately the heart, are flooded with the energy of Divine Love.

From the point of view of the person who desires to learn more about the art of trusting others, it would seem that there has to be first of all a breaking down of the false confidence that relies totally on the managing ego. The stress[26] that accompanies isolated self-sufficient patterns of behavior can be alleviated by whatever type of relaxation response works best—mental, physical, environmental, or a combination of all three. Regular exercise, proper diet and nutrition, creative use of imagination and memory, distancing oneself from life's immediacy, and recalling the relativity of all temporary life forms can all be helpful in learning the letting-go process. Once a break has been achieved in the circuit of reactive striving, once the preconscious has surfaced, once anxious controlling tendencies are released, tied-up energy is also released. It can then flow out in constructive thought and activity. One's sensible/responsible heart can open to situations that include vulnerability and risk. As Ellen found, once the heart is touched, one can stop scheming and planning and worrying. One can, instead, open oneself quietly to the Spirit and his ways, which infinitely surpass our own.

What have been for you the most satisfactory ways, either ancient or modern, of attaining a certain stilling of focused consciousness? Do you find your body stiff and tense at times because of stress? Do you suspect that the difficulties you have in feeling relaxed could be lessened if you were more inclined to "let go" from time to time? Did the shift as you described it have anything to do with moving away from control by the ego and toward a less focused mode of consciousness?

CHAPTER 7

LOOKING AGAIN AT
THE TRUST SITUATIONS

Look at how your event was coconstituted as personally
significant, not only by the "external" meaning of the situation, the cultural modes that surrounded it, but also
1. by its "internal" meaningfulness;
2. by involving lived time and interpersonal space;
3. by being intimate rather than merely social;
4. by being a problematic or crisis situation involving
   some stress;
5. by forcing you to become reflective, perhaps about a
   transcendent horizon.

"Lived" Situations

In the original study each participant was asked to describe a situation
in which he or she experienced trust in someone. They were told to
reflect on the ongoing stream of their already lived through experience
and describe the limited time and space that had gestalted for them as
"interpersonal trust." In focusing attention on this one segment or pulsa-
tion in their total life stream, they demonstrated that interpersonal
phenomena experienced by human beings always emerge in an immediate concrete situation that is embedded in a larger world of meaning.
Each one's trust experience emerged from an immediately relevant
space/time context, from what we might specify as the "world" of business associates, of teaching colleagues, of prospective marriage partners,
of conscience in relation to the Creator. These concrete encounters, in
turn, were inevitably influenced by still larger worlds of meaning constituted by the culture or society, the time in history, the particular socioeconomic and political freedom available to them, the racial, sexual, and
class structures in which they found themselves. Bill and Carl, for example, were undoubtedly influenced to some extent by competitive pres-

sures in the dog-eat-dog business world. Pressures from the rapidly changing religious scene in America, with its controversies about educational goals and objectives and the prevailing anxiety about seminary life itself, were implicit in Alan's situation. The decisions of both Donna and Ellen were bound to be swayed somewhat by the conflicting notions in our society regarding marriage, sexual morality, family life, professional commitment, and the liberation of women. Moreover, each person was influenced to some extent by the current prejudices, family instability, social injustice, change and anxiety, threats of nuclear disaster, conflicts over conformity, values and public opinion, inflation, alienation, and all the other stresses and frustrations of contemporary life that contribute to the total field of experience that modified still further his or her situation. Even though an analysis of all these factors is outside the scope of this limited study, they are implicit in every description of experience here considered.

We have already noted that insofar as the immediate concrete situation shaped each person's style of trusting, it also governed the meaning of the other person to some extent. The other person for Bill and Carl existed in the business world context, which carries a different meaning from the lived context of romance, shared values, and permanent commitment where Donna encountered John. Clearly the differences between the culturally structured modes of settling a business deal, considering a marriage proposal, deciding whether or not to have an abortion, and talking things over with a colleague point to the variety of situation-oriented behaviors possible in an interpersonal trust experience. However, it would be a mistake to characterize any interpersonal situation strictly according to its "external" meaning. To do so would be, in the opinion of Alfred Schutz, to remain merely in the point of view of an outside observer; would be to miss the inner or "lived" intentionality of a situation, and its meaning for the experiencer as well.[1] The sections that follow attempt to penetrate the lived meaning of what each person had to say in the taped interviews about the situations they had described in their write-ups.

Lived Time and Interpersonal Space

Each person's total personal life stream of undifferentiated experience, continuously flowing and changing, with its temporal structure of present "nowness" and accompanying retentions and protentions,[2] seems to find its fundamental unity by referring back to the transcending self that lives through these successive stages.[3] We saw earlier that this self is a situated lived body[4] whose underlying synthesis is lived time.[5] To illustrate the latter point, we have only to recall Donna's distinction between standard or clock time ("we had known each other only three months") and the lived time ("but our friendship had grown so much in such a short time") she experienced before and during a moment of interpersonal trust. When thinkers like Edmund Husserl speak of lived time as the underlying synthesis of a lived situation, they mean that the situation is modified by the lived body with its immediate actual "now," its retentions of "just now," and its protentions of "then."[6] So every one of the situated trust experiences carries a comet's tail of embodied memories from the trusting person's past and his or her embodied intentions for the future.

Within this understanding of the lived body as center of time coordinates lies the key to comprehending how the people who wrote descriptions of an experience of trusting were able to recognize that experience amid all their other life experiences. They were able to remember their body as having lived this experience at least once before, and to refer to that same embodied self as having "done it again."[7] Even though experience is essentially an ongoing flow, it is possible for us to pick out from that flow one discrete segment and, by reflecting on it in terms of the lived space and time involved, to recognize ourselves as having behaved in certain meaningful attitudes that can be identified as belonging to a trusting situation. Not only past behavior, however, but also, as we have seen, the trusters' future projects gave meaning to their trust experience. Thus the real meaning of each situation has its origin "in the inner time consciousness [of the person], in the duration of the ego as it actually lives through its experience."[8] This means that we will discover the real meaning of trust situations only if we have access to their lived temporality, which is the trusting persons themselves.

In the suggestions offered for persons writing descriptions of a situation in which they trusted someone, we noted that it is preferable for the two to have been in face-to-face contact, at least part of the time. This directive insures at least some moments of shared space and time, of what Alfred Schutz calls "vivid presence," between them.[9] In everyday life it is only in the moments when two persons share time (what Schutz calls an intersection of *durée* and cosmic time) and space (bodily proximity) that an intentional field of feelings, language, gestures, and so on springs up "between" them. In such a moment both the vital/functional body-subject and the consciously transcending intention to trust, communicable by words and reason, are present in a living relation. Interpersonal trust relies on such personal communications between persons, and not simply on the more doxic level of vital affinity that may underlie it.

Of what does this "between" that is so essential to interpersonal trust consist? Or, perhaps a better question: Where can it be found? It can be found in the lived space that exists when two persons who retain the fullness of themselves as personal, unique fields of presence, as relatively free centers of insight and decision, and who remain "other" even though they are in lived relation, come together in a face-to-face encounter. An encounter that is predominantly prepersonal or even impersonal would not yield a truly personal phenomenon like interpersonal trust. Just as we have recognized that trust is founded on, but structurally distinct from, "doxic confidence," so the interpersonal aspect differentiates it from a relationship in which one person may structurally be object instead of subject for the other. It is this quality of what might be termed *mutual subjectness* that must be preserved if an encounter is to be truly interpersonal or "between" persons. Allowing the other to remain other, without objectifying or overemphasizing identification with him, is a quality evident in the descriptions of Alan, Carl, Ellen, and Donna. At times Carl perceives the other in a semiobjectivistic manner, isolating him by confining him to his role as "lawyer," and at one point the romantic aura that surrounds Donna's situation almost automatically minimizes "otherness" and maximizes the prepersonal tendency toward fusion.[10] Thus the interpersonal aspect of the trust situation depends very much not only on the styles of presence appropriate to the situation and its context, but also on the quality of personal presence, of ability to be the responsible subject of his or her own actions that each truster is. Yet this is not all. The intersubjective flow may also be blocked if the truster confines his or her response to the merely social or functional level.

Two Responses: Social Reliability and Intimacy

Referring to the trust in self that underlies man's ego-functional life, writers on Eastern religions have drawn attention to the need for a lively sense of this self that underlies the phenomenal (ego) personality. They have shown how easy it is for people to lose centeredness in their true self when they lapse into the ego modes of pragmatic competition and anxiety for "the outcome of their deeds."[11] Taoists, for example, refer to the possibility of renunciation of ego modes by those who know the nature of the basic life force (Tao), and who know that it will sustain them if they will only stop thrashing and flailing and trust it to buoy them and carry them gently forward. Western Christianity, especially in its mystical tradition, also counsels people to abandon themselves to the flow, to trust in the power of divine energy to uphold and carry their lives. Christianity, however, is an incarnational or worlded spirituality. Its emphasis is also on doing, on bearing fruit, on involving oneself in the situation. Indeed, at times its main focus seems to be on involvement, on being in situations on the functional rather than the transcendent dimension of life. Especially in the post-Renaissance era, which one writer has characterized as an "ego revolution par excellence,"[12] Westerners have tended in the direction of large-scale restoration and exertion of the ego's executive functions.[13] Our situatedness in this Western culture shapes our approach to persons, events, and things in the direction of both resisting these realities and attempting to cope with them.[14]

Not only does our situatedness in the contemporary Western world shape us. As relating human subjects, we also codetermine situations by the quality of our response to them. The field of presence brought to a situation by a would-be truster immersed in modes of the ego or merely empirical self tends to call forth from the other a trustworthiness in terms of merely social or functional reliability. Here in the Western world it is not at all difficult to lose the lively sense of the real or true self that underlies the phenomenal personality or identity. Unable to renounce the ego's claims to finality, we all too readily lapse into ego modes, gearing into a predictable, controllable, manageable, and functional "world of deeds" that, unlike the unpredictable world of the unconditioned, is verifiable by proofs. This world can best be described as one of socioeconomic or functional reliability, of what some would call "merely social trust." In this world belief lies not so much in persons themselves as in what they can do. This social trust or functional reliability may also be based on a prior "doxic confidence," but it is not yet truly interpersonal trust, because in its insistence on predictability and control, it does not allow the other to be "other." This merely social level of trust is not yet a situation where mutual subjectness is preserved. It is not yet a situation where the person as transcending presence can allow the other also to be a free subject, and thus unpredictable and out of his or her focused ego control.

Admittedly, a certain degree of functional reliability, of social trust in the other's ability to function for the subject (as friend, lawyer, husband, or miracle worker), does underlie interpersonal trust. Nevertheless, all said in their interviews that if the other had failed to function for them (if he had failed to sustain their project, in other words), they would still have trusted him. Interpersonal trust seems to belong to the realm of personal being that exists beyond the "typifications" of everyday pragmatic consciousness.[15] In this realm one does not relate to the other merely as a type or merely in his social role or persona; rather, one looks to the radical subjectivity of who the other is on the level of transcending self or spirit. This knowledge of the other does not appear to be merely a cognitive intellectual understanding. It is, instead, a kind of knowledge of the other that Alan called "knowledge of the heart." It could as well be described as intimate response to the other.

Throughout his writings, Alfred Schutz speaks of the interpersonal aspect of situations as varying in degrees of intensity from anonymity to intimacy. He says, "I do not experience partners in all We-relations with equal intensity, nor am I equally intimate with them."[16] He goes on to point out that although both sexual intercourse and casual conversation are instances of the We-relation (or interpersonal encounter) in which the partners are face to face, the degree of directness and depth of personal involvement vary radically from one experience to the other. He says further that the degree of intimacy depends on how "nakedly" or central-ly we know the other person, on how willing we are to share our inner life with another.[17] Besides knowledge of the other's inner life, Schutz contends that intimacy is expressed by feeling "at home" with others, although he later qualifies this by saying that the category of intimacy can continue independent of the face-to-face relationship. A fourth inference Schutz makes about intimacy refers to knowledge of the inner life of the person: he says that intimacy is higher the nearer such knowledge brings us to being able to interpret what the other means and to forecast his actions and reactions.[18]

Evidently the degree of intimacy in a situation depends very much not only on one's knowledge of the other but also on how much the other is willing to reveal or share of the internal knowledge that only he can have about himself and the loves and desires of his heart.[19] External behavior does not always reveal these hidden motives and projects. A man observed chopping wood can be clearing a path, cutting some fire-wood, building a house, or working off a rage. Only he can tell you for sure. The taped interviews confirmed this point. Only Ellen, Donna, Carl, and Alan themselves could reveal the meaning of their internal project, of the concerns that were central to their existence at the moment of trusting. Donna told me that a sharing of central concerns was clearly initiated during the trust experience when she and John revealed to each other the desires of their hearts. Ellen explained how she had opened herself and her predicament, with all its possible meanings for the future, to the merciful gaze of God. Believing that God somehow reveals his central concerns to people if they are willing to pay attention, she men-tioned her own desire to know what his project, his will, the desire of his heart, might be for her in that situation.

Obviously the intensity of the sharing of personal concerns varies from situation to situation: one expects more intimacy between lovers than between businessmen. However, at a certain point, when there is hardly any sharing of central concerns, hardly any internal relation between the two persons, the situation has moved from being one of intimacy to one of anonymity, from being a Thou-orientation to what Schutz calls a They-orientation. At this point a necessary element of doubt enters into what

is now a merely social relationship of functional reliability between contemporaries.[20] It seems that as the degree of anonymity increases, the
situation moves past the level of functional reliability and becomes one
of mere doxic confidence, where the trusted other is a type, not a fellow
human being, and his inner horizons or where he is going in his life are
of absolutely no concern to the person who perceives him.

Such doxic confidence, while precluding intimacy, seems to preclude
also the recognition of shared values as central to being, as horizons of
meaning fulfillment to the two persons who are also the projects of their
inner lived time. We conclude that although a high degree of intimacy is
not absolutely essential to identifying an interpersonal situation as one
of trust, some situations (such as that of Bill, with its limited repertoire
of possible behaviors and its pragmatic focus on his individual project)
allow for and encourage so little sharing of central concerns that the term
intimate ceases to be operative in describing them. The degree of intimacy
involved in an interpersonal trust situation is one of the necessary conditions that gives it personal significance for the person who trusts.

You may find it interesting now to look for the point on the intimacy—
social reliability continuum that characterizes your trust experience. Does
this point characterize many of your interpersonal relationships? With
whom do you share central concerns?

The Stress Factors Involved

Interpersonal situations that tend to evoke a response on the ego-
functional level and situations that call persons forth in a more intimate
mode of presence to the other both involve certain kinds of stress for the
average person in today's society. This was not always so. A recent TV
special on the topic of stress showed one of our early ancestors, a caveman, being threatened by an attacking tiger, a typical situation for him.
Instead of fleeing with adrenalin-powered energy, he hurls his club and
rids himself of both his attacker and the surge of fear-induced adrenalin
brought on by the incident. The scene switches to a modern office, with
the same man, now in button-down business apparel, being attacked
verbally by an extremely critical female boss. In this emergency situation,
he, too, experiences a surge of adrenalin useful either for "fight or flight"
response. His more civilized situation obviously forbids a physical response. He can neither flee from this tigress nor hurl a club at her. Yet
inherent coping mechanisms urge him to action. There is an unhealthy
buildup of chemicals in tense muscles, especially if his normal behavior
pattern happens to be Type A.

In looking at openness moments as they gestalt, we noted that most
differentiating moments involved some conflict accompanied by the nor-

mal stress of trying to cope with whatever loss of balance the situation seemed to offer. Usually tension is resolved as the person integrates otherness, newness, or whatever, and the ongoing flow of growth proceeds. This flow can be blocked, however, if the person lives a pattern of absolutizing vital/functional reactions (e.g., of having to cope immediately on a vital/functional level after the manner of the caveman). In our society these reactions, once set in motion, have little or no outlet. The normal flow of energy can also be blocked by rigidified encounter patterns arising from the person's need for mastery and control, by his or her exaggerated impulse to move against (fight) or away from (flight), or to defend against any possibility of change in self or situation. When the heart is set in these defensively reactive patterns, even a slight conflict between the way reality presents itself and the ego's compulsive need to dominate brings stress and tension to the body and mind. All the situations we have been considering so far in this book are the types that could have evoked responses on the ego-functional level. Each person could have chosen to cope by "thrashing and flailing." The fact that they did not opened the way for an experience not only of trust but also of intimacy.

Even in interpersonal situations, however, predispositional reactive patterns are usually responsible for some measure of felt tension. The fact that all five of these encounters took place within the human condition means that they partook of a situation that was essentially finite, and thus contingent, uncertain, somewhat insecure. Because of human materiality and the limited freedom it embodies, the other person always remains essentially "other." A vague awareness of the social abyss of incarnated differences, of unpredictability and possible betrayal, underlies every interhuman encounter, no matter how compatible. Since the human heart is rendered anxious by insecurity, and feels powerless in the face of ambiguity, average inhabitants of the Western world are naturally inclined to control their fears of relating by attempting to do away with the unpredictable "otherness" of the other. To this end, we have evolved an array of functional modes of relating, modes described by Karen Horney[21] and many other analysts as neurotic obstacles that interfere with our presence to one another as persons.

With this in mind, we can look again at the by now familiar trusters and perhaps more easily recognize where the core of their individual conflict, especially as regards intimacy, was located. As Horney puts it, all of us, in the anxiety of our struggle to be secure in the world, are tempted to replace the actual imperfect self with an ideal self we believe is more acceptable to others. The illusory "search for glory" that ensues sets up a conflict between this ideal self one would like to be and the real self one actually is. To further conceal our vulnerability and imperfect creature-hood, we repress our original sensibility and resort to techniques of control that will preserve the illusion of success and perfection for the ideal self. Denial of one's own human limitedness takes forms related to "mastery" (aggression, competitiveness, willful domination of others and situations), "love" (compliance, overdependence, external agreement with others and situations), and "freedom" (withdrawal, detached avoidance and lack of involvement with other people and situations).[22] How did these stress-inducing attempts at autonomous self-sufficiency emerge for the five very different people we have been considering?

First, we have Alan with his mixture of compliant need to please (Mister Nice Guy) and aggressive need for self-assertion ("I guess I did feel that I was the only one who really knew how the seminary program should be handled"). Then Bill, the self-confident smooth talker whose externally agreeable manner concealed his drive to succeed and his need to control the other's every move. Then Carl, the most withdrawn of the group, whose escape routes "away from" others were effectively cut off by the patient Mr. B. Carl's aggressive need for mastery in the business field was almost overruled by his even greater need to avoid involvement in a rather messy human and legal situation. Next Donna, warm and friendly bundle of compliant need to move always "toward" others, to appeal, even seductively if necessary, to the doxic level of their confidence in her. And finally Ellen, like the others, finding security in denial of her human poverty, while at the same time clinging to the illusion of spiritual success. Yet, for all but one of these men and women, the flow of life "between" them and the other was allowed to go on. Jolted out of embeddedness in doxic confidence, in spite of tension, they transcended the merely functional response in situations that bore personal significance for them.

The Crisis Moments Revisited

Overriding even the tendency to be vaguely apprehensive about the other's intrinsic "difference" is the fact that we are inserted via our bodily anchorage with others in a common world or situation that is intersubjective in character. Our doxic confidence in the taken-for-granted existence of the world "as it is . . . as I experience it" is akin to what Schutz and others called the natural attitude. Maurice Natanson comments that to live in the natural attitude is to live believingly in the world with an unsophisticated commitment to its intersubjective character.[23] In this commonsense, unquestioning confidence in the others' "thereness" we live in a more or less unthinking presence to them. Familiar others can be, and often are, experienced as unvarying, unquestioned objects in the environment. They are there the way the wallpaper or the floor is there.

This doxic character of confidence in others is at the very root of our social system and is indeed necessary for sanity. As Martin Plattel puts it:

> Socio-economic society is based also upon mutual trust; in trust I rely upon the butcher, the cab-driver, and many other citizens, I trust that the engineers have constructed the bridge solidly. This form of hope is directed to the obtaining and having of something. My "functional" trust is rationally justified because it is the other's interest also that he acts in a reliable way.[24]

Embedded as they are in the obviousness of everyday routines, most people (unless their pact with the world is already seriously disturbed or unless they are fixated and unable to transcend beyond the structures of embeddedness[25]) do not stop to question the relative ambiguity of their everyday doxic confidence. This perceptual faith[26] in "the others," this invisible rooting of interpersonal trust, is never given in experience. Trust in this sense can never be approached directly as an experience. In the ordinary course of events, persons who "trust" in the sense of doxic confidence, or even count on the other's functional reliability, do not reflect on the fact that they trust. They do not question this positive natural tendency, so it never emerges for them as figural. They never stop, that is, and think "I am trusting."

However, in everyday experience a moment may come when the taken-for-granted *doxa* is disturbed. Common relevances may break down, one may come to the limit of what one can count on, the world may present itself as temporarily "up for grabs"—and everyday confidence in the other becomes problematic because of its personal significance.[27] The trusters had unique ways of experiencing this personal significance—this problematic aspect of the concrete limit situation in which they found themselves. The ability to point later on to a situation of interpersonal trust in their experience came, not from their everyday doxic mode, but rather from a reflective moment of awareness of having had a problem with trusting someone. Martin Heidegger refers to the hammer that breaks, that fails to operate in its normal everyday manner, and thus shifts consciousness from the forgetfulness of merely using an object to reflectiveness about its properties.[28] Similarly a moment of lack of confidence or certitude in relation to another can cause a break in doxical confidence, a disruption in the taken-for-granted relation to the other as unquestioned object in the environment, to, in fact, that environment itself.

Ellen, Donna, Alan, and Carl each described such a moment of reflective breakthrough or transcendence of the natural attitude. For each, the situation described was a moment of challenge to their routine self-complacency. For each, the problematic situation signified a kind of personal crisis where some aspect of their project in life was at stake, momentarily up for grabs. In this limited situation all described their reactions to being tested. They recounted what they did first (their attempts to control the other person, to withdraw from the situation or to rationalize it) before deciding to trust the ambiguous, partly anonymous "other." From what they had to say, we can see that in some way each "internal marginal situation"[29] produced feelings of not being able to cope, of anxiety about not being completely in control of either self or situation. For each, the challenge came mainly in the form of letting go of former ways of doing and being. In order for trust to emerge, each seems to have been required to give up the illusion that he or she could handle things alone.

Perhaps the person whose story exemplifies most clearly this gradual progression is Ellen. Before this jolt to her "taken-for-granted doxa," Ellen felt good about herself. A well-thought-of, competent, and respected Catholic nurse, she was secure. She knew where she was going and had managed to make something of her social world, and to pile up spiritual riches as well. Safe in the sight of the God she imagined, Ellen had never glimpsed her inner poverty, had seldom faltered in her self-esteem. True, she sometimes escaped into overactivity, and occasionally she found herself resisting occasions for growth and change. But on the whole her conscience was clear. Then came the moment when her sensible/responsible heart was shaken to its roots by the situation she described. Paralyzed by fear not only of God's judgment on her but even more of the loss of esteem in the eyes of others, she had a momentary humbling glimpse of her very ordinary self, a relatively powerless and somewhat shallow creature who needed forgiveness and who could not possibly "handle this thing" alone. From the midst of her inner conflict, a conscience-stricken Ellen recognized the truth of who she was. In so doing, her human weakness opened to God's trust of her. She allowed that healing trust to emerge "between" herself and the Other.

Ellen's experience touches on the intuitive wisdom of recognizing God's loving providence in all events, a wisdom that seems traditionally to be granted to those who are humble.[30] It also points to the need for a faith vision of reality and of history if one is going to become capable of seeing all that happens in the context of its ultimate horizon. Ellen herself connected this possibility of trusting in invisible reality with her insertion into a community of faith for whom the Scripture, especially as proclaimed in the liturgy, offers a viable view of the world and its meaning. Without these other believers, Ellen would not have been aware of this mysterious transcending horizon that encompasses and carries all that is and everything that happens. She would not have been tuned in to seeing the meaning of her experience in a Christian context, nor would she have been able to accept it and let herself be formed by it. Her trust in God's continuing presence in her small history had been nourished by others who helped her to see this presence in the larger events of history, especially in the central events of Creation, Incarnation, and Redemption. Conscious membership in the new people of God provided a framework for trusting in the midst of an ambiguous "sacrament of the moment."[31]

CHAPTER 8

A NEW LEVEL OF BEING FOR PEOPLE WHO TRUST

In the experience you described, can you point to a moment when

1. something happened as you freely assented to your heart being touched;
2. you became aware of the other's "already there" presence as initiating subject;
3. you moved from a state of relative isolation to a new relatedness with others;
4. you felt less rather than more anxious;
5. though vulnerable, you were confident?

The Heart Is Touched

In the opinion of many contemporary guides of the human spirit, one of the most creative changes that can happen to a person is to "break out of his precarious adaptation to a single rigidly maintained level of functioning . . . [which frees] him to move from one mode of existence to another . . . [in his] quest for ever increasing degrees of personal freedom and self-fulfillment."[1] The possibility of moving from one mode of conscious existence to another arises from dimensions of human consciousness that range "from Western man's standard, technological mode of experience to the satori of Zen masters, from dreaming to wakefulness, and from the normal to the paranormal."[2] Human beings are relatively free to shift from one mode of consciousness to the other.[3] In so doing, they may also shift from one level of functioning to the other, as their attention is drawn to various "finite provinces of meaning."[4] We have already discovered that there is a lived type of awareness below the level of objective or positing consciousness.[5] There is also what William James calls our "normal waking consciousness."[6] At the service of the pragmatic self as it gears into the everyday world of practical concerns, this mode of consciousness comprises what van Kaam describes as the functional mind and will.[7]

There exists for each human being also a "transcending consciousness": a possibility of reflectively appraising reality that goes far beyond the limits imposed by the comparative "sleep" of the other conscious modes. Gabriel Marcel points to the open-ended possibilities available to the aspiring transcendent mind when he writes:

> . . . we are literally arched over by a living reality; it is certainly incomparably more alive than our own, and we belong to it to an extent, unhappily a very limited extent, to which we release ourselves from the schematizations to which I referred. . . . The great service that philosophy should render us . . . would be to constantly increase our awareness, even this side of death, of this reality which quite certainly surrounds us on all sides, but from which, thanks to our condition of free beings, we have the awful power systematically to withhold ourselves. . . . On the other hand, insofar as we allow ourselves to give ear to the solicitations . . . countless in number, even if slight in substance—which come to us from the invisible world, then the whole outlook undergoes a change; and by that I mean that the transformation takes place here below, for the earthly life itself is at the same time transfigured. . . .[8]

With this reminder of the human spirit's capacity for freedom, for being present to "more than" the limits of its embodied perception seem to allow, we enter into a still more profound possibility that opens up for persons who trust. Not only is a human consciousness capable of awakening to the transcendent Mystery underlying all of life; the human heart itself is able to be touched by and respond to this gifted aspect of its experience.

Looking once again at the written descriptions, we see that the initiative seems to have come mainly from the other. Alan's friend "stopped in" to see him. The trusting moments that ensue come about without any conscious effort on Alan's part. Carl also "finds himself trusting" the dogged Mr. B., who persists in his questioning in the face of Carl's resistance. John asks (Donna) "to marry him," bringing about a crisis moment for her, a moment of responding to initiative from beyond herself. For Ellen also, the initiative is clearly with the Other, who gifts her with inspiration from Scripture and from the Holy Spirit at a time when she is "feeling at the end of her rope." All agreed that somehow a whole gestalt of time, place, persons, and expression came together as an unplanned gift from beyond themselves. Reflection on the process during the course of this study helped them to recognize its nature as gift.

In recalling how tension had departed from both their bodies and their minds at this juncture, they agreed that a parallel loosening of the ego's frantic clutch, a letup in effortful striving, also occurred. Our discussion of the effects of stilling the focused consciousness provided an opportunity to examine what happens when there is a slowdown of vital/functional capacity. Each recognized a momentary pause in the functioning ego's "business as usual," a pause that opened them to the evocative power coming from reality. The heart, responsible/sensible core of affects and emotions, in a moment like that is vulnerable. Hierarchized preconscious modes of loving persons, things, and events of its world become spontaneously present to new directives. No longer so rigidly enclosed in feelings, reactions, and stressful patterns proper to the natural attitude, the tranquil heart is better able to dialogue with reality from the authentic and original orientation of its loving will. Open to divine inspirations as well as transcendent aspirations,[9] such a heart can be touched. Only now can something really transformative happen for the whole person. Only now, when the integrating center of one's being is open to transformation, can we say there will be a real change, a change that is formative[10] of both person and world.

In the process of human growth, each time such a shift occurs, it is possible to be somewhat aware of it, to detect in a more or less felt way whether it truly reflects the unique directedness of the foundational life form that underlies it. Certainly from our conversations I gathered that Ellen and Alan, and to some extent Donna, were open and receptive to what went on at this "heart" level of their experience. They recognized both its conscious and its preconscious aspects. They were interested in sharing some of the ways they had found helpful for tapping into the preconscious or lived self, which they now saw as preliminary to transformation of the heart in the direction of trusting. Convinced by the structure of their own experience, they did not, however, confuse what they could achieve on their own, in terms of methods of relaxation and meditation, with what they could only learn to wait upon, to allow to come upon them gratuitously as the result of another's initiative.

Before leaving the realm of the heart, which represents the limited yet free presence of the entire human being to reality in all its aspects, we must look more closely at the fundamental willing or primary orientation of that heart. Sooner or later, we must become aware of our fundamental attitude toward the uncertain reality of ourselves and the world.[11] According to theologian Hans Kung, we are all continually forced, whether we reflect on it or not, to make a decision about our fundamental reaction to reality as a whole. This decision colors our attitude toward ourselves, other human beings, society, and the world in general. It is a "life decision," a "fundamental choice" of what the world, society, people, and I myself mean to me; a "fundamental option" on which all my individual options, the whole complex system of my views, opinions, convictions, and expectations, are based; a "primary resolution" that affects all my perception, feeling, thinking, and action, and in regard to which all my other decisions are secondary. Reality itself does not exert a self-evident yes or no. The whole is not transparent. I am faced here with a matter of trust or mistrust where I stake myself without security or guarantee. I am faced here with a fundamental and unavoidable decision of the heart. It is on this primordial yes, this foundational trust of the human heart in the unity, truth, and ultimate goodness of reality, that the possibility of particular decisions to trust another are ultimately based. In their moment of waking up to the uncertainty, the ambiguity, the "otherness" of the other, all of the interviewees acknowledged their awareness of incertitude. It was the kind of incertitude that evokes decision or action. Each felt called upon, and also free, to decide to overcome or negate his or her natural attitude of basic confidence or basic skepticism. There was for each a reflective questioning of "Will I or won't I?", an anxious moment of decision possible only to human subjects who are at least somewhat free to risk the consequences of their personal acts.[12]

New Awareness and Perception

How, then, does the primordial yes of one's heart get translated into a concrete trusting response to a fellow human being? We begin with the change that we have seen taking place in the truster's conscious awareness. Of what does the truster become more aware? We have pointed out that the initiative for these experiences of trust was "already there" in the truster's world, in the other who was trusted, before any of the subjects of the study began trusting. Reminded of Merleau-Ponty's remark that "man is but a network of relationships and these alone matter to him,"[13] we see that one of the implications of being a human being is a certain doxic confidence in that network, in that "already there" interpersonal situation. Gabriel Marcel speaks of this already there subjectivity as "intersubjectivity," referring to it as "the presence of an underlying reality that is felt, of a community which is deeply rooted in ontology; without which human relations, in any real sense, would be unintelligible."[14]

Marcel calls this underlying unity that ties people to one another "the realm of existence to which the predisposition *with* properly applies, as it does not apply . . . to the purely objective world."[15] Seeing this dimension as a foundational structure of the world that must be acknowledged because it is given, he describes it as a "mystery" we are within rather than a "problem" we confront, a mystery that comes with being humans whose intrinsic structure "is already, and in the most profound sense, genuinely intersubjective."[16] I do not believe that any of the trusters became consciously aware of all this. Usually this dimension remains hidden beneath already established schemes of reference that allow people to see only what they are prepared to see. However, on the prereflective level of fundamental feeling, Marcel points to a preconscious responsiveness most people have toward a "much vaster reality which transcends the order of obvious and apparent relationships between persons."[17] He compares this common feeling of "participation" in the vaster reality of intersubjectivity to the kind of immediate response that a peasant has to the soil or a sailor to the sea—a response that transcends both utility and gain.

This responsiveness cannot be worked at or accomplished. It is simply there. At certain moments it may be discovered, uncovered, revealed as an experience persons are already *in.* We are reminded again of the fish who discover they are already in the water. We are also reminded of what Alan, Carl, Donna, and Ellen said about their new awareness of the trustableness of the other person as having emerged from a taken-for-granted obviousness. They just "found" themselves "in" interpersonal trust, which revealed itself to reflective awareness from the until now unaware doxic confidence they already had in the other person. Their perception of the other shifted from viewing him as taken-for-granted object or semiobject to perceiving him as to-be-trusted subject. This lived shift indicates a distinct break from merely natural-attitude intersubjectivity, where an eminently pragmatic motive governs and there can be a tendency to anxious distrust of the other as possible competitor. The other as subject is infinitely "more than" simply useful object or even skilled competitor. He, like Carl's lawyer, can address the one who trusts on many dimensions of his or her existence at the same time.

In shifting from the natural attitude, the perceptual consciousness of those who trusted seems to have been transformed from a stance of focused, purposeful calculatedness into a kind of "releasement" or meditative presence to the other. In commenting on this difference, Martin Heidegger mentions that "releasement towards things and openness to the mystery belong together. They grant us the possibility of dwelling in the world in a totally different way."[18] Similarly, these men and women who trusted seemed to shift from perceiving the other in terms of "How can I use him in his reliability?" to simply being open to or dwelling with the other's quality, the inner horizon of the mystery he was. Marion Milner addresses a somewhat similar distinction in her autobiography when she tells of the shift she was able to make between what she calls "narrow attention" and "wide attention." The first involves attending to whatever seems likely to serve one's personal desires. The second attends to something, yet wants nothing from it. As she learned to relax into the second mode of perception, Milner claims that she learned to perceive, not through her head only, but with the whole of her body and past life also.[19]

Heidegger, Schutz, and others warn that the predominantly ego-functional modes of contemporary Western consciousness make it prone to the rubricizing and categorizing tendencies of the natural attitude. Such a consciousness does not find it easy to shift perceptions to what is "already there" to be trusted in the other and his horizon. Carl had perhaps the least felt knowledge of his own change of heart toward the other person. He could, however, describe well his own perceptual shift from the merely ego-functional mode. He explained that prior to the shift, his rigid perception had been a kind of "blindness." He had only been able to perceive the other in the narrow horizon of his own needs. The fact that the other's initiative, his insistence and persistence, precipitated a break in Carl's static, rigid setup was an important element in the transformation. After Carl "dropped his bias," his perception of the entire situation changed. He no longer calculated how to dump his problem on the lawyer, but relaxed and widened his view of the other as dwelling in larger, richer horizons from which he himself also could be said to come forth.

New Relatedness to the Community

New perception on the part of the person who risks trusting another breaks him or her out of former blindness. It allows the other person, and the community of values he or she represents, to emerge as affirmable, as warranting a response of yes. It gives the trusting person access to an "already there" intersubjective nexus of directives for his or her life. This mediation of a community's values by one of its members who is trusted becomes evident in Alan's explanation of his basic reasons for being able to trust his friend. He felt that he had already said yes to the tradition out of which his friend was speaking—the two thousand-year-old Gospel revelation that they both shared and that formed the basis of their lives. During this experience Alan awoke to the fact that his friend embodied values and directives they both believed in. In his friend's care, Alan dimly, but nevertheless really, sensed the caring presence of the God of Abraham, Isaac, and Jacob, in whom he basically believed and for the sake of whom he had originally entered upon their shared ministry.

The communities, large or small, to which people belong exert an extremely powerful though often unrecognized influence on those who give them allegiance. This influence is often mediated by fellow members, on whom they are inclined (as we will see even more clearly in the next chapter) to bestow a trusting yes. This affirmation, probably in the

nature of a vote of doxic confidence, is natural and appropriate; it characterizes the stance of each one of the trusters prior to the trust experience.
The comforting familiarity of this stance of prepersonal togetherness can,
in fact, give rise to the desire to resist the other's and the community's
"otherness." It can tempt someone of Donna's compliant temperament
to remain in a sort of "fusion,"[20] not allowing differences to come to the
fore. Yet we have seen that real trust fully acknowledges the other's right
to be different, to be another subject who can challenge and criticize and
ultimately remain "mystery." Trusting does not consist in compulsively
moving toward the other in unfreedom. Nor does it imply totally uncriti-
cal fusion with the different communal groups to which one may belong.

On the other hand, it is possible to turn away from the community, to
cease to experience it fully, to choose withdrawal, to "close my eyes, to
stop up my ears, live as a stranger in society, treat others, ceremonies and
institutions as mere arrangements of color and light, and strip them of
all their human significance."[21] All who trust are capable of losing the
grounded feeling that belongs to intersubjectivity, that makes them aware
of being interconnected with others. Carl, who was temperamentally
inclined to this type of solipsism, mentioned the effect that the shift to
a trusting stance had on him. He spoke of switching from isolated attempts to solve the problem by himself to "joining" his lawyer and
sharing a common effort with him. In a somewhat similar way, a realistic
and balanced trust of the group or community does not imply movement
against or away from, but rather a crossing over or chiasm of mutual
support and helpfulness "between."

Freedom to be "with" the group or community, to creatively confront
mutual differences while at the same time agreeing upon points of unity,
can impel members to realistic trust of one another. It follows that a shift
in the direction of such freedom is needed before members can intelli-
gently take responsibility within the community; before they can commit
themselves to it; before they can make it the locus for personal decisions
that issue into actions reflecting the deepest options of their heart. Even
in Ellen's experience of a shift in her relation to God, we see a similar
pattern. There is neither "fusion" of two subjects into one nor flight into
the independence of introspective isolation from the Other. Rather, Ellen
finds herself drawn out of her complacent tunnel vision in the direction
of a much wider vision of reality. Opening herself to the initiating self-
communication of the mysterious Lord of history, she trusts herself to a
love "already there" in her own personal story. The ambiguity inherent
in recognition of the other as unpredictable subject of his own acts does
not disappear, but neither does it paralyze the sense of intimacy "between." Ellen's situation does not change, but she sees it with new eyes,

as part of the Other's plan. She is willing to "be with" that plan, sharing concerns that are central now to both.

Abnormal Anxiety and Lack of Relatedness

Everyone who grows up in the human condition experiences anxiety from time to time. Anxiety is the gift that comes with freedom. The cud-chewing cow in the meadow is probably never anxious. But then neither is that cow free to take responsibility for past actions or look forward to the unknown future. Immune to the problems that are part and parcel of human spiritual potential, it has no experience of that anxiety Søren Kierkegaard called "the dizziness of freedom." This particular anxiety stems from the human capacity for transcendence. Understandably, then, one of the most crucial questions in contemporary psychotherapy is whether the therapist should aim at helping clients gain freedom from anxiety or helping them confront anxiety experiences in order to enlarge their freedom. The issues that trust research can illumine in relation to the theory and practice of psychotherapy are many. Only one concerns us here: how anxiety and the need for trusting relations are rooted in the human capacity for reflective awareness and freedom.

One way of alleviating the anxiety accompanying the rigid purposefulness of the merely natural attitude is to shift to more relaxed openness, to a dwelling mode that perceives the other as multidimensional—as addressing one simultaneously from several different horizons. The shift to a more relaxed, more trusting stance, from relative isolation toward human closeness, is sought by therapists who daily confront the patient's loneliness and schizoid modes of being in the world. In fact, new discoveries are constantly being made regarding the connection between the origins of anxiety and people's lack of trusting relationships with their world.[22] Andras Angyal is one therapist whose consistently stated aim is to restructure the client's dialogue with the world away from a neurotic, anxious gestalt toward a healthy trusting one.

Though he acknowledges the striving ego's propensity for "autonomy," he also emphasizes the fundamental desire for what he called "homonomy." He bases his entire therapeutic approach on this even stronger human propensity for a sense of trustful belonging to something greater than the self.

Angyal traces abnormal or neurotic needs for security to the child's original separation from at-homeness (or trust) in its world. He speaks of the client's basic conflict as being between the freedom to live in a pattern of trust where the world feels like one's home, and the anxiety and lack of freedom experienced when everything is chaotic and threatening, when one lives in the loneliness of having lost one's home. In elaborating on this "theory of universal ambiguity," he tries to account for the primordial no to their world that people are sometimes forced by circumstances to utter:

> One outlook, while not indiscriminate optimism, reflects the confidence that "supplies" for one's basic needs exist in the world and that one is both adequate and worthy of obtaining these supplies. The neurotic belief is that these conditions are not available or that they can be made available only by extremely complicated and indirect methods. Thus, in one way of life, the two basic human propensities function in an atmosphere of hope, confidence, trust or faith, if you like. In the other, the propelling forces are the same, but they function in an atmosphere of diffidence, mistrust and lack of faith. Phenomenological concepts such as hope, trust and faith have not yet achieved a clear position in systematic theorizing, but no one can doubt that these states, as well as their opposites, do exist and are extraordinarily potent irrespective of whether or not they can be translated into current psychological concepts. Confidence and diffidence, conviction and doubt that human life is liveable in this world, marks the "real divide," the point at which our path bifurcates and our life acquires its dual organization and its basic existential conflict.[23]

Other therapists agree that people whose trusting relation with the world has been disturbed are in need of a restructuration toward health that parallels what the research describes as a transformation of perception and a shift in interpersonal relatedness. These therapists' descriptions of anxiety itself also parallel our findings regarding the relationship of anxiety, trust, and freedom. Ernest Schachtel, for example, describes anxiety as an "embeddedness-affect," an expression of the individual's anticipated or actual loss of the feeling of at-homeness in a situation. He views anxiety as an impotent or helpless experience of unfamiliarity, of the unknown state of being that occurs when we leave a particular constellation of embeddedness where we trust and are trusted. In other words, being jolted out of doxic confidence into any new venture requiring the power to decide and act (freedom) opens us to risk (anxiety) as we move out of our familiar environment (trust).[24]

Two cultural analysts, Karen Horney and Erich Fromm, complement the more genetic approaches to anxiety by seeing it as basically an alienation from oneself and others that is not only a personal maladjustment but also a result of the nature of contemporary Western civilization. Horney describes "basic anxiety" as the child's feeling of being isolated and helpless in a potentially hostile world with which he tries to cope in various ways.[25] Fromm, a social psychologist, sees man as needing to escape from his primary dependence on and security with parents and parental community. However, the price of that freedom is isolation and insecurity.[26] Finally we have the opinion of psychotherapists like Hellmuth Kaiser and Jan Ehrenwald.

Ehrenwald contends that the contemporary patient puts his or her trust in the presence and contagious quality of the therapist's conviction of personal freedom to change the patient, whom he sees as also capable of deciding to change. He calls this the mutual "myth" that exists between patient and therapist.[27] The patient who enters treatment with proper expectations and trust in whatever approach the therapist uses is more likely to break out of the vicious circle of neurosis than one who is unable to find anything about this other person that he or she can trust. Hellmuth Kaiser found his clients' universal anxiety-causing conflict to be rooted in their fundamental desire to avoid facing their essential separateness from others. In a "delusion of fusion" with the therapist, clients attempt to deny their essential uniqueness because it makes them feel alone in the universe.[28] Kaiser, like other therapists, recognizes that in the process of therapeutic change people also tend to move from a state of not being at home—from being isolated and alone—in the direction of renewed doxic confidence. They also grow in capacity for intimacy with the other and for an increasingly nonanxious perception of themselves and the world. Evidently a trusting relationship, even when it emerges in a situation of very limited freedom, can be a potent factor in overcoming anxiety.

Risking with a New Heart

Human freedom and the heart's decision to risk are the underlying themes of this chapter. That risk is central to the experience of interpersonal trust—is, in fact, one of the major findings of the study on which this book is based. Why this centrality of risk? Where does it originate? Are shifts, however slight, in the direction of trusting another human being inevitably accompanied by a sense of "suffering uncertain danger, harm or loss?"[29] In terms of the descriptions of trusting, this would seem to be the case. Risk was alluded to in some way by each person who trusted. It was always connected with the bodily situatedness of the truster, with a felt recognition of the essential fragility, the vulnerability of his or her embodied existence. Like anxiety, risk seems to be located primarily in the lived body of both the one who trusts and the one who is trusted. The feeling of risk originates in the relaxed, undefended body that is exposed, insecure, open to attack from what is other. There is always the possibility that in a situation characterized by mutual subjectness the other may use his freedom against me in unpredictable ways. Anyone who has experienced lying in the "sponge position" after a yoga session will understand this feeling of bodily vulnerability.[30]

Psychic vulnerability was also an issue for each truster. Carl experienced little feeling of risk as long as he was able to perceive his lawyer somewhat objectivistically as a controllable "dumping ground for problems." However, as soon as he shifted to seeing the other as subject not to be controlled and manipulated, but as really free to do him in with his questions, Carl admitted to feeling vulnerable. He and the others agreed that letting go of defenses, whether physical or mental, and really perceiving the other person in his concrete reality without abstractions or categorizations can leave one feeling very vulnerable indeed. Allowing the other to emerge from the wider horizon of personal freedom seems to make the would-be truster more or less anxious about increased vulnerability. Only when Carl could no longer maintain the doxic confidence of his pact with the world just as it was did he turn in desperation from his lonely ego-functional attempts to cope with the situation. In other words, he had to be almost forced by the poverty of his own resources to look beyond himself before he would take the risk of seeking out and trusting the uncertain other.

Many popular guidebooks are devoted to the art of coping, of managing by oneself, of avoiding all forms of vulnerability.[31] Our culture decries defenselessness, dependence, loss of personal control. As a society, we are fearful of being duped or taken in. We are anxious when the other threatens our personal myth of independence and self-sufficiency.[32] As Ernest Becker points out, human beings tend to deny recognition of the limitations of physical existence. When forced to such recognition in moments of apparent vulnerability, we become victims of what Erik Erikson terms "ego chill."[33] He describes this metaphysical anxiety as a sudden awareness of our possible nonexistence, and of our "utter dependence on a creator who may choose to be impolite." William James and William Johnston, among many researchers on human religious attitudes, also see a connection between attitudes of dependency and surrender and the elements of risk involved in our relation to Divine Otherness.[34] Man's recognition of his inability to "save himself" has throughout history driven him to risk the unknown in a search for an Other in whom he could place his trust.

Returning to the descriptions, we find that the experienced risk of uncertain danger, harm, or loss varied in intensity according to the situation, the biography, the consciousness, the future project, the style and value horizons, and the reflectivity and decisiveness of the person who trusted. One might think that Ellen's or Donna's situations were most obviously significant in that they appeared to ask the greatest long-term risk. However, a talk with Alan disclosed that because of what he brought to his situation in the way of sedimented meanings from his personal past, the risk to his self-image may have been every bit as intense. The risk intensity seems to vary also in accordance with the degree of detachment demanded of the trusting person. Each in some respect had to give up a familiar certainty. In order to move onto a new level of freedom and love, of deeper awareness of the true self, comfortable routines of perception and action had to be given up, well-worn defenses and illusions had to be dropped. Old directives with which they were comfortable had to be let go as new and transcendent directives were welcomed and acted upon.

In Ellen's case at least, this acceptance of new directives from beyond herself involved a change in her entire outlook on the world, a change that involved not only her head but her heart as well. This *metanoia* touched her deepest sensibility as well as her transcending responsibility. She came through a real crisis of death to her old way of life and embraced a risky decision in a kind of rebirth on a new level of being. Her newly illumined heart was more open to all the possibilities and even pneumatic inspiration "already there" in the reality that confronted her. In meditative presence to her situation, she was able to appraise its deeper meaning for her, trusting that it was ultimately an expression of God's personal love for her. Her ego, no longer isolated from the flow of created and uncreated divine energy, became the servant of this larger life. No longer out of contact with the Transcendent Source of her life, her decision-making process became anchored in her heart. She was able then to unmask the false directives coming from the culture and from her own rigid expectations of herself. In attentive openness to the Holy Spirit and to God's love for her as manifested in and through this concrete, rather messy human situation, Ellen, in her trust of that underlying love, was really free.

CHAPTER 9

APPRAISING THE OTHER
AS TO-BE-TRUSTED

Try to describe the "lived" knowledge you had of the
other's particular appeal, including
1. what in the other person turns out to have the elements of a trustworthy "style" for you;
2. what you saw in the lived world of the other;
3. what appeals ultimately to you about the value horizon
   of the other;
4. what that might mean about your openness to the transcendent.

The Other's Trustworthiness

In speaking of our body's perceptual access to the world of things,
events, and people, Merleau-Ponty describes a kind of natural perception. He says it is not a science. It does not posit the things with which
science deals. It does not hold them at arm's length in order to observe
them. Rather, natural perception "lives with them." He compares this
perception to the primary faith (or doxic confidence) that binds us to the
world and gives us a prepredicative or lived knowledge of the things and
events we meet in everyday life.[1] Natural perception of this kind is operative toward persons also. When you trust someone, you do not begin by
positing the other as trustworthy because of what you rationally observe
about him "at arm's length." Rather, you begin with the knowledge you
have of him from your experience of living with him. Here you have a
much richer source of knowledge than mere facts about the other. There
is much "already there" to be trusted in the situated concreteness of the
other. It can only emerge for one who would trust, in terms of what the
lived openness or closedness of the truster's natural perceptual field will
allow.

The lived other, then, appears as perceived figure surrounded by a complex margin or "fringe" of thoughts, feelings, sensations, and relations that make him or her trustable for any one person or group of persons. In speaking to the complexity involved in perceiving another person, William James draws attention to the fact that the perceiver takes in not only what is focal to his experience (the other person) but also, and simultaneously, his or her own field of consciousness, which contains

> . . . sensations of our bodies and of the objects around us, memories of past experiences and thoughts of distant things, feelings of satisfaction and dissatisfaction, desires and aversions, and other emotional conditions, together with determinations of the will, in every variety of permutation and combination.[2]

We recognize this "fringe" that contextualizes the other from the discussion in Chapter 6 of the lived body-subject as ground of both perceiver and perceived. It is in this living relation on the radically intersubjective level that an experience of a fellow human being who can be trusted originates. However, the meaning of the other always exceeds what the trusting person can perceive of him as visible appearance. It can be very helpful to have an understanding of the invisible horizon that coproduces the other as trustable for this particular person.[3]

In trying to catch hold of the "something about the other" that made it possible to trust him, the trusters invariably mentioned aspects of the other that resembled their own favored modes of being. These aspects usually reflected the other's affirmative stance toward them. What each trusted in the other seemed to be almost an extension or incarnation of themselves. You might say that the perceived presence of the other awakens a certain echo in the one who trusts, a momentary welcoming response to that particular style of being in the world. It is as if the one who trusts were responding to a solicitation or appeal that the other "already" is. Each unique truster is attracted by or tunes in to a particular atmosphere or aura of the other that he or she can identify. Nice guy Alan, for example, trusts his friend's kindness and gentleness, while skeptical Carl commends his lawyer's ability to question him and "get at the roots." It is interesting to note that the style of the person whom Alan trusted was very unlike the style of the person trusted by Carl. The invisible quality of to-be-trustedness is somehow announced in a unique way for each trusting person as it appears or happens in the context of everyday life.

In commenting on this "mute texture of experience," Merleau-Ponty reminds us that in a work of art the style inheres in the visible work, yet remains invisible itself. It would seem that something similar is true with regard to the trusted person. In the written descriptions each writer seems to be pointing to a certain style, invisibly inherent in another person, that makes him or her appear as to-be-trusted. It was as if this invisible meaning of to-be-trustedness inherent in the visible appearance of the other was, at the same time, a hidden aspect of the truster's own perceptual consciousness. We are reminded of Merleau-Ponty's contention that only for persons who already belong to some extent to the world of those who trust and are trusted can there be this prepredicative "chiasm" or crossing between the one who trusts and the one who is trusted.[4] Moving from here to foundational formation theory, we discover how the heart on the level of primary willing becomes increasingly inclined in the direction of a trusting yes to reality's directives. After reflective appraisal, such a heart is more likely to transfer its affirmations gradually to the empirical level of decision and trustful action.[5]

The trusted person, then, is never merely "given" as "just any trustworthy person." He or she is always coconstituted as trustworthy-for-this-particular-truster by the person doing the trusting. A similar dynamic seems to apply to many of the communities to which people give their loyalty. People tend to trust a group of others whose style of trusting is closest to their own. As to-be-trusted themselves, they identify with a group or community that, in turn, affirms them, that implicitly affirms their mode of trusting as being likable and good. However, because this circular system is rooted in the ambiguity of the lived body, it is always difficult for those who trust to put their finger on the "something" that allows a person or group to emerge for them as trustable. This preact dimension of trust is more easily lived than thought about. Theoretically, it consists of tentative appraisal,[6] not only of directives from the conscious, preconscious, and infraconscious dimensions of one's own inner life, but also of relevant transconscious aspirations and inspirations. Moreover, it includes directives flowing from the surrounding people and situations, as well as from the wider context in which all are situated.[7] Though the appraisal process seems enormously complicated when we survey it in the abstract, it is a constant feature of every person's concrete daily life, and on occasions of lesser intensity is performed at lightning speed on a preconscious level. People just know immediately whether they trust or don't trust a person, a group, an idea, or a process. They can't explain why, but they know when "something about the other" evokes a provisional yes. Usually they also instantly recognize their provisional no in relation to a perceived person or group.

The theory of Edmund Husserl and others regarding the experienced object and how it gives itself in the life-world to those who perceive it may be helpful in pinpointing what it is that people sense when they recognize trustableness "again."[8] Husserl begins his analysis of the object of experience in the life-world by seeing it always as a structured relationship of data plus context that fulfills the sense of what he calls "the same." For instance, he would see a certain identifiable trustworthy type or style as repeatable, even though the "manners of its sensible exhibition" (the concrete particulars of data and context) "were different." In terms of interpersonal trust, this could mean that each appearance of the other who is to be trusted might even correlate with a different sense for those who trust (seeing, hearing, etc). Or it might present a different aspect to their view (loving, accepting, seriously concerned, etc). No matter, it always points back or refers in some way to aspects of the whole (other person or group) that do not appear but that persons who trust can anticipate as being part of "the same" type of whole (structure) that they recognize from past experiences as trustable-for-them.

When someone is trusted, then, he is experienced as a whole (structure) prior to his parts. That is, when we trust a person or a certain segment of the community, we experience the quality of what is other— physiognomy, style as a whole, or synthesis prior to our experience of the other's separate parts. This visible sensible structure imparting the other's trustworthy style or physiognomy—this inexplicable "something" about the other—*is* the way the trusted object first gives itself to us. And to further add to the impossibility of clear definition, we note that persons who trust perceive the other in terms of their own project or interest, their own inner system of situated relevancies. Carl's interest in another who is a competent lawyer differs right from the beginning from Donna's interest in someone who will marry her. Conceivably your interest in a certain group could differ widely from mine. We could both find the same group trustworthy, yet it would be for different reasons. So the other is never definable as a typified structure that invariably means to-be-trusted for everyone. The trusted other or group is a sensible whole that emerges from a framework (or fringe) of anticipated satisfaction that particular trusters expect him or it to fulfill. Thus the trusters' interests, their central modes of existence, their expectations or anticipations of the other, are highly influential for the trusting process. The "sense of the same" recognized in the object of trust points to invisible aspects of the other that refer back to the whole gestalt of meaning that the other is for the one who trusts. This "sense of the same" also points to aspects that are uniquely relevant or meaningful to the intending trusters. Just as there is a certain way in which persons intend another as trustable-for-them, so, too, is the other revealed as capable of fulfilling these intentions. The relations between the consciousness of the person who intends the other as trustworthy and "the same" whole structure of inner and outer horizons of that other emerge as an internal one. We understand now that when persons trust someone or a group, they come into internal relation with a whole structure, a theme in context that corresponds to the lived intention that they are. How else do people come to affirm and trust the more or less invisible charism, the sense of things, the ideals and vision, the feeling about reality, the common spirituality of the groups and communities they join and even commit their lives to? But more of this in the next section. At this point we conclude that people who trust can reflectively recognize this "same" basic structure as it occurs for them as relevant "again" in the stream of their experience, even though the external situation and sensible elements of this particular recurring gestalt may change each time the moment of trusting another person or group happens.

The Lived World of the Other

Some years ago I was involved in a study designed to explore the "lived worlds of meaning" in which different people carried out their lives. With the help of a young couple, Laurie and George, I spent several months actually participating in what had been until then an unknown realm for me—the "world" of persons whose primary interest is in psychic phenomena. I talked and ate with Laurie and George, participated in some of their daily activities, went to meetings with them, read their books, and met their friends. In sharing their daily space and time, I discovered that although we lived in the same world, because of our different orientations, interests, and ambitions, we also lived in "different worlds." Their topics of conversation, the way they furnished their apartment, the magazines and books they liked, the kinds of people they chose to associate with, though very similar to mine, were somehow also different. Their rationale for eating and sleeping (or sometimes for not eating and sleeping) and other aspects of bodily care was specified by their ambition to attain goals of consciousness expansion and psychic powers that I had never seriously considered. Even our shared interest in meditation turned out to reflect the different worlds of meaning that contextualized them. Yet both they and I, out of perhaps widely differing motivations, desired to remain open to whatever might be initiated in our lives by this other dimension that was the "already there" ground of our prayer.

When I finally asked George for a description of trusting someone (I was just beginning to do pilot studies for my research at this time), he wrote about his experience of trusting a wise and technically sophisticated psychic whose view of the cosmos and extrasensory reality resembled his own. At about the same time, I received a description of trusting from a young Trappist monk, who told of how trusting his abbot was the same thing for him as trusting in God. What amazed me about the two descriptions was their external resemblance as compared to the difference in lived worlds that they represented. Both men had chosen to pursue a life-style that set them apart from the average person in our society. Both felt comfortable about receiving advice and even commands regarding how. they should live their lives from an older, wiser man. Both trusted this other human being because they saw him as "data in context," as Husserl might say. Both regulated their daily use of space and time, their meals and conversations, their reading material and associations with others, according to the larger horizon represented by this other person. Both spent a fair number of hours daily in prayer and meditation, attempting to be present to the source of their respective overarching "worlds of meaning."

Analysis of the descriptions, however, demonstrated just how far apart the apparently similar lives, and thus trusting experiences, of these two persons were. The trusted other for George was the admired product of years of personal struggle and striving in the psychic field. This guru had "made it," and as George described him, he was quite conscious of his personal achievement. His advice to George consisted in suggestions for actualizing his and Laurie's psychic possibilities, combined with encouragement to learn to use wisely any healing or paranormal powers they might develop. Success in the field depended on the effort they were willing to put forth. The initiative was theirs. The abbot, on the other hand, saw himself as one placed by God in a position that, without the help of divine grace, would have been an impossible one for him. Conscious that his monks basically belonged to God, he tried to help them become daily more aware of the loving initiatives of God in their lives. The style of his presence as to-be-trusted other depended completely on the context or "world" of faith in God's love.[9]

This notion of the influence of lived worlds is common to many twentieth-century thinkers, including William James and Alfred Schutz.[10] Both these men draw our attention to the way in which stylistic "subuniverses" of the shared everyday world are capable of being lived by certain persons as *the* order of reality in which they act and make decisions. They claim that various "orders of reality" (James) or "finite provinces of meaning" (Schutz) can not only claim the attention of human beings, but can structure their style of living in all of its dimensions. Certainly the faith "world" claiming the attention and affirmation of the young Trappist profoundly influenced the style of his trusting as well as the recognizable "sameness" of the other whom he trusted. The sensitivity of George and Laurie to the world of paranormal and psychic phenomena provided a no less powerful coloration to the inner meaning as well as to the external style of the person they were able to find trustable. This insight from James and Schutz also helps clarify one of the more puzzling aspects of Bill's experience.

Both thinkers contend that the ordinary world of everyday life ("the world of sense" for James, the "paramount reality" for Schutz) is what claims the major part of the average person's natural attitude or pragmatic attentiveness. When people tend to live exclusively embedded in this attitude, the other stylistic subuniverses of everyday life—such as the world of science and abstraction, the world of mystery and madness, the worlds of the supernatural and the interpersonal—are simply not available to them. Yet each of these worlds can be lived by everyone as the order of reality to which their trusting can refer. Bill, at the moment he described himself in relation to the other, was not available to any but the world of the natural attitude—the paramount reality of the world of business. In that world, it is achievement, not interpersonal relations, that counts. Note that in the other descriptions the other as trusted not only represents but in a sense becomes "world" for the one who trusts. Alan, Carl, Ellen, and Donna intend a human world that accepts them as they are, as having value and as being worthy of love. The trusted other, in his own situated style, fits these intentions, fulfills these expectations, and so becomes a lived physiognomy of the world as trustworthy for these trusting people.

The discovery that what we respond to as trustworthy corresponds to aspects of our own personal presence found to be "already there" in the physiognomy of the other has many implications. For instance, we realize that the level of openness to reality we are presently living will have a lot to do with the level of meaning in the other that will be allowed to emerge. We recognize the importance of living in an attitude that lets the other *be.* We hope to be present to more of the "fringes" of the other's style. We hope to glimpse more profiles from the fund of possible meanings that can emerge from him in our regard. We try, then, to live on the level of *being* rather than *having* in relation to the others in our life. We see the difference living this way only for a moment made in Ellen's relation to God. Something more always opens up when we apply our understanding of "style" as pretrust correlate to the continuum of possible ways of living our life.

People inhabit worlds of meaning ranging from the concrete to the abstract; from the vital to the transcendent and pneumatic; from anxious concern for purposes to purposeless, relaxed acceptance; from rigid adherence to immediately experienced social reality to an attention to finite provinces of meaning that transcend the merely cognitive or even affective realm. We have perhaps more appreciation for influences stemming from the cultural network of persons who trust. Their situated ethnic, religious, and customary stock of knowledge makes their style of trusting unique, yet at the same time guarantees its participation in general, intersubjective structures. We see clearly that a trustworthy style inheres in the "flesh" of things. It is earthy and solid. It belongs first of all to the world of everyday life.

Value Horizon of the Other

A person's "horizon" can be equated with the limits of that person's lived world of meaning. When we say that the other appears against a horizon, we mean that like a figure on a ground, the experience of another person or group always implies an experience of their larger meaning ground as well. For Husserl, this ground or meaning horizon that accompanies every perceived other divides into external and internal "fringes" of marginal acts and contents that surround both participants in a trust encounter. People who trust perceive the other against an external background of the world and the given circumstances of his participation in it (e.g., they see a doctor against the external ground of his office in a professional building with his certifying credentials on the wall and a manner that is friendly and professional). They also perceive him against a horizon of the less visible internal anticipations of him that they bring to the situation (e.g., they need to be vaccinated and expect he will be able to do this because he has vaccinated a friend of theirs who recommended him). The past and future ground of the doctor to be trusted intersects here with the past and future ground of the would-be patient.

If the patient needs only routine care, a relatively isolated profile of this other person as reliable for the general public will suffice. The other's background is presumed to be acceptable. His entire horizon would not likely be examined in order to open up a *presence* to the truster that the figural function he performs does not contain. However, when a more than routine functioning is expected, when the visit to the doctor has the personal significance of committing a serious health problem to his care, then the larger horizon of the doctor becomes important. What can the patient expect of this person above and beyond the level of the merely vital/functional? Is he a person of integrity? Has he kept up with his field? Is he dedicated as well as competent? Is he a man of faith? How will he react in an emergency? What kind of "other" will he be if one is ultimately called to trust him with one's life? All these are questions addressed to the value horizon of a to-be-trusted other. The answers to this type of question convey a lived sense of the other's presence that represents not merely the given but also the chosen dimensions of that other's life.

It is the fact that they have usually been freely chosen that makes value horizons so important to the trust process. The philosopher Max Scheler regards human beings as predisposed to respond differently according to their personal *ordo amoris* or hierarchizing of the world of values. Persons who prefer the vital values of control would rank first the values from that end of the ordering continuum. Beyond science and health interests, Scheler would rank aesthetic, intellectual, moral, and cultural values. Then would come what he calls the values of holiness connected with religion and the sacred. Scheler's theory posits these differing worlds of value as the already-there contexts or horizons that persons apprehend or fail to apprehend by means of positive or negative "feeling states." People, according to Scheler, tend to rank their choices along a continuum of sensible and vital to religious and spiritual values. They choose (taking into account certain aspects of the givenness of their situation) which of these worlds they prefer to be open to; which of these worlds they live toward as "ultimate" for them.[11] It is on this level of intentional or transcending consciousness that the other's ultimate value horizon comes into question in a personally significant situation.

Each one of the four in his or her own way viewed the other not as an isolated figure, but rather as emerging from a ground or whole or horizon. This value horizon addressed each one of them personally in such a way that they could respond affirmatively. They did not merely see the other against the isolated horizon of their own ego needs (the lawyer as merely useful and conciliating for Carl; the fiancé as merely dependable and pleasurable for Donna; the friend as merely confirmatory and agreeable for Alan; Christ as merely problem solver for Ellen). Rather they were able, momentarily, to distance themselves from the immediacy of their own pragmatic focused presence. They were able to allow the other to appear against the more fundamental ground of the invisible reality that represented "the choice of their heart in the face of the ambiguity of existence."[12] Carl recognized that his lawyer emerged from a context of rich human and legal experience that extended far beyond Carl's immediate need of him. Donna reached for a transcending intersubjective horizon she called God as ground for this experience of human love. Alan not only described the deeper value horizon he shared with his friend, but also claimed that it was the explicitly religious aspect of this horizon that made it possible for him to trust the "origins" of his friend's unexpected behavior toward him. Ellen, unable to find anyone whose horizon was totally trustable for her, turned in her distress to Jesus Christ, whose lived horizon was the Source of all love in the universe, his Father, the Holy Trinity, the Mystery of the Godhead itself.

For each of them, the experience of interpersonal trust seemed to demand reflective awareness of a horizon that is "more than" the taken-for-granted natural world of appearances. This horizon transcends the person's own self-interest. It allows both the person who trusts and the other or group who is trusted to emerge from a valued invisible whole that is "already there" for both of them. The truster's presence is to both a figural aspect of this whole (the other person) and to the whole itself (the other's ground or horizon). The implications of this double presence in trust to both figure and ground are far-reaching, as will be seen in the next section. Moreover, without this double presence, it is doubtful that an experience of trustful commitment would ever take place. This does not mean that the horizon of all experiences of interpersonal trust is explicitly religious; it simply means that you do not trust another in isolation from a horizon or context, both internal and external. However, it does seem that trusting another person or group is more humanly possible when the truster's life view includes the larger horizon of a whole that is essentially good rather than hostile, that can be experienced as gift rather than curse, as "cosmos" rather than "chaos," as calling for a response of yes rather than no, as inducing feelings of security more than anxiety, that involves the possibility of identification with an infinite someone rather than complete dependence on one's isolated self.

Trusting the Transcendent Other

During the interviews Ellen was the most articulate about the change that took place in the quality of her relationship with the Other whom she trusted. She was quite frank in acknowledging that prior to the experience she described, she had not been a terribly trusting person. "You might describe me as sort of cool toward other people. My relations with the other nurses and even my family were cordial, but I didn't get really close to anybody. I guess maybe I tended to see them as critics or competitors or something." As far as her relationship to God was concerned, "Well, I guess you could say I was pretty cool toward him, too. I was a typical Catholic. From catechism, from readings during the liturgy, and from a good Scripture course during nurses' training, I had a fair amount of head knowledge about God. But I wouldn't describe it as a personal relationship." I gathered from this that although Ellen's baptism had given her the basis for intimate participation in the Trinitarian Mystery, the earthy solidity of God's love for faithless creatures in which the two thousand-year-old tradition to which she belonged was rooted had not yet penetrated her natural attitude. A vivid sense of this faithful love had not become "heart knowledge" for her. Yet there had been in her bones since childhood a positive "fringe" of thoughts, feelings, and sensations surrounding her somewhat distanced perception of the Transcendent Other.

In one of our interviews she showed me a small book on prayer that had been helpful for her at the time of her crisis. The following quotation had seemed to speak directly to her condition. The author is addressing people crippled by anxiety at the recognition that they, by their own free choice, have made serious mistakes, have sinned. He says:

> Of course, we must sometimes acknowledge sins and mistakes and we must try to learn from them; but we should not foster the kind of worry that leads to despair. God's providence means that wherever we have got to, whatever we have done, that is precisely where the road to heaven begins. However many cues we have missed, however many wrong turnings we may have taken, however unnecessarily we may have complicated our journey, the road still beckons, and the Lord still "waits to be gracious" to us. (Isaiah 30:18)
> ... We must be prepared to leave it to him to play his part, trusting even when we do not see, and knowing that, on the one hand, we are not justified simply because we are conscious of no sin, and on the other hand, even if our heart does condemn us, "God is greater than our heart" (1 Jn. 3:20).[13]

"At the end of her rope," unable to count on her usual ability to "solve things for herself," Ellen found herself in a crisis. "I pride myself on always being able to handle emergencies [at the hospice] and I really had planned how the next few years of my life would go. And there I was, not only about to become a sort of public scandal in the eyes of everyone, but also I felt for the first time like a real sinner. Usually in a crisis I managed to stay together. Yet here I was, falling apart. Those few words really got to me. Could it be possible that this experience of not having all my ducks in a row was giving God an opportunity to intervene in my life?"

In this "transcendence crisis" Ellen moved from *having* a spotless reputation to *being* vulnerable before God. Relaxing her clutch on the immediacy of her social predicament, she was able to be more attentive to the "order of reality" where the mystery of her existence was to be discovered. As her pride form was broken open by shame, as she lived with the humbling realization of herself as "just an ordinary sinner," Ellen was forced to confront her own sense of disappointment in herself, her own temptation to self-hate. "So I started to read the Bible with new eyes. What stood out for me most about Christ was that he especially loved people who were sinners. He said he really came for them. I felt I needed someone to love me in spite of what I had done or was tempted to do." What interested me in Ellen's words was that the very attitude of merciful love and compassion she admired most in Christ could actually have described her own central mode of existence. What Ellen trusted in the Christ of the Gospels was a quality that resembled her own mode of being in the world. She responded to this "sense of the same." She anticipated finding it in Christ, and identified, in her own unique way, with his revelation of the providential love and mercy of God.

This horizon or meaning world of the Other whom she trusted was only able to emerge for her when the axis of her interest no longer centered completely around herself. At this point she was in a process of self-transcendence, shifting her interest and awareness to the "value world" of the other. Christ's horizon of his Father's merciful will encompassed a lived world of meaning that was already attractive to her. In two-dimensional presence to Christ, she was able to commit herself and her worries to him in a trust that she did not yet have for any other person. She "just knew there and then" that she could trust him. "I didn't need proofs: I didn't need to read a whole lot of convincing reasons why I could. I just could." When people have lived in this world for a while, as Ellen had, experience tells them what in the world really matters to them. More aware of the possible location of their heart's treasure, most can recognize the appealing style of "the same," the affirmable relation of "data to context" when it appears in their lives "again." They respond to something about the other that evokes affirmation, that touches their hearts before it convinces their minds. We can only commit ourselves to others, to a transcendent Other, of whom we have a knowledge that is "lived."

CHAPTER 10

NEW POSSIBILITIES FOR INVOLVEMENT

As you felt your attitude shifting in the direction of a positive yes or a realistic no on one level, there may have been
1. a feeling of risk accompanied by an inrush of memories, imaginings, or anticipations;
2. a feeling of commitment to new action;
3. a receptive element to your willing;
4. an anxious feeling accompanying the new action;
5. the realistic decision not to trust.

Risk That Leads to Action
People have all kinds of theories about swimming. Some say you should learn the strokes beforehand. Others advise certain exercises on dry land to strengthen muscles you'll need to use. Ultimately, though, all agree that you can only learn to swim by jumping into the water. You must take the risk of committing yourself to the water, entrusting your body to its "already-there" uncertainty. There is no other way to experience the delight of swimming, and of being sustained by cool, wet waves. You have to get right in and try it. In so doing, you find that the initiative is not entirely with you—it is also with the water. The water makes swimming possible by challenging you to commit yourself and showing you in practice what its meaning for you can be. In a somewhat similar way, you cannot learn to trust others without leaving the dry land of your isolation and getting involved with other people. Your yes to them means you are willing to risk the consequences of this involvement, even to the point of changing your behavior, of acting in a new way.

The following is a description of the risk experienced by a young waitress named Frances in a frank conversation with her mother-in-law after her first quarrel with her new husband:

During the early days of our marriage I felt that I could probably pretty much trust my mother-in-law, but the question really never came up until the day after Jim and I had our first big disagreement. Actually there was a real liking between the two of us. But that afternoon when she asked how things were going with Jim and me, I really felt threatened, sort of caught with half my clothes on.

I remember thinking, "Should I tell her the truth? What will she think, how will she react when she hears that I can't get along with her son? That it was mostly my fault? I'd really rather pretend that nothing has happened. I don't want her to see the situation as it is, or me as I really am. Once I tell her, I won't be able to hide as well again. It feels like a sort of final step . . . she'll know for sure."

Well, for some reason, I don't know exactly why, I just found myself telling her. The stream of words just came out of me. She sat there with a sort of understanding little smile on her face. At first I felt she was really going to be disappointed in me, and I hated to lose the closeness that was between us. But when I had finally laid it all out and she began to speak, I felt somehow that we were even closer than we had been before. I wasn't alone in my problem any longer. Somehow she was with me . . . we were together and she understood my side as being worth consideration. I felt so relieved and comforted. I had let someone into a very private part of my life and it felt okay. I was no longer so afraid of what she might think of me as a daughter-in-law. I felt it was all right just to be myself as I was. From that time on, I've always been honest with her, even when it's difficult.

This description illustrates graphically the risky feeling of jumping into the water. The writer compares the internal vulnerability she feels to that of her own exposed body "with half my clothes on." She also points to how in the presence of the other, a new and unaccustomed place opens up for the trusting person to move into in an increasingly self-confident and surrendered way.

Reading her description, we have the impression of reviewing much of what analysis of the other descriptions revealed about the pattern of interpersonal trust. We find that for her also, the emergence of trust rests on a basis of doxic confidence in the other person (e.g., "I felt that I could probably pretty much trust my mother-in-law"). At a critical moment, the day after the first major marital disagreement, Frances finds herself jolted out of this natural confidence into reflectively facing a personally significant problematic. Should she risk exposing her hitherto concealed self to the view and grasp (control) of the other? In this moment of reflective awareness brought on by the situation itself, she foresees not only the risk that faces her but also the consequences of that kind of vulnerability. She comments, "Once I tell her, I won't be able to hide as well again." Moreover, she experiences the consequences in a bodily way. They are not merely thought about but actually *felt*.

Restructuration in the direction of risk always seems to involve at least some bodily tension. The reader senses it in Frances when she hovers between telling the whole truth about the disagreement and keeping her own responsibility for it safely hidden from the gaze of the other. As she makes herself vulnerable, letting down ego defenses and cracking open the armor of anxious tension; as she lets go of ancient "musts" and "shoulds" that wall her in an ideal self reserved for the public gaze, we realize that she no longer controls the reaction of her mother-in-law. She can no longer attempt to predict how the other will use her freedom. The mother-in-law is now really "other" in the sense of being free. The initiative in the interaction comes from her.

Like the others who described an experience of trusting someone, Frances implied that the risk belonged more to the realm of yielding to the heart's fundamental orientation toward truth than to the realm of keeping things hidden and thus under control by executive willing.[1] She, too, "found herself trusting." She did not plan or will her trust. It just happened, like a gift that is accepted rather than rejected. She "found herself telling" her story. Somehow she was able in the presence of this trusted other to do something, to act in a way that had not been possible before. She discovered within herself a new possibility of acting: "I had let someone into a very private part of my life and it felt okay." And: "I wasn't alone in my problem any longer . . . from that time on, I've always been honest with her." In the understanding presence of the other person, she was indeed able to step forth into a new space that opened out between the two of them. The lived space between them seemed to become less as she experienced the shift in interpersonal relatedness. The new space that opened up was a comfortable, at-home place where one can be oneself and feel understood and cared for.

No longer alone, Frances was able to move again, this time through the creative tension[2] of telling the truth about herself in more or less relaxed presence to the other. This new way of being was not a mere regression to former doxic confidence. Rather, it was a lived experience of new freedom, of new closeness, of new openness, of a new flexible way of "being with" another person. It has parallels in the reports from the other four. In risking trust, Alan was able to take another point of view and own his negativity. Carl relaxed paralyzed mental capacities, got rid of the boxes in which he had categorized the other, and found solutions instead of building up defenses. In becoming confident of herself, Donna was able to take the new and significant step of "committing her whole life." They were able, in other words, to come to a final appreciation[3] of the other person as emerging from a to-be-trusted value horizon. In the light of these values, they were able to make what was for each one a formative choice of concrete directives. The choice of each heart fostered action or, to say it another way, bore fruit in each one's life.

Ellen's experience is particularly rich in this regard. In her new heart knowledge of the Other's trustableness, she decided to risk wholehearted honesty about her condition. She decided to have her baby and accept the consequences this action would inevitably have for her life. In deciding this way, she was undoubtedly following the basic inclination of her heart, the directives she had incarnated from her entire Christian heritage. Yet the actual situation with its societal pressures plus her own desire to be approved, to willfully be in control and not to forfeit her other life choices, offered a lot of resistance to this inclination. She needed a period of dialogue with her own limitations, not a forceful act of the will. She needed to focus on God's love for her more than on her duty or on what other people might say or think. She had to beware of the temptation to absolutize the willpower self at the expense of the deeper self. At the moment when it would have been "just as easy not to trust," she, like the others, had to be willing to let something of her ego-functional self die as she faced the consequences of an inner attitude of yes.

The concretization of her decision not to have the abortion was aided by Ellen's memory, imagination, and power of anticipation. Besides the paragraphs on Providence quoted in the preceding chapter, Ellen told me that phrases from past Scripture readings, including the one "for those who love God all things happen for good,"[4] came back to her. Her appraisal was also helped by recalling her church's opposition to abortion. She had been able to move beyond the merely societal or even merely subjective view to ponder what her situation might mean in the sight of God, to wonder how such a seeming disaster might serve the true end of her life. She was able to imagine, from her own experience of other apparently impossible situations turning out to be possible, several alternative ways in which she might deal with all the practical problems she would be facing. The power of this realistic imagining convinced her that there is help to be had in the world from others. She also mentioned that she looked forward to eternal life and that this anticipation was a powerful encouragement to "hang in there" in terms of her faith stance. Open to the call of the still-to-be-realized, she was able to see what is not yet, and to believe in "more than" what was visible and obvious to her at the time.

New Acting and Commitment

Anyone observing the people who wrote the trust descriptions would not really have seen much in the way of action. Alan would have been listening to his tapes and talking with his friend. Carl's behavior would have been similar as he talked with his lawyer, and Frances's as she talked with her mother-in-law. Ellen's Other Person would not have been visible, but Donna's would have been there both to talk with and embrace. Acting is never merely a species of visible, public behavior, however. It always embodies invisible intentions, it is always temporally oriented, and it is always defined by the subjective meaning given it by the actor as well as by its total context.[5] We have already discovered that each of these experiences of interpersonal trust was contextualized by a larger situation or relationship with the world that gave it a particular internal meaning for each truster. The considerable shift in inner attitude and approach undergone by each was not immediately visible in terms of outer behavioral change.

Interpersonal trust is more than just an inner attitude, however. Putting trust in another is precisely the gesture of making a commitment.[6] The words "I trust you" like the words "I love you" have a performatory quality. Not only do they express the truster's presence to the other, but they are themselves an action in that they change or reestablish the nature of the relationship between the two persons. They do not simply value or approve the other as trustworthy. They carry the willingness of the one who trusts to commit him or herself to the other, to actually put trust in the other in such a way that something really is at stake. There is an element of personal risk involved here. Interpersonal trust is never merely a detached observation *about* someone. It partakes of the nature of a "*deed* that establishes or sustains the bonds that constitute the crucial dimension of the person."[7] In uttering the words "I trust you," one commits an action that carries with it the notion of promise. I trust that the other will in return do what he or she has promised. Trust is a task that must be carried out in practice. Directed not only from the past but also toward the future, interpersonal trust resembles the larger action of which it is one dimension.[8]

Ellen and I talked at length about this performative aspect of her trust in God and her lack of trust in other people. She said that she felt her experience had brought her to a new level of presence to God. She had discovered that the underlying ground, support, and goal of human existence was loving and merciful, contrary to her previous expectations. From what she said, I gathered that this discovery had been integrated into the ongoing life of presence she was not only to God but to everyone and everything else as well. "No big miracle happened," she assured me, "but with this new outlook I did find myself more willing to trust other people, to get more personally involved with them. When in your heart you begin to realize that infinite goodness and love is at the bottom of things, then you are more inclined to say yes even when you crash up against difficult people and anxious-making circumstances." As I see it, Ellen and the others were more ready to commit themselves in human projects and service to others after life had given them the opportunity to experience a moment of interpersonal trust. Can you describe any commitments to new actions that followed upon your decision to risk trusting someone? Did it last?

The Kind of Willing That Was Involved

Just as the new possibility of acting opened up by interpersonal trust was seen to be one aspect of the larger action and situation in which each person who trusted was involved, so, too, the decision implied in this acting was part of the larger project that he or she was, as willing or intending consciousness. According to philosopher Paul Ricoeur, at the heart of intending consciousness, at the heart of every lived project, is what he calls "receptive volition."9 After tracing the history of volition (willing) in philosophy through Aristotle, Augustine, Descartes, Kant, Leibniz, and Spinoza, Ricoeur indicates the location of the radical question of will or volition. He maintains that it lies in the tension between conceiving the highest degree of human liberty as the independence of human choice, and the discovery and comprehension by Spinoza of that "interior necessity" that is the deeper and more profound horizon of all human choices. In the introductory chapter, we noted the centrality of the human heart, calling it the sensible/responsible symbol of the entire human person. In his notion of receptive volition, Ricoeur draws our attention to how this notion, in revealing persons to themselves as possibility of acting, reveals also their original rooting in the world as field of their *practice* before it is a view for their theoretical reason.

He speaks of the way in which motivation places will or volition in a living relation with the person's bodily spontaneity. In stressing this "point of passivity or of receptivity at the heart of volition,"10 Ricoeur makes a correlation between the affective volitional intendings of the person who trusts (responsibility) and the corresponding givens or necessities of his or her world, body, and surrounding community of persons (sensibility). In a commentary on Ricoeur's thinking about the will as "receptive volition," Alden Fisher asks:

> Is the highest degree of human liberty to be conceived as the independence of human choice, as man's power of deciding for himself, or is it, on the other hand, the discovery and comprehension of an interior necessity, one which is deeper and more profound than any choice? . . . Must not the necessity in question concern the relation of man, of the concrete human existent, to

some existent (ultimately personal) beyond himself? . . . [an] internal relation between himself and a transcendence . . . [and] will it not be the case
that man may adhere to this relationship freely and voluntarily? But this is
perhaps to touch one of the profound mysteries of human existence in the
precise Marcelian sense of the term . . . a mystery which concerns not the
unintelligible, but the supra-intelligible.[11]

Although not every person who took part in this study would agree to call
it "God," there is no doubt that their experiences pointed to an initiating
mystery as horizon. Trust happened. It came as a gift. No one could have
planned or predicted the circumstances in which it would emerge. Its
reception seemed to depend on their own condition of openness to it, on
their willingness to "let go" or surrender the clutch of their respective
egos.

In this sense, their primary consideration in the trust experience was
not the *doing* of anything. It was rather *not* doing, letting go, allowing the
other to emerge as to be trusted. They had to shift from the level of doing
something to the other to the level of simply being in the presence of the
other; from the realm of making something happen to the realm of
allowing it to happen. The positive activity of the will was not figural at
the moment of trusting. They seem to have been primarily open to the
reality of the other rather than trying to manipulate or control this reality
in any way. Their activities of decision making or willing as described in
the interviews reminded me less of what the psychologist Leslie Farber
calls "secondary willing"—a relatively conscious, isolated effort that
presses toward a particular objective—than of "primary willing"—a direction or way whose object is not clearly known by the person.

Farber makes a useful distinction between what he calls the "two
realms of the will":

> In the first realm, will itself is not a matter of experience though its presence
> may be retrospectively inferred *after* this realm has given way . . . the first
> realm [is the one] in which will is joined to all appropriate human capacities
> —mental and physical, intellectual and emotional—to form a seamless whole
> enclosing me that pushes in a particular direction at the same time that the
> direction in the world enlists my will and faculties wedded to it . . . it moves
> in a direction, rather than toward a particular object . . . a way whose end
> cannot be known . . . a way open to possibility, including the possibility of
> failure. . . . All other freedoms are derivative of, grounded in, the freedom
> of the first realm.
> The second realm of the will . . . is experienced during the event.
> . . . I can distinguish its presence . . . the course of the will in this realm is
> relatively isolated. . . . Since this will presses toward a particular object—
> rather than a direction, as in the first realm—it can be said, roughly speaking,
> to be utilitarian in character; I do this to get that which has its utility

. . . in other words, the end of the will's exertion is anticipated to some degree before I begin . . . the face of the object willed by will of the second realm is known in some fashion from the beginning, and therefore there is a discrete, tangible, visible, and temporal end to the willing of this realm.[12]

Farber adds that the problem of the will lies in our recurring temptation to apply the will of the second realm to those portions of life that will not comply but will rather become distorted under such coercion. For example, he says, "I can will knowledge, but not wisdom; going to bed, but not sleeping; eating, but not hunger; meekness, but not humility." He might have added, "I can will reliability in the other, but still not really trust him." Trust, a phenomenon of the first realm, cannot be willed or brought about merely by the effortful striving of secondary or merely vital/functional willing.

In Farber's description of the conscious pressing forward toward an objective of secondary willing, it is possible to recognize something of the utilitarian character of what we have called "functional reliability." In it, stress is on the predictable outcome, on the end result. The other is relied on because the one who trusts has proof that he will come through—that he has the situation under control. There is no possibility of failure, as there is in Farber's description of primary willing. There is no risk, no open-ended possibility, no ambiguity or uncertainty, as there is in the realm of primary willing. Yet it was just this problematic aspect within the trust experience that carried with it the risk element. It was this aspect that called forth a reflective response from the persons who would trust, that made them choose (on the level of primary willing) to affirm the other as trustable for them.

In the unfolding of each of these experiences of interpersonal trust, there was a moment when it would have been just as easy *not* to trust the other; when it would have been easier to remain in the natural attitude of either doxic confidence or skepticism; when the prereflective level of spontaneous identification or skepticism was most immediately available. In order to transcend the natural attitude, the one who trusted had to choose a reflective appraising stance that was distanced enough to see beyond the immediately apparent goodness or badness of the other and that included the horizon of value affirmation. This integrative stance implied a decision of yes to the other from an inner attitude that affirmed him in his finitude as positively good. It took a chance that the other would live up to positive rather than negative possibilities. It took the form, with Ellen, of active receptivity to God's loving presence. This shift to reflective awareness, this selective attention to the affirmable aspects of the other person, this opting for the self as subject who transcends the natural (ego-centered) view of the world, pointed also to the "volitional" element of the receptivity involved in interpersonal trust.

Creative Tension in the Face of Uncertainty

To act means to move in the face of uncertainty—to risk. Action necessarily implies embodiment in a world of concrete people, events, and things. It has consequences over which the actor often has little or no control. Even when the person making a decision to act is reasonably sure that he or she is not being moved merely by anxieties, impulses, striving ambition, or cultural pressure, and even when this person has dialogued realistically with the concrete circumstances of his or her situation, there is always the possibility of error. As long as we are relatively free to decide, to channel our life energy along new lines of concrete life, there will always be some anxious tension accompanying the decision-making process. This tension can be creative, however. Creative tension does not have the connotation of mental, emotional, or nervous strain. It refers rather to a lively interplay between extremes that is fruitful for life and development.

It is the very structure of the human being as limited and hence ambiguous freedom that opens the experience of trusting another person to the tension of risk. For Merleau-Ponty, "ambiguity" has the sense of rejecting the clean-cut distinction between the different aspects that constitute one and the same reality. Just as for him, knowing is permeated with nonknowing because the knowable is so ambiguous, so, too, in its most fundamental sense, the experience of trusting is permeated with nontrusting because the trustable other is human and therefore also ambiguous. "Ambiguity is of the essence of human existence" according to him, "and everything we live or think has always several meanings."[13] Thus in the shift away from doxic confidence, in natural skepticism about the other, there is always room for doubt, for incertitude, for the tension that accompanies confronting the contingency of human finitude. Even though the other for Alan and Donna emerged from an ultimate value horizon, they felt inclined to avoid, resist, or deny the surrender of trusting with its accompanying personal vulnerability. Ellen's reasons for resisting trust were somewhat different, but her feelings were very much the same.

In trusting another human being, you have to approach the other as multilayered whole. The other is neither totally trustable nor totally untrustable. You need an approach characterized not by the either/or mentality, but by the more realistic both/and. If you see only the negative possibilities of misplaced trust, you will try to avoid making any decision in the direction of trusting. If, on the other hand, you look only at the positive possibilities, you may blind yourself to the reality of the other's ultimate human unpredictability. The temptation to isolation or fusion has been called by Fritz Perls, "a suspense between catastrophic and anastrophic expectations." He notes that people who are asked to define risk taking tend to see only the negative side. If this were the only side to risk taking, people would have nothing but catastrophic expectations, and would tend to avoid risk completely. But reality is also capable of fulfilling our anastrophic or positive expectations. In risk taking, says Perls, "you have to see both sides of the picture. You might gain and you might lose."[14] For him, human risking always involves both/and. His description of "leaving the secure reality of the now to jump into the future" in risk taking echoes our description of deciding to trust as leaving the dry land and jumping into the water.

Creative tension, then, includes living the tension between the now and the then without filling in the gap, without coming to closure with the plans and techniques of making sure that belong to the level of functional reliability. The open-endedness of such living makes a demand on the creative imagination of the person who trusts.[15] Once more we are reminded of how difficult it is to prevent the will from attempting to take over the work of human imagination.[16] We are reminded of Bill who, in order to avoid the anxiety connected with risk, the tension involved in openness to interpersonal encounter, did not become vulnerable. He protected himself from unpredictable "otherness" by adhering to the routines of the social paradigm. He neither found himself acting in a new way nor laying himself open to a radical change of attitude. He managed to escape almost all the tension and risk involved in the kind of trusting experienced by the other five persons.

Thus it is possible in situations of so-called trust to avoid almost entirely the performatory aspect of trust—and with it normal human risk and creative tension. We can choose, for example, to live on the merely social level of acquaintanceship, ignoring intersubjective reality in favor of social selves or anonymous typifications.[17] We can also refuse to allow the other to be "subject," turning him instead into controllable "object." Living entirely within the confines of our limited horizon, we can become indifferent to interpersonal encounter.[18] It is also possible to make blind, unrealistic attempts at fusion because we idolize or idealize the other;[19] or to retreat into solipsistic isolation,[20] paralyzed by the ambiguity of the human condition or by distrust of our own evil inclinations.[21] Emmanuel Mounier describes the effects of habitual mistrust of others:

> But habitual mistrust is more of a danger signal than a simple, protective reaction. It is no longer solely an instinctive spasm but already a form of

human avarice. It refuses to others that credit from man to man which is a sort of anticipatory homage to the effects of generosity . . . to refuse one's confidence is not only to refuse a feeling, but to refuse effective help. Mistrust is not the lucidity it claims to be; it is the countenance of avarice . . . it is lack of inner availability, and, strictly speaking, an inhospitality of the heart.[22]

In that light, we have no other choice than to attempt, in spite of all the obstacles, to open ourselves to more trustful living with ourselves, with the others, and with God.

Freedom to Say No

For all that has been said so far against lack of trust, we now have to admit that distrust can also be a sign of health. Without a ratio or balance of trust and mistrust, without a capacity for healthy skepticism that avoids the extremes of unreal blind trust and retreat from all trusting relationships with finite human beings, our lives would not be truly human. In fact, as the research has demonstrated, trust actually arises out of the possibility of mistrust. Interpersonal trust is not simply a reinforcement of doxic confidence. With mistrust, there is a moment of real break in embeddedness, a reflective moment of thoughtful presence to reality that opens up the possibility of moving in several different directions. This healthy skepticism or warmhearted realism is sometimes the lived origin of the creative moment when trust reclaims the to-be-trusted already there in the world and in fellow human beings.[23]

For example, in the midst of their experience of the other, the trusters were able, in spite of affirming the overall physiognomy or whole that the other presented, to say no to certain partial elements of that other's reality for them. Alan mentioned that on other matters he disagreed with the opinions of his friend, because "he was often wrong." Donna certainly said yes to John's meaning on the deeper level of their ultimate destiny as man and wife. Yet on the practical level, she uttered a resounding no to his awkward attempts to fix things around the home. Ellen was frankly unable to find any other human being equal to the personally significant act of trust she needed to make at that moment. Yet she admitted that because God's ways are not our ways, she had problems saying yes to parts of what seems to be his will for her. In relation to her loyalty to the dedicated nursing group at the hospice, she also had reservations. This segment of the community attracted the yes of her total person as no other group ever had. She trusted its charism of compassion, which so closely resembled the spirit out of which she wanted to live her own life. She agreed with its general outlook on reality, with its ideals, with the Gospel horizon from which it derived its strength. Yet Ellen also sensed here the no in every yes. In her experience, no human being or group ever merited an unqualified yes, a total surrender of herself.

Trust implies affirmation of an overall physiognomy or style, a whole that remains "the same" for the one who trusts. It does not imply total agreement with all parts of that whole, whether the trusted other is a fellow human being or a group. Trust of another, then, may not be identical with assent to, for instance, this other's particular political, social, or economic opinions. Trust does not inevitably mean identification with all segments of the particular community with which one has cast one's lot. Individual members, for instance, may not all live up to the standards of the group. Moreover, sometimes a feeling of distrust may signal the unblinking recognition of how, on a very deep level, the subjective meaning or intentionality of the other or the group differs so radically from one's own that it is impossible to affirm even partial aspects that are obviously positive. Thus it is possible to trust your own distrust, to be thoughtfully present to your almost instant skepticism about the other's "style." There are evil and crime in the world. There are dangerous and power-hungry people. There are unjust bureaucracy and hypocrisy, racism, prejudice, apathy, conformity, untruth, and paternalism. The person who absolutizes trust without a balance of reflective distance may be almost pathologically out of touch with reality. Interpersonal trust calls for awakening to a more realistic appraisal of the world in its many-splendored diversity.

Each person finds here the basic option of either relying on dull, meaningless guaranteed safety, or freely choosing to risk trusting while living in the whole of reality in all its contradiction and ambiguity. The latter course is the truly human one. However, in view of our finite/infinite structure, trusting is only possible against a horizon that includes not only our finite self but also the infinite desire that each of us is. We live in a society whose world view suppresses or denies transcendent meanings, and this can be an obstacle to the flow of created and uncreated spiritual energy among us. Failing to progress through the various maturational stages can block our spiritual growth and development. Encapsulation in the pride form can also isolate us from the sources of energy. In the following chapters, we will look at these three obstacles to the flowing pattern of openness moment-actuation-integration.[24] We will see some of the ways in which the flow becomes blocked, when life is not allowed to be formative, when people find themselves embedded in deformative aspects of the human condition.

Part Three

THREE
APPROACHES
TO THE
HUMAN CONDITION

CHAPTER 11

CULTURAL OBSTACLES TO TRUSTING

Take a look at the society in which you live and see whether you detect
1. a certain alienation of persons from the ground of trusting solidarity with others;
2. an overemphasis on ego modes of prediction and control;
3. an inability to live comfortably with persons whose race, class, or sex makes them ambiguously "other";
4. a repressed but nevertheless real desire for a trustable horizon in which to live out certain marginal events.

General Absence of Trusting Relations in Society

Human societies with their relatively limited world views, their built-in ways of thinking and appraising, their collective strivings and emotion-laden attitudes, provide natural, historically based contexts for the persons or groups who are their products. Since everyone lives in a culture or societal situation of some kind, everyone is influenced to some degree by what van Kaam calls "historical-cultural pulsations."[1] The culture of persons who trust is the "already there" ambiguous framework of their decisions and actions. Inevitably they share in both the vision and the blindness that characterizes the particular time in which they happen to be living. They also share in the relative ignorance of that society regarding its ultimate horizon and destiny,[2] as well as in its collective illusions about how to reach that destiny and obtain its own fulfillment.[3] To the extent that their culture represses or ignores the transcendent dimension and lacks a world view adequate to transcendence crises brought on by the inability to trust, most people are likely to remain embedded in the natural attitudes offered by the media and popular culture to which they are exposed during their lifetime.

A survey of contemporary sociological and psychological literature on the topic of trust between people reveals an interesting phenomenon. Trusting relationships in contemporary North American culture are referred to mainly in terms of their absence. Touching on this theme of the massive mistrust of our age, Martin Buber traces the "existential mistrust" of contemporary man to the teachings of Freud and Marx. He indicates that both psychological and sociological traditions must be examined in order to come to an understanding of the deeper problematic that the conflict between mistrust and trust conceals.[4] It is not possible within the focus of this chapter to attempt an analysis of that deeper conflict, anchored as it is in the ever-present threat of nuclear war, environmental, economic, and political disaster. Nevertheless, even a brief look at a reality like contemporary alienation can open up the relationship between the exploration of trust as undertaken in this book and the problems of contemporary society as presented in current sociological literature.

Some sociologists see alienation as based mainly on the person's socioeconomic situation. Thus we find a writer like Erich Fromm arguing that the category of alienation is at bottom a category of sociology rather than of metaphysics.[5] He contends that men's separation or estrangement from, and consequent mistrust of, other persons arises from present evil social conditions rather than from the alienation from self and others that is a basic feature of the finite human condition. Fromm exemplifies the belief of many social thinkers that the condition of estrangement and mistrust between man and man, being essentially of socioeconomic origin, will disappear when a decent human community is built. One of his critics, John Schaar,[6] agrees that after the research of Marx, Durkheim, James, Dewey, Cooley, and Mead, no one can deny that social structure affects personality structure. He would also agree that trust between persons can be, and is very much, modified by socioeconomic and other aspects of the situation, both immediate and total, in which it occurs.

However, the social context is not the only context that needs to be considered in an analysis of interhuman trust and mistrust. Schaar points out that Fromm, and theorists like him who see character as primarily molded by social structure, seem to miss the point of the person's relative freedom to choose, to decide, to risk acting in the face of uncertainty. Such theorists need to see trust in a new light, not as mere doxic confidence or social reliability, but in its most human and spiritual dimensions, as truly interpersonal. Thus in analyzing the general absence of trusting relations in society, one cannot simply refer to their dependence on a certain social context or condition. One must probe deeper. Moreover, one should not expect to solve problems related to lack of trust by means of sociological techniques alone. The necessary conditions for an experience of interpersonal trust are not limited to any societal framework. As we have seen from the research, conditions for trust are horizonal, in both the external and internal sense, to a merely sociological approach. Trust that is truly interpersonal is conditioned by, but not confined to, the alienating conditions of its immediate social context.

In examining how other social psychologists approach dyadic trusting, we find that they speak more of anxiety and fear than of trust and love as characterizing the larger cultural context in which the experiences take place. Karen Horney notes that a hostile world may be coconstituted by the child's projection of anxious reactions to difficult family experiences on the world in general. Thus the distrustful person's all-pervading feeling of being lonely and helpless in a hostile world is not solely a function of the society, but reflects his or her own basic anxiety, hostility, and distrust as well.[7] Another well-known commentator on the contemporary scene, Kenneth Keniston, in speaking to the theme of alienated youth in an alienated society, points to numerous examples of pervasive distrust due to chronic social change, social fragmentation, familial conflicts, decline of a positive myth, and other alienating factors inherent in contemporary North America.[8] In fact, there are countless critics pointing to the anxiety-producing and even "mad" aspects of our social situation.[9] They see it as evoking, if not outright neurosis or psychosis, then certainly problems of competition, fear of failure, emotional isolation, and distrust not only of others but of ourselves as well. They seem to agree that our twentieth-century society offers us a sense of reality or world view that includes at most a limited possibility of trusting other people.

Some point to the fact that we tend to search for security in two disjunctive realms: the intimate primary grouping of the family-neighborhood cluster, and the rational sector comprising bureaucracies such as factory, government, and financial enterprises.[10] For those who have no access from the small-scale family grouping (where attitudes of trust can be nurtured) to the large-scale economic and political systems, trust is confined to the personal or private world, while the public world becomes the terrain of individualism. Is it possible to live in mistrust all day and suddenly trust in the evening? Many see this cleavage between personal and public life, and the confining of trust to the former, as a mutilation of the human being who abandons part of his or her life to falsehood and individual isolation.[11]

At least part of the absence of trust in our society seems to stem from a lack of a commonly held value horizon. People lack awareness of the underlying reality of intersubjectivity that founds the living relation between them. Yet it is the human community itself that provides not only an alienating context but also an "already there" possibility of belonging to something greater than the isolated self.[12] The literature on institutionalized oppression, on racism, sexism, poverty, and the impersonality that results from a lack of face-to-face meetings, speaks to the anonymity, to the loss of mutual subjectness in society's vast institutions. In dealing with the emancipatory implications of allowing the mutual subjectness of a trusting relationship to prevail, a revolutionary like Paulo Freire sees the possibility that, in restoring a lived perception of the other in small face-to-face communities, we can emancipate the ego from embeddedness as object to being subject of its own action. He is interested in freeing people from oppressive social structures via a process of "conscientization."[13] Since interpersonal trust can be experienced only when people are co-subjects, this type of trust is seen by Freire as the indispensable precondition for revolutionary change. It is also very much sought after in current international relations. Negotiations for international peace revolve around questions of trust and mistrust, cooperation and competition, sharing and generosity. Answers to these world questions depend to a large extent on the decision a society makes regarding its general outlook and world view as it meets the ambiguous situations of daily life.

Predominance of Social Reliability

Reflecting on trusting, sociologist Burkhart Holzner describes two basic types of socially structured experiences, which he then applies to the behavior of trusting. The first is the experience of mastery and control that Schutz portrays when he describes the world of working as the field of domination. The other is the stance and experience of openness and risk-neglecting vulnerability that occurs in total solidarity flowing from an experiential stance of "surrender." Holzner concludes:

> It is clear how in these two attitudes of trusting the element of risk is treated rather differently. In trust as confidence and the ability to control, risk becomes implicitly acceptable because trust is precisely in the ability to manage it successfully; in the attitude of trusting and surrender, risk is accepted as the potential of being hurt, an inescapable open vulnerability. One may put it differently: Trusting can be in the truth of control and prediction or in the truth of love and belonging. It is clear that the former is the more distinctly modern modality of trusting.[14]

He seems to be saying that contemporary persons are caught on the level of "social reliability," the taken-for-granted level of predictability based on doxic confidence. In his view, this level lacks risk, vulnerability, personal significance, mutual subjectness—the essentials of the interpersonal trust gestalt.

Social critics speak of the alienated consciousness of post-Renaissance, postindustrial man in such a way that we are reminded of the distinction made previously between the functional level of living engendered by a rationalistic theory of society and the personal styles of coexistence proper to the more personalistic idea of a community. Those critics stress contemporary persons' need to be liberated from the narrow single vision offered by the horizon of the empirical ego.[15] They strongly suggest a liberating revolution for those who have reached the horizon of technocratic society and are sundered from the wider dimensions of the Eternal Mystery in an alienated urban industrialism.[16] Theodore Rozak, commenting in the 1970s on the "secularization of consciousness," pointed to the diminishment implied in the contemporary loss of transcendent energies following the adoption of scientific objective consciousness and the Renaissance ego revolution. Peter Berger echoes his thought:

> As there is a secularization of society and culture, so there is a secularization of consciousness. Put simply, this means that the modern West has produced an increasing number of individuals who look upon the world and their own lives without the benefit of religious interpretation.[17]

This shift from the security of the taken-for-granted plausibility structures of Christendom constitutes one more challenge to people's confidence in reality as trustable. Human certainty and trust in the other is no longer derived from an external socially shared and taken-for-granted world, but must be dredged up from within the subjective consciousness of the individual. Berger also indicates that in trust, people somehow leave behind the merely empirical frame of reference. The act of trusting is itself a "signal of transcendence" demanding a larger horizon than that which appears for the secularized consciousness.[18]

According to Robert Ornstein, there are two major modes of human consciousness that function in a complementary way.[19] In the West, the dominant mode is the analytic rational mode of consciousness, which views reality in its parts and is analytic, rational, linear, and verbal. Our society deemphasizes and even devalues the more holistic, arational, nonverbal modes of consciousness. But interpersonal trust emerges in a situation whose horizon of consciousness includes the nonfunctional orientation. Trust belongs to situations that are not altogether governed by the pragmatic, natural attitude of competition, with its consequent mistrust and functional anxiety. It can emerge when the personal prevails over both the prepersonal and the impersonal, and where there is risk in trusting the ambiguity of the unpredictable other. Yet the priority of the functional life in our society seems to have led to a contextualizing of people's lives that tends to coconstitute them as less and less able to deal with the tension and risk involved in interpersonal trust. Trust is difficult if not impossible for many in such a society.

Lack of Trust in "Otherness"

Along with the tendency to escape or avoid the ambiguity and tension involved in interpersonal trust, there is in many people a disposition to mistrust strangers that is traceable to the experienced precariousness of human life. The more unfamiliar the conduct and belief of others, the more people are likely to feel that they must be prepared for inimical intentions.[20] The literature on prejudice and racism testifies to this inability to tolerate ambiguous "otherness" with its mixture of both positive and negative, good and bad. The authoritarian personality in the "attitude-toward-people interviews" of the classic study scores low in trustingness (openness; considering people essentially "good" until they are proved otherwise) and high in distrust-suspicion (seeing people as threatening; victimization; survival-of-the-fittest ideas; the world as jungle).[21] It seems that if the horizon from which the other emerges does not contain an invisible system of possible fulfillment for the person who trusts, the other, no matter how trustable he may be in himself, is not trustable for the prejudiced person whose rigid personal horizon does not admit a very wide range of difference, of the unfamiliar. On the other hand, people whose value horizon is less narrow do not so easily reject others who are superficially unlike them, but are able to find elements of "the same" in a greater number of people.

In his description of the tolerant personality, psychologist Gordon Allport says that such a person can live with ambiguity, with the creative tension or anxiety involved in confronting both the negative (unfamiliar) and positive aspects of to-be-trusted others. Tolerant persons have a broader perspective, the result of previous retentions from the family atmosphere of acceptance of minorities and fairly diversified personal experience of encounters with others who are different.[22] They see others as person (as subject) first and feel less threatened by the individual differences they find in other people. Authoritarian or nontrusting persons, on the other hand, cannot live with ambiguous situations. They move at once toward establishing the closure of a dogmatic security system. They need always to feel able to predict and control the other, who threatens their security by his very "otherness." Lacking self-trust, they seek security in outer defenses and authority.

The role of inner security or self-trust in the experience of interpersonal trust warrants much further attention and research than were possible in this study. Beginning with the early dependent relationship of mother and child, Ian Suttie, for example, theorizes that all people originally have a trusting and affiliative philosophy of life—an inner security that orients them toward being at ease with all sorts and conditions of human-kind.[23] What happens, then, to this early healthy affiliative possibility? Why do so many of us develop dependent or authoritarian relationships later in life? Again, why in the presence of others are so many of us tense rather than relaxed, defensive rather than vulnerable, preferring security to risk and narrowness to breadth of perspective?

Another strategy people use to lessen the anxiety of confronting "otherness" is the practice of reducing the other to social roles or stereotypes. Current confrontation between the male and female stereotypes and the resentment it is arousing in our culture may be a case in point. By remaining strictly within the limits of the social paradigm or situation that calls forth merely social reliability, men and women, for the sake of avoiding some of the risk and tension that come with interpersonal trust, may be reducing one another to less than full humanity. Issues of power and its relationship to trust/distrust become thematic here also. Such issues are dealt with in the literature coming forth from the women's movement, as well as in studies on prejudice and group affiliation (in-group versus out-group) and on conflict and cooperation.[24] One discovery made by members of dominated minorities is that trust is the single thing they can withhold from the other who dominates them.

Events Where Trust Is Tested

The literature of social psychology is replete with articles and books engendered by humanistic psychologists or members of the Human Potential Movement on all aspects of the group learning strategy known as the "laboratory approach."[25] This latter is an umbrella term for sensitivity training, encounter, T-group theory, and so on. Based on the principles of group dynamics, this approach is aimed at solving problems created by the defensive climate prevailing in our society and what its practitioners see as the consequent failure of most people to achieve their full potential. It consistently concerns itself with the establishment of "trust" between members of dyads or groups. Concentrating on techniques for exploring and manipulating the feelings and interaction of group members, experts in this type of learning attempt to create an atmosphere that they describe as a trusting one.[26]

According to Sigmund Koch, the Human Potential Movement uses some of the most intricate and delicately contoured words in our language—*openness, honesty, awareness, freedom,* and *trust*—in a "simplistic, mechanical, repetitive, and incantatory" way because its underlying image of the human being is so impoverished.[27] In presupposing an ultimate theory of the human being as merely "*socius:* man as an undifferentiated and diffused region in a social space inhabited concurrently by all other men thus diffused," the Human Potential Movement, Koch argues, "obliterates the content and boundary of the self or the inner life by transporting it out of the organism . . . into the public social space" of the group. Because of its overwhelming belief in the growth-releasing potential of self-exposure, the "laboratory approach," according to Koch, tends to reduce trust to the function of facilitating a self-stripping performance in the group situation. Commenting on the often-used device of letting someone fall backward and be caught by another in order to test his or her trust of that other, Koch says that this may serve as a screening device for detecting psychopaths among the presumptive catchers—but that the faller would have no warrant for regarding the catcher capable of playing this meaningless game as therefore a trustworthy recipient of later psychic confidence.[28]

After remarking that all other methods in the copious armentarium of encounter groups have the same garbled relationship to the notions of which they are the purported realization, he proceeds to describe their impoverished use of the humanly precious word "trust":

> In encounter group parlance, "trust" is that homogeneous, gelatinous enzyme secreted by a group that catalyzes the process of self-exposure by decreasing the apparent risk-contingencies. The person will "let himself be known" because his share of the collective ambiance of trust gives him a sense of safety. . . . I will spare the reader a serious analysis of "trust" and merely indicate that it is no simple notion. Even in the sense that our groupers have somewhere in mind, "trust" . . . is not an undifferentiated global matter.[29]

Koch then brings forth some of the many-leveled distinctions with which we are by now familiar, and offers an apt criticism of the above-mentioned example of trust used in encounter groups as a nonverbal communication method. He concludes:

> . . . The "operational" (or essentially mechanical) definition of trust conveyed by this example exhibits, in especially witless fashion, the deficiency of most so-called "operational definitions." . . . These are essentially definition by "symptom," and cannot be expected to hold for the relational pattern of symptoms actually constitutive of a reasonable abstract or general concept.[30]

Obviously such an operational definition could never apply to interpersonal trust because it fails completely to reflect the movement from embeddedness in doxic confidence, through the momentary tension of reflecting on the problematic of "otherness," back to a relaxed state that being no longer mere doxic confidence, has become truly interpersonal trust.

When theorists like Carl Rogers[31] make extensive use of the word *trust*, they are usually referring to the level of doxic confidence, or at most to the social reliability of someone who plays the game according to the rules—e.g., who catches persons when they fall backward. We do not find here the lived constellation that includes at the same time risk of vulnerability, creative tension combined with relaxation, mutual subjectness that includes focusing on the central concerns of each person, a nonfunctional style, and reflective appreciation of the lived value horizon of the other. Since these theorists apply their theories to the more functional dimension of life—to organizational and administrative fields like business management, this lack of essential conditions may be conceivable. What is not conceivable is confusing this functional "trust" brought about by techniques with the gifted moment of living relationship that characterizes an experience of interpersonal trust.

On the other hand, certain techniques can and do have a relationship to the experience of interpersonal trust. It is possible that a generalized confidence in the other as an element of one's anonymous engagement in the world may be induced via relaxation, not only of social environmental stress, but also of one's tense muscles and nerves. Studies of anxiety reduction through physical relaxation techniques do indicate ways of lessening hypertension and restoring a sense of trust on the grounding level of doxic confidence.[32] Moreover, as Ashley Montagu reminds us, human beings do gain a sense of basic security from being physically touched, held, and stimulated.[33] In fact, many books are appearing whose authors, aware of the importance of tactile experience, link the techniques of massage and other forms of stimulation through touch to the development of the individual's ability to have confidence in himself and the world.

However, it takes more than relaxation and security on the vital or even the ego-functional or personal level to come to the inner attitude of playful letting go and letting be that characterizes interpersonal trust. Gustave Bally is said to have discovered that just as animals must have a sense of security to really play, so men must have a sense of being loved. In the heart of man there is a longing for loving encounter in which one's freedom will be acknowledged and affirmed. In order to play most creatively, one needs to develop a sense of trust, not merely in oneself or in the other, but basically in the world that opens before one.[34]

Even though most of the psychological research being undertaken confines the understanding of trust to the levels of doxic confidence and social reliability, there is evidence that a restructuration of experience in its interpersonal and even transcendent dimension can break through these taken-for-granted levels. This breakthrough usually comes about in the moment of reflective presence to a problematic situation. Of over one hundred descriptions collected for this study in various pilot projects, every one described some sort of personally significant situation such as tension and loneliness, a failure, a quarrel, a family crisis, a social misunderstanding, and various other "ego-desperate" moments when the truster, experiencing his own resources as inadequate, felt a need to reinstate a disrupted trust or deepen an ongoing confidence in the other. It seems the phenomenon of trust only becomes focal through its disruption.[35]

Karl Jaspers labels such marginal moments "limit or boundary" situations. He describes them as situations that go with existence itself, like walls that we run into, walls against which we crash. They never change, except in appearance.[36] They are in the events of life as it gives itself to us day by day. Clearly such events in their marginality did happen differently for each person in the trust study, according to what each brought to the event in terms of biography and the like. For Carl, the situation became personally significant when he reached the point where he could not handle his business affairs by himself. For Alan, the obviousness of a friendship became problematic at the moment of threat to his self-image. For both Donna and Ellen, in different ways, their whole life project was at stake in the moment of breakthrough from embeddedness in the natural attitude of relying on the other. In other words, the marginality of the situation for each truster varies with the risk for him or her that trust involves. The social process literature sees this externally, in the sense that a life-or-death matter objectively entails greater risk. However, it fails to take into account the *internal* horizon of the person's personal vulnerability and limitations.

If we look at current research being done on the phenomenon described as burnout,[37] for example, we see how in a culture where people operate primarily on the functional level, the transcendent implications of this marginal event can be completely ignored. The term *burnout* refers to a progressive loss of idealism, energy, and purpose. It is found mainly among managers and professionals, especially in the helping professions, and the literature relates it to on-the-job stress, aggressiveness, ambition, and unrealistic anxiety regarding success. The Type A behavior pattern is seen as the root cause of many of the symptoms that characterize burnout, but even workers with a different approach experience this disillusionment, frustration, and loss of enthusiasm. It is not only prevailing work conditions and stress that are at fault. More blameworthy, in fact, is the meaninglessness that pervades our culture—the inability to consciously root one's project in a horizon of meaning that transcends the self, that makes ultimate sense in terms of one's primordial decision to undertake a commitment of service to others. When one encounters resistance and frustration of immediate plans, when one sees the inevitable failure of part if not all of one's projects and ambitions, when one becomes conscious of negativity and evil in the world, one needs to be able to trust in God's providential ongoing formation and love of oneself and one's world. Otherwise in the words of van Kaam, one's "social presence"[38] easily becomes eroded. The heart goes out of one's commitment and all that is left is the routinized conditioned behavior of another "burnt-out case."

Thus our commitment to the service of others in the culture can in times of difficulty take on the character of a marginal event where the horizon of our life-as-trustable is put to the test. The way in which the men and women of any given culture confront death is another such event. Peter Berger describes death as "probably the most important marginal situation . . . [which] radically challenges *all* socially objectivated definitions of reality . . . [and] radically puts in question the taken-for-granted 'business as usual' attitude in which one exists in everyday life."[39] According to others who have reflected deeply on death as the ultimate moment when trust is tested, the level of trust that makes sense to the dying person is always the level that we have been describing as "interpersonal." The moment of death seems to be experienced as a lived breaking away or detachment from the purposefulness and calculation of the "natural attitude" that characterizes life in the world. It is a moment that calls for a meaningful value horizon, an otherness that corresponds to the dying person's own most trusted ultimate values. Indeed, particularly in our culture, the breakthrough of death, with all its ambiguity and darkness, does set a priority on the experience of interpersonal trust.[40]

CHAPTER 12

DEVELOPMENTAL ASPECTS OF TRUSTING

What maturational period were you in when the incident you described occurred? If, for example, you were involved in a "passage" from one phase to another, i.e., middle-age crisis, or were facing a predominantly functional period, such as the thirties,

1. how did the conflict between your empirical self and your real self emerge?
2. can you trace the "good enough" basis in the past for your present trust capacity?
3. do you detect natural anxieties in yourself regarding security or the future?
4. do you find yourself stuck in a certain developmental stage?

The Present Empirical Identity

Closely allied to the world view of a culture or society are the ways the persons in it view the processes of development and maturation, of growing up and growing old. All kinds of values are attached by various societies to the different phases of these processes: the vital, expansive, curious, unformed time of childhood; the idealistic, rebellious, dreamy poetry of youth; the young adult's struggle to get ahead, to make good, to find a spouse, raise a family, succeed in a job or career; the middle-age responsibilities of caring for others and using power in the service of others that coincide with aging and facing one's limits; the gradual onset of old age with infirmities of the body and the desire to hand on what has been learned to coming generations. In some cultures, the older and more experienced one is, the more one is revered as an asset to the tribe or society. In others, the opposite is true. In twentieth-century North America, to judge from popular images in the media, our society bestows its favor on people in their early thirties—that is, those who have attained the stage of young adulthood but have not yet moved on to what is known as middle age.

As van Kaam points out,[1] this is the time when physical prowess and energy are high, when one is probably most productive as a member of the work force, making a substantial contribution to the economy and to society. Ambitions may motivate the executive will into exclusive focusing on achievement, both in work and in social life. Aspirations from an earlier period of life may be forgotten as competition and perfectionism take over. The lived style of young adulthood resembles the culture that produces it. The empirical current identity a person has attained by age thirty points both forward and backward, into the future and back to childhood. The present self of each person who wrote a description of having trusted someone is, as we have already seen,[2] coconstituted as social identity by the very fact of having been born into a human family. This insertion via the family into a culture means that prior to any choosing, persons are assigned a certain provisional role or identity. So each person is automatically identified from the beginning as the oldest or the youngest, the most like his father, the slowest, the strongest, or whatever vital/functional tags awaited him or her at birth.

When children learn to talk, they insert themselves into the symbolic order, referring to and identifying themselves with the "me" who had been thus constituted by the family and significant others.[3] They unquestioningly take over attitudes, gestures, habits, and language from the community that surrounds them. For instance, in our culture, boy babies grow up under a very different set of expectations and hopes than do girl babies. This difference becomes a matter of concern when it leads to a history of unjust treatment and exclusion of one sex from the goods that society has to offer.[4] Besides absorbing the culture's general sexual orientation, children also take in its unspoken functional and more personalized assumptions. The more pragmatic the character of these assumptions, the more likely it is that children will model their self projects and life projects in that direction. Recall Alan's present identity or "nice guy" social self; Donna's ambition to always play the role of "peacemaker"; Carl's need to "succeed in business by mastering the situation"; Ellen's project of preserving her role as the "perfect nurse."

Present empirical identity, then, rather narrowly articulates the person's presence to a world of practical purposes to be accomplished, of merely partial aspects of the whole. It limits his or her modes of operation to the more pragmatic ego-functional order. It does not encompass either the whole person or the horizon of the transcendent aspiring self.[5] Yet one's present identity does tend to organize one's world and confine one to the limits of the vital/functional body, which takes the initiative in standing out over against the immediacy of practical concerns. Bill exemplified this functionally oriented style of presence. Involved in the typical concerns of the young adult to make an impression, get a job, and pursue a career, he was also at a stage in life when the invisible transcendent meanings of any situation may be repressed in favor of the immediately visible task at hand.

Fortunately, even for persons like that, there usually comes a moment that forces each one to reflect on whether or not his or her present identity corresponds to what thinkers throughout the centuries have called the real or the true self. In Chapter 3, we pointed to this underlying soul or foundational life form of whose existence most people are unaware. Yet each of the stages or periods of human maturation can be valued as a necessary step in the process of unveiling this hidden but nevertheless real and unique foundational form of the person. A Christian perspective on the veiled image of God seeking to be released and to permeate the whole of each person's life[6] makes possible a transcendent/pneumatic view of the person's developmental history as well. In this horizon, each period of life, whether it be childhood, youth, adulthood, or old age, becomes a gift and a challenge. Each phase will have a value in itself. Each will be worth living fully as a preparation for the next. Christians, as they pass from one stage to the next, are not formed only by what the culture says. They can freely choose their attitude toward both past and future passages. They can fully live their present age in the trust that it, too, is simply a part of the life process leading to the final unveiling of the unique image of God "already there" in the depths of their being. The inability to define oneself in terms that transcend one's empirical identity, and thus accept and live gracefully each maturational stage as it comes, can constitute an obstacle not only to trusting but also to living one's life to the full.

The Past as Basis for Trust

Embodied doxic confidence, the basis of any person's capacity for trusting, presupposes a more or less normal physiopsychical development. Certain psychosomatic preconditions must be met if the personal innate dispositions in this regard are not to be impaired from the beginning.[7] Before birth, hereditary obstacles such as congenital abnormalities, physical limitations, or depressive predispositions may be passed on to the child. There may also be intrauterine influences in the form of the mother's nutritional deficiencies or diseases, her age, her emotional state, or her addiction to certain drugs. There may be injuries from the birth process itself. The baby may also lack organic resilience, intellectual endowment, or coordination, or may simply have problems with bodily sensitivity, tempo and rhythm, activity and vigor. All these things can complicate the earliest stages of the trust/mistrust phase of development. Emotional deprivation may be experienced in the form of maternal neglect or pervading family anxiety; illness, accident, dietary deficiency, or poor housing may constitute obstacles to the infant's physical well-being, to the sensible feeling that "all's right with the world."

This basic sense of the world, this vital predisposition of basic at-homeness or basic alienation that develops in infancy, is regarded by developmental psychologists as the fundamental basis of the person's later attempts to trust others. Following Erikson, the majority see this earliest orientation toward basic trust or basic mistrust as corresponding closely with everyday notions of optimism and pessimism.[8] Stressing past retentions of people's temporality, developmental theorists give detailed descriptions of past encounter history, especially as regards reactions in infancy to mothering persons, doctors, and strangers. Evidently they all agree on the importance of those early feelings of situatedness in a community of others who do or do not make the world a stable place that can be relied on to fulfill one's needs. They cite this primordial sense of the world as dependable situation, as the first component of a healthy and confident personality.

In relation to this emphasis on the interformative dialogue between the developing person and the community, the developmentalists are aware of the influence of the child's cultural heritage on his or her trust capacity. They point to the effects of universals like systems of family life, language, emotions, use of time and space, and taken-for-granted assumptions of the subculture to which the growing child belongs. They examine its attitudes toward sex and other interrelational questions, and are critical of the disrupting effects of low status accompanied by prejudice and discrimination, which can jar the child's unfolding sense of trust in a basically friendly world. They claim that just as there is no adult (and therefore no person who trusts/mistrusts) who does not embody a vital predisposition, so is there no adult (or truster/distruster) who is culture-free. The vast bulk of developmental literature, however, is devoted to the origins of basic trust in the relationship of love between the mother and child.

Through harmony with the maternal environment, they see the child as being bodily in touch with a whole invisible world of persons, events, and things. Like the person who trusts and the trusted other, the mother and child, by virtue of the harmonious mediation of their lived bodies, share a primary intersubjective "whole" or world. Although they would not use this terminology, the developmental experts testify to the mute harmony or chiasm between mother and child, whose result is the doxic confidence described by Erik Erikson: "Love and hunger . . . meet at a woman's breast, thus preparing the great alternative of basic psychosocial attitudes, trust and mistrust, which the maternal environment must balance in favor of trust and thus a lifelong hope in benevolent fate."[9] Other psychoanalysts variously describe the newborn infant as being "symbiotically identified" with the mother, undifferentially "embedded in the environment of the mother," clinging to the familiarity of this "embeddedness affect," and later defensively attached to the mother by "safety and security needs."[10] Prereflexive confidence in the mothering "other" is further described by Angyal as the original unity, the sense of belonging or "homonomy" that gives the trusting person a sense of the world as his or her home.

The concept from phenomenology that comes to mind here is "body memory." All the literature on the importance of maternal care in the earliest years emphasizes the significance of the touching, handling, fondling, and cuddling that happens to the baby, particularly when it is being held and breast-fed. The infant's awareness of the touch of the mother's body constitutes its first object relation; it is the quality of this first skin-to-skin contact with the world that remains with it and provides an essential source of comfort, security, and warmth long after the actual moments of contact have passed.[11] It is partly from this experience that the person's primordial openness or mood, his or her basic predisposition, is said to arise. This vital tending, this bodily feeling or innermost mood that shapes a person's "sense of the world's presence," is captured first in the lived body that "remembers" its primordial pact with the world in a way that the conscious mind cannot. Thus the relating body becomes the source of doxic confidence, of basic trust; therefore a better understanding on the part of psychoanalytic theorists of the concept of "lived body memory" may be in order in the study of early object relations and their influence on later experiences of trust.

This first naïve confidence is what opens children to the world, giving them access to its richness by relieving the anxiety that accompanies exploration of what is new and unfamiliar. Psychoanalysts argue that the child who is relatively free from having to seek mother substitutes is able to risk moving out into other relationships with his or her world. Yet this freedom is still very immature and untried. Eventually the child must give way to the adult who, having faced some crises, has moved to a new more mature level of trusting. The level of bodily synthesis opening onto an "already there intersubjectivity" provides a basis for, but is not identical with, the lived experience of interpersonal trust between two mature adults. It is also clear that very few people in our society have had a perfect foundation of doxic confidence on which to build. Most people who are functioning and relating in the world at present have had a "good enough" basis, but no one had an absolutely flawless mothering environment. We should not be surprised to find ourselves with some experienced "holes" to be filled, some restless longing in our lives for "more." For most of us, trust in life has emerged within a somewhat flawed human condition, as a gift that grows through being practiced in a broken world.

In speaking of the obstacles to the flow of divine life energy that can be engendered by deformative developmental history, Adrian van Kaam focuses on the "withholding of the foundational formative triad of human and Christian faith, hope and love."[12] He says that this withholding in regard to the dignity and mystery of the child's foundational life form manifests itself early in life: parents or significant others are unable or unwilling to show genuine faith, hope, and love in vital and functional acts and gestures that manifest to the infant that he or she is worthwhile and loved. Whatever the causes of this withholding, its effects are devastating for the child. He or she may spend a lifetime struggling with excessive need for vital manifestations of love and acceptance. Not only are the person's relations with other people affected; his or her capacity for trusting confidence in God's love may also be diminished. Moreover, van Kaam points to possible deformative reactions and responses to this withholding in terms of perfectionism, attitudes of withdrawal, fear, and subservience or demanding behavior. Both he and the analysts agree that psychotherapy may be necessary to dispel these people's illusions and to provide them with the faith, hope, and love they have been missing since childhood.

The Future, Anxiety, and Security

When psychoanalysts think about trust, they tend to focus mainly on the past. Yet, as dialogue between necessity and possibility, human beings must also be seen in their freedom to grow toward the future. Infants, if they are to develop, must leave their mothers, must at a certain point separate from their state of embeddedness in the mother-child relation. There is much in the psychoanalytic literature about the anxiety engendered by this separation. Psychoanalysts see it as the first or "nuclear" conflict in human life. Described variously as a struggle between embeddedness and growth, between desire for homonomy and striving for autonomy, between embeddedness affect and activity affect, between safety needs and growth needs, the fundamental life conflict turns out to be essentially between basic trust and basic mistrust. At the origin of all human anxiety, according to these theorists, is the first great separation experience of birth. Anxious, tense mothers who, by withholding the fundamental triad, cause the baby's separation from trusting security in early infancy, are blamed for unconsciously engendering later anxiety in the growing child.

A fairly large number of psychoanlytic theorists see trust, in the form of security between mother and child, as an absolute necessity for later growth and development.[13] However, in speaking to the question of whether lack of security due to deprivation of maternal care in childhood can result in future neurotic disturbances, J. H. van den Berg says there is no evidence as yet, even from authorities like Spitz and Bowlby, for the widely accepted opinion that this *should* be the case.[14] Still, no one would deny the findings of either Freud or Erikson on the necessity for a predominance of bodily based basic trust (or doxic confidence) over the anxiety-provoking vulnerability of mistrust.[15] Freud recognized the tremendous significance of the first dependencies and entanglements in infancy and childhood, and Erikson widened this recognition to include the influence of society. However, neither man seems to have questioned his conclusion that the mothering person is the sole source of this basic trust; that she alone is responsible for the infant's sense of the world's presence as affirmable or not.

Erikson himself admits that the mother does exist in a broader invisible horizon of her own past experiences, the values of her society, and the enveloping world view shared by members of that society. He comments:

> Biological motherhood needs at least three links with social experience; the mother's past experience of being mothered; a conception of motherhood shared with trustworthy contemporary surroundings; and an all-enveloping world-image tying past, present and future into a convincing pattern of providence. Only thus can mothers provide.[16]

Obviously both mother and child exist in a larger horizon, a whole or ground against which the mother is only figural and from which she, too, receives her meaning. So there is room here for a basic self-experience of identity for the child in terms of his or her lived connection to the whole, as well as in relation to his or her lived connectedness with the mother. As the mother is figure against an invisible horizon of meaning, so, too, is the child, although his or her experience of the whole is implicit in the earliest years. One has the impression that many mothers in our society, where popular psychology penetrates everywhere, are laboring under a false sense of guilt for not having been able to personally provide this "whole" for their children.

The experts have left the impression that the mother, in isolation from her own ground, has to be the absolute, irreplaceable, ultimate horizon of her children's existence. In giving such an impression, they also absolutize the consequences of separation from, or unhappy experiences in relation to, the maternal environment. Caught in a dimension that might be termed *absolutized ego psychology,* these writers are unable to see that there is no strictly causal or determined explanation for either trust or lack of trust. They seem not to suspect that there may be a horizon or context that goes beyond that of mere sociopsychological explanations. The basic experience of both infant and adult includes the possibility of belonging to a whole that is greater than any of its isolated parts. Otherwise the entire realm of religious and mystical experience can be precluded or simply reduced to a manifestation of the unconscious search for a mother or father figure.[17]

Following this first conflict, children must face the inevitable process of separation or distinction between the ego or "I" and the world, sometimes called the "no" stage. Again, anxiety emerges as children struggle with conflicting desires to cling to the familiar (breast, mother, home, neighborhood) and to strive for the new (eating and walking alone, venturing beyond the known people and places, going to school, making new friends). If the earliest relationships have produced a prevailing feeling in the children that the world is alien and not their home, but rather a hostile, anxiety-provoking environment where one must always be on the defensive against threats to one's security, children will automatically distrust the new and strive to avoid risk. They may become fixated in one stage and never move toward the future by fulfilling its maturational tasks. Anxiety over the change that accompanies moving from one maturational period to another may become an obstacle to growth.

Like risk, this anxiety over maturational changes is rooted in the body. As people mature through the growth stages of childhood and adolescence toward middle and old age, their bodies undergo a series of shifts. The well-known "crises" of adolescence and middle age, for example, focus on responses to bewildering bodily changes announcing a marked increase or decrease in vital/sexual or functional energy. An experience of illness can have the same effect, and meet with similar responses ranging from curiosity and confusion to resistance, denial, and even flight. Immature people tend to deny or artificially cover up vital changes. A typical response to the transcendence crisis of middle age, for example, consists for some contemporary men and women in a desperate escape into youthful clothing, occupations, and mannerisms. In the face of cultural dislike of growing older, they are unable to trustfully accept this new life stage and deal with it in the horizon of God's providential care for the entirety of their personal historical lifetime. This inability to trustingly affirm vital changes in one's life parallels the inability to accept other forms of newness, whether events, persons, or things. Yet it is these very situated changes that afford the openness moments in which we can grow to new stages of awareness and integration, in which our hearts can be touched by a New Creation.[18]

Van Kaam draws attention to the fact that the formative community in which persons grow and develop may err not only on the side of with-holding the foundational formative triad. It may also err in providing too much direction, an excessive protection for the unfolding human beings in its care.[19] Out of their own anxiety and distrust with regard to vital impulses and functional ambitions, or out of an excessive need to domi-nate and control all details of formation, a family, a subculture, an ethnic, or a religious group may engender compulsive perfectionism and other deformations in their young people. Abiding distrust of one's vital spon-taneity and alienated compulsive ambition for perfectionistic success are typical consequence of this erroneous view of formation. We find the consequences of these unfree approaches to human growth and develop-ment lived out by anxious adults, whose fear-ridden lives bear witness to the narrow horizons of their original formative/deformative communi-ties. In the next section we will look more closely at how obstacles to growth and appraisal against a truly transcendent horizon arise mainly from fixation on the vital/functional level of development.

Maturational Fixations

Different modes of appraisal accompany different maturational phases. Infants, for instance, are guided in their reactions to people, things, and events by the demands of their body's organismic needs. They live on the level of what the analysts call oral incorporation. They want to swallow the world, or at least put as much of it as possible into their mouths. As they grow, children's appraisal of what is good for them is guided for the most part by what their parents have told them to do or not to do. A stage beyond mere vital absorption, young children are permeated by the ex-pectations of their parents, whom they desire to imitate in as many ways as possible. Schoolchildren have reached a still further stage in that they are directed in their choices by the social situation as well as by their playfellows and schoolmates. However, this level of appraisal still origi-nates on the more or less vital/functional dimension of their existence.

In adolescence, people reach the stage where they can begin to select more independently from reality as it presents itself to them. Although still very dependent upon what others think and say, adolescents and young adults are more consciously aware of themselves as separate per-sons whose individual vital and psychological makeup must be taken into account. This more personal, though still somewhat functional, level of appraisal opens them gradually to transcendent participation, to allowing for the appeal of transcendent aspirations and pneumatic inspirations. If the flow of development is not blocked or fixated at any stage, eventually human hearts reach the point where they can be touched by God's love as the motivating force for their decisions and actions. Each phase with its mode of appraisal has its place and meaning in the history of personal spiritual formation, just as each chronological developmental phase is the necessary launching pad for what follows.

Unfortunately, it is possible, as van Kaam has indicated,[20] for persons not to develop, not to allow the flow of development to continue in their lives. Human beings can and do become fixated on any one of the pre-transcendent phases of appraisal. As adults, they may live out their human and Christian life on a level inferior to their chronological age and responsibility. With mind and will weakened by the quasi-foundational pride form, they may exalt and totalize partial wholes or "little beyonds" at the expense of the larger whole or Great Beyond.[21] In living through the various maturational stages, it is possible to become fixated on the motivations peculiar to each. Thus at the age of forty a woman may still be trying to act as "cute" as she was at the age of six. Or a fifty-four-year-old man may still be attempting to prove his athletic prowess in competition with men half his age. It is difficult for adults to take seriously these aging "girls and boys" who are unconsciously afraid to let go of the unintegrated strivings that functioned and gave them satisfaction in the past.

It is interesting to speculate about what might have happened if Alan had been unwilling to let go of his youthful "nice guy" image; if Carl had insisted on ignoring the limitations that were part of his own midlife crisis; if Donna had been so locked into adolescent fantasies that she was unable to imagine herself moving into the adult roles of wife and mother; if Ellen had let herself be directed by the culture's opinions about women over thirty-five having babies. In other words, crises of transcendence are often contextualized by the maturational phases the person undergoing them is in at the present moment. Thus some aspects of the conflict experienced during the openness moment of trusting may be traceable to the life stage of the truster. Perhaps also, Bill's lack of conflict is traceable to the fact that he was totally locked into the functional mode characteristic of people in their thirties.[22]

In any case, it is apparent that like any other foundational attitude or disposition, trust takes a lifetime to mature. The naïve, untried doxic confidence of the child must meet and overcome serious crises in the course of human development. Mature trust will correspond to the increasingly independent and wise appraisal that accompanies the integration process as it gradually unfolds in the truster's life. One of the greatest obstacles to the development of a trusting attitude lies in the possibility of becoming encapsulated in the defensive "character armor" that accumulates with each developmental stage. This buildup of protective attitudes, a necessary part of human experience, has the power to obscure the original spiritual being under layers of vital/functional "security directives." As the Gospel reminds us, one can easily lose track of one's real self in the welter of precautions one takes to preserve it.[23]

Thus the psychosocial identity that developmentalists like Erikson see as evolving from the basic trust acquired in infancy is not yet a perfect expression of the "core" or foundational form of that life. In fact, some of the unintegrated leftovers from past developmental periods and crises further obscure the "image of God" that lies hidden deep within each of us. Some developmental psychologists have recognized the need to turn to the more transcendent nature of human existence. They see clearly that we are not only formed by our world, family, and society. Even in early infancy, we also form our environment by the quality of our relation to it. They know that a consciousness that trusts and loves actually has a different environment,[24] and is more likely to experience breakthrough moments of trusting and being trusted. Thus we have studies, like that of Carroll Davis, that stress the emancipatory quality of reciprocal trust between parents and children.[25]

Davis demonstrates that there must be a balance between freedom involving independence, confidence in self, and emergence, and care or control that involves dependence, confidence in the security of parents and home, and reliance. She points out that in a really trusting relation, children must not be seen as objects. As growing children relate to their parents, they remain subjects of their actions because they are trusted by their parents. Here we have an excellent illustration of the circle or "chiasm" of trusting. At the same time, Davis continues, because of parents' care, children are able to be dependent in a good sense, relying on others whose love for them is sure. Always, though, in this example of interpersonal trust the other (the parent) respects the child as subject. In fact, between them mutual subjectness exists. And so here again, we return to the initial idea that the fundamental dynamic of trusting, as of all spiritual life and growth, lies on the side of freedom, on the human capacity for "more," on the transcendent aspiration at the core of our being. It is this desire or love in the human heart to move beyond itself, to participate in the life of others, that lies at the root of our trust not only of the others but of the Holy Other who is God.

From approaching the human condition in terms of cultural obstacles to trusting and in terms of the findings from developmental psychology, we learn that everyone who has lived in this culture and has gone through any maturational stages at all lives with some anxiety. The anxiety takes different forms. There is the fear of being isolated and helpless in a hostile world, the fear of not being able to cope, the worry over having to gain ego control over others. To maintain the image of his or her ideal self, everyone from time to time, indulges in some illusions about how best to manage in relation to reality. Everyone has a favored method of feeling secure, a psychosocial identity characterized by certain encounter tendencies. Sociologists, social psychologists, psychoanalysts, and psychotherapists continue to point them out, and to suggest ways in which we can become more free in relation to these obstacles.

All great spiritual traditions also contain an image of the person and a concept of his or her situated freedom in regard to the obstacles they see inhering in the culture and developmental processes. All seem to agree that one important element in the process of freeing oneself for transformation is an awareness of one's unfreedom. Convinced that the source of transformation is rootedness in Divine Being, these traditions speak to the obstacles to spiritual unfolding discoverable in the chains of childhood, the prison of superficial social life, the trap of falsely conceived adaptations to the social self and the ceaseless longing of the ego for security. They point to the threefold danger to spiritual growth of isolated introspection, deterministic fatalism, and a nonreflective closed world view bereft of Mystery. The Christian tradition (that of the undivided Church[26] and the Fathers) echoes this warning against dominance by historical, vital, or functional dimensions of the self at the expense of the unique freedom of the whole person to respond to transcendent and pneumatic longings and inspirations. The next chapter turns to that tradition for a third approach to the human condition—a condition in which the experience of trust is always situated.

CHAPTER 13

BEYOND THE PRIDE FORM

In this final look at your trust experience, can you get in touch with

1. some of the ways in which the pride form blocks the flow of energy in your life;
2. how you tend to avoid differentiation and become one-sidedly fixated on the vital/functional level;
3. the true identity that is yours beneath the social self;
4. the ways in which what you learned from reflecting on your trust experience coincides with or differs from what Ellen learned from reflecting on hers?

The Conflict That Blocks the Flow

In Chapter 5 we looked at the dynamics of the ongoing flow of life, at the way in which events happen and are incorporated into a pattern of openness-actuation-integration. We also looked at the element of conflict that gives an event the character of an "openness moment." There is, however, underlying all our encounters with events, people, and things a deeper conflict that the Christian tradition sees as existing between the autarchic pride form and the Christ form,[1] between the counterfeit or false self and one's true identity as a child of God. Aelred Squire points to this conflict:

> . . . By the very fact of having been born at all, we are involved in a state of tension between two apparently incompatible facts. On the one hand, simply as human, and not as monkey or cat, or even rose, we have a special and unique sublimity. . . . The biblical apprehension of this situation, as seen through the eyes of the New Testament, is that all that God has made is good, and very good but only man is, as St. Paul says, "the image and glory of God." . . . Yet, on the other hand that it is necessary to add an observation which would seem to be a direct denial of all this was as clear to St. Paul as . . . to any ordinary, honest man. . . . If it is in any sense true that man is the image and glory of God, then this sense must take into account the

inescapable fact that something has evidently gone unaccountably wrong with him. St. Paul's way of saying this explicitly refers the matter to its context within the doctrine that man was made in God's image when it declares that we all "fall short of the glory of God." . . . The sin situation in which we are all alike involved, though its effects upon us individually may be varied, is that in which we became involved by the mere fact of being human . . . it is a situation of disharmony in which we find ourselves . . . in being pushed and pulled hither and thither by one's own uncontrolled and often uncontrollable drives. The Fathers all agreed that human nature is profoundly wounded by the Fall, but they are equally agreed that it is not destroyed by it. Hence the experience of deep disharmony in those who become aware of their true possibilities, their true selves.[2]

Most people are not aware of this underlying disharmony or conflict between their actual sinful self-encapsulation in what van Kaam calls the pride form and the divine form of Christ pushing to be unveiled and released in the depth of their souls. Yet the presence of the pride form as a block to the flow of formation energy[3] can be detected in the very bodily rigidity of proud people, whose entire energy is absorbed in camouflaging of their actual selves under counterfeit forms of their own devising.[4] Such persons become obsessed with the need to be perfect in some way, either by appearing to be totally in control or by complete absorption in the pursuit of self-chosen goals. A recognizable example of the takeover of the pride form is the compulsively "holy" person. These people prove their exalted status by setting up and adhering to a self-chosen holy schedule of duties and practices that sometimes succeeds in completely blocking out from their lives initiatives other than their own.

Along with dominance of this self-encapsulating pride form, van Kaam mentions several other reasons why people ignore their true possibilities, their true selves as images of God referred to by Squire.[5] He says that people fail to recognize themselves as transcendent presence because they share in the illusions of autonomous fulfillment and self-esteem common to their culture. He notes that their life energy is mostly invested in the limited vitalistic and functionalistic pursuits that culture offers. People tend to escape the anxiety involved in confronting ultimate life questions by becoming involved in partial outlets for competition and by taking refuge in the comparative safety of the taken-for-granted answers of a society that has repressed the demands of the Transcendent almost entirely. Van Kaam is clearly indicating the dimensions of human pride as it tends to ignore other levels of fulfillment in favor of absolutizing vital impulses and functional ambitions. Cutting persons off from dialogue with the rest of reality, pride gives an illusion of ego autonomy, an illusion of self-sufficiency apart from the grace of Christ. Its opposite, humility, is the basis for the acknowledgment of dependence on God, the basis of our trust in him as Transcendent Other.

Human beings discover the depths of this conflict in themselves, this alienation from their true identity and life call, when they begin to become aware of how their lives are dominated by the spirit of competition, the pull of consumerism, the impact of affluence and sexual freedom, subtle and not-so-subtle directives from the media and other avenues of public opinion that surround them every day. Christians with recourse to a Gospel-based community strong enough to confront the self-actualizing directives of contemporary society are fortunate. From within the wisdom of a two thousand-year-old tradition, they are more likely to discover the distortions in their own isolated impulses, ambitions, aspirations, and even inspirations. With this objective criterion, and illumined by the Spirit, they are better able to question the structures of the present self, its underlying attitudes, perceptions, feelings, and motivations. They are perhaps less likely to cling to the narcissism of their particular defensive profile of sin. They are less inclined to resist admitting their own limitations in the face of their tradition's teaching about the God whose deepest initiative toward them is the love and mercy incarnated in his Son.

In our pursuit of our illusion of what will make us happy and secure, we exist in a tension between sensitivity to the messages from our deepest selves and the directives prompted by the specific ways in which the pride form searches for glory and autonomous self-fulfillment in our lives.[6] This anxious struggle for security in the midst of contingency, fear of death, and ultimate nonbeing prompts many of us to seek safety in an idealized self. Although ultimately alienated from the true self, the apparent success and external perfection of this counterfeit self can help suppress the anxiety of finding oneself alone and friendless in a hostile world. The appeal of mastery, of love, and of freedom can give the illusion of safety to fallen vulnerable creatures unable to trust that the Creator will be merciful. So we embed ourselves in the familiar and avoid differentiation and new life. Or we disown normal limitations in an abnormal striving for power and prestige. Forgetful of our transcendent destiny, we reduce ourselves to the lowest common denominator of what "they"—the group, the media, the current opinion makers—think and say. Caught in a "tyranny of shoulds," we have very little freedom to risk, to open ourselves to reality, to let life and the Other emerge from the salvific horizon of the eternal divine plan.

These dynamics of the pride form become operative at moments of incarnation, when we begin to actually *do* what we have been thinking about. When a person like Bill, for instance, actually decides to find a job in a certain firm, he has to imagine what he needs to do, how he needs to act during the interview in order to get the job. In his imagination, he rehearses what he will say, anticipates how he will dress and act in order to make a good impression, tries to predict any difficulties that might prevent him from mastering the situation. These are all the typical precautions that accompany a normal job-seeking interview. However, for an abnormally anxious mistrustful person, these precautions could become excessive. Such persons might become so preoccupied with coming off well during the interview that they would try to absolutize prediction and control. Fearful of looking unprofessional, they might rigidly organize their dress and facial expression into an artificial, somewhat frozen solemnity. In their anxiety to guard against an impression of ineptness and inefficiency, they might overdo precision and punctilliousness. In their total self-preoccupation, they might keep their gestures and speech stiff and rigidly correct. Their total control would prevent the other person from emerging as anything more than a filler of the role of "employer." In other words, lack of trust in goodness beyond the self can lead to an absolutizing of what van Kaam calls "security directives."[7] All one's energy becomes tied up in defensive maneuvers to protect the self from the overwhelming and presumably hostile "other." As a result, there is not only total forgetfulness of one's own identity but also lack of recognition of the richness inherent in the being of the other. This exaggerated picture gives some idea of the way in which the normal flow of energy can be blocked by fixation in attitudes that stem from an unwillingness to humbly accept and live the human condition as it is instead of as we would have it be.

Resisting the Differentiation-Integration Dynamic

Obstacles to a life of trust and wholeness arise, then, from exaggerated striving on the vital/functional level. Undisciplined vital impulses and functional ambitions need appraisal in the light of Divine Otherness. As was suggested in Chapter 6, living merely on the level of embeddedness in the lived body has many negative aspects. Although the infant's trust of the world is rooted in its "body memory," mature trusting must transcend this vital dimension. Otherwise all one's adult appraisals of reality will tend to be unbalanced, oriented in the direction of security and self-preservation, fixated on a pretranscendent level. In this context, we might ask whether Ellen's original decision to engage in sexual activity was the result of a lack of integration of her sexuality within the wholeness of her project of existence. Certainly all five of the trusters, as partakers in the fallen human condition, were somewhat blocked in the differentiation-integration process by the pride form as it manifested itself in their particular life situation.

At a certain point in the research project, as I mentioned once before, it became apparent that the trust described by Bill did not coincide with the trust described in the other write-ups. Since he stood only to gain from the situation, Bill was not personally vulnerable, as was plain from his statement, "Even if I didn't get the job, I felt privileged to be so close to it." That both he and Mr. M. were protected by the social paradigm from the unpredictable elements arising from "otherness" was evident from the fact that "we talked and asked questions of each other and generally discussed what responsibilities were involved" and a third party was there to "attest to what was actually said or promised or assumed, and later on perhaps clarify what might have been misunderstood." Bill's anxiety arose more from the chores of meeting ritual social expectations ("I was anxious to do and say the right thing") than from the feeling of personal risk that comes from launching a new action or laying oneself open to a radical change in attitude. Because Bill held the other up as an ideal ("I felt I wanted to be like him"), he almost canceled out the "otherness" of what Mr. M. expected or wanted. In this particular situation, then, Bill escaped almost all the tension and risk involved in the kind of trusting the others experienced.

Bill was also the most functionally oriented in his approach. He took the initiative in the experience. He seemed to see the other person as an object or means for him rather than as an end in himself. His presence to the other differed significantly from that of the other people. He failed to establish an intimate, and thus truly interpersonal, relationship with the other. He did not experience any significant break in his taken-for-granted life-style. He trusted mainly in the predictable elements about the other person, and he trusted them in the functional pragmatic horizon of his own project-to-be-accomplished. Bill did not describe a dawning awareness of trusting the "already there" trustableness of the other. He neither seemed significantly changed by the encounter nor emotionally moved by the experience. There is no evidence of his having come to a new possibility of acting, or of having made a decision or experiencing tension in this regard. There is, in other words, an almost total absence of experienced risk in Bill's description of a situation of interpersonal trust.

Bill is not a caricature. He is simply an average twentieth-century person caught in the typical deformative dispositions of our time. He could not even be described as a Type A personality.[8] He does, however, live out many of the character traits typical of people in their thirties. He is very ambitious. Ideals of mastery and control lead him to functional overexertion. He is not reflective or receptive in approach. He is not interested in interpersonal intimacy. Rather, he is interested in achievement. He tends to objectify and even use the other. He has little time in his life for openness to the Transcendent. Because he has not remained in touch with his deeper self, he is encapsulated in a horizontal life-style. His trusting resembles the style of social reliability that may have been fairly appropriate to the situation in which he found himself. Nevertheless, the dynamics of this interaction between two human beings could never be seen as facilitating attitudes or responses that would be helpful for either in terms of their relationship with the Other who is God.

What would have facilitated Bill's encounter with the human other and also prepared his dispositions for relating to the Divine Other? First of all, Bill's thought processes tended to be somewhat one-sided. His style was informative,[9] mainly issue oriented and directed to the mind. His goal was a functional grasp of the situation in a linear progressive fashion. He achieved knowledge about the other in the Heideggarian manner of calculative thinking. In contrast, the style of formative thinking is an experiential, open style that stirs the heart as well as the mind of the thinker. In its openness, it tends to be receptive to more than simply the obvious facts about the other. In its availability to the powers that pervade the universe, this manner of thinking discloses transcendent meanings about the other, yielding a lived knowledge, an emotional insight that appeals to the heart of the knower, to his or her sensible, responsible core, to the deeper motivations of decision and action. The natural center of integration, the heart needs to be awake in relation to its differentiated interactions with the people, things, and events of the world.

In us all, however, is a natural inertia or resistance to what is other, to what is new, to change, detachment, risk. The temporary loss of balance that accompanies large or even small crises of the new and unexpected discomforts us. We are inclined to resist the conflict, to escape the tension, unless we have some trust in the underlying providential direction of this life. Escape from differentiation may take the form of withdrawal into the interior life, where people not only barricade themselves against threats from the outer world but against the initiatives of God as well. Other people resist differentiation by escaping the demands of the inner life, by getting overinvolved with people, groups, and various worthy causes simply to avoid facing a new and unexpected glimpse of themselves as they really are. Out of a desire to evade the task of integrating the new into the ongoing transcendence they most truly are, they become addicted to drugs, alcohol, social activism, or workaholism. This resistance is rooted in the by now familiar dynamics of the pride form— isolation from vital sharing and dialogue, plus functional self-sufficiency, whose one-sided emphasis on security and defenses further conceals the already one-sided image of God hidden in the depths of the soul. Only those who trust that they are loved can dare to move out of this state and risk an honest appraisal of their own vital/functional fixations, the pulsations of the surrounding culture, the present phase of their own maturational life, and the predominant modes of relating it discloses.

Substituting the Social Self for True Identity

One of the main problems for twentieth-century North Americans is that they have grown up in a culture that suppresses the Transcendent dimension. Most people reach adulthood ignorant of the fact that their restless hearts were created for transcendent and even pneumatic fulfillment. They are ignorant of the potential they are for being open to the Spirit of God, for participative union of likeness to the Trinity. They do not perceive reality or their own life of dialogue with ordinary reality as an opening for Christ to come more fully into a world that can only reach fulfillment in that loving relation. The dimension of life where formation has taken place for most people is the functional. We find all kinds of opportunities in the culture for formative processes that foster education in this dimension, especially in its social articulation. People in the West have learned well the lessons of individualism and capitalistic achievement. Competition is encouraged and rewarded. Functional ambitions to succeed, to come out ahead, to "make it" by taking control of one's own destiny, are caught from as well as taught by role models and paid experts.

When education and formation remain strictly on this level, there is throughout the entire culture a natural blockage of the flow of divine created and uncreated energy. This blockage is a result of the substitution of the social self for one's true identity as transcendent uniqueness. Deprived of true identity, people find it more difficult to feel at one with others. How can you trust people who appear to be, not fellow aspirers after mercy and justice, but simply competitors striving to save themselves first? In the absence of a transcendent sense of the unique worth of each person as emerging from the horizon of the Holy, there is only the functional level, with its coping and encounter mechanisms as defined by psychoanalysts like Karen Horney. In van Kaam's terms, vital and functional strivings originating in the pride form both weaken and obscure the appraising mind and will. As adults, people make decisions on the basis of outworn and unintegrated partial life directives belonging to earlier periods of development. Not only is their perception of reality distorted, but their perception of God's initiatives in life is also weakened or lacking.

Thus an entire group or community can become absorbed in the narrowness of immediacy, with its one-dimensional point of view and its evasion of the unexpected. To retain their trustworthiness, social groups need recourse to revealed sources and a wider communal myth or world view that provides a context of mystery and depth. Without these, they are subject to the same misplaced trust in the natural attitude as are individuals. A collective need for security rooted in the pride form can drive a group to withdraw in fear and isolate itself not only from other people but from the God whose love they doubt. A community that is unable to love and trust others cannot risk any kind of involvement with others that would open it to vulnerability. The need to control and dominate not only drives individuals to live on a level of functional relatedness with others; it also stops the flow of life between groups, both large and small, whose possibilities of trusting have to find their ground beyond the level of merely functional presence to one another. This is not to suggest that the vital/functional dimension be discarded. Rather, it must be integrated into the intentions of the transcendent and pneumatic presence of both individuals and groups. In the resulting creative tension of immanence-transcendence, vital energy is preserved and integrated into the individual and group efforts to reach out beyond the self in acts of love. This reaching out in love and respect to the totality of the other despite differences and strangeness cannot be separated from the trust in the other's true identity that is its necessary condition.

A description by Thomas Merton catches, in a situated moment "in Louisville, at the corner of Fourth and Walnut," this necessary realization of hidden glory, of the to-be-trusted point in others, the deepest ground of our trust in them:

> In Louisville, at the corner of Fourth and Walnut, in the center of the shopping district, I was suddenly overwhelmed with the realization that I loved all those people, that they were mine and I theirs, that we could not be alien to one another even though we were total strangers. . . .
>
> . . . It is a glorious destiny to be a member of the human race, though it is a race dedicated to many absurdities and one which makes many terrible mistakes: yet with all that, God himself gloried in becoming a member of the human race. "A member of the human race." To think that such a commonplace realization should suddenly seem like news that one holds the winning ticket in a cosmic sweepstake.
>
> I have the Immense Joy of being . . . a member of a race in which God Himself became Incarnate. As if the sorrows and stupidities of the human condition could overwhelm me, now I realize what we all are. And if only everybody could realize this! But it cannot be explained. There is no way of telling people that they are all walking around shining like the sun. . . .
>
> . . . Then it was as if I suddenly saw the secret beauty of their hearts, the

depths of their hearts where neither sin nor desire nor self-knowledge can reach, the core of their reality, the person that each one is in God's eyes. If only they could see themselves as they really *are*. If only we could see each other that way all the time. There would be no more war, no more hatred, no more cruelty, no more greed. . . . I suppose the big problem would be that we would fall down and worship each other. But this cannot be *seen*, only believed and "understood" by a peculiar gift.

Again that expression, *la point vierge* (I cannot translate it), comes in here. At the center of our being is a point of nothingness which is untouched by sin and by illusion, a point of pure truth, a point or spark which belongs entirely to God, which is never at our disposal, from which God disposes of our lives, which is inaccessible to the fantasies of our own mind or the brutalities of our own will. This little point of nothingness and of *absolute poverty* is the pure will of God in us. It is so to speak His name written in us, as our poverty, as our indigence, as our dependence . . . it is like a pure diamond, blazing with the invisible light of heaven. It is in everybody, and if we could see these billions of points of light coming together in the face and blaze of a sun that would make all the darkness and cruelty of life vanish completely. . . . I have no program for this seeing. It is only given. But the gate of heaven is everywhere.[10]

In a sense, all who wrote a description of trusting someone had, in that experience, passed through the "gate of heaven" that is potentially present in every human situation. All had glimpsed something of the infinite "otherness" of the stranger. All had recognized, consciously or unconsciously, the presence of "more" in another human being. All had tuned in to this transcendent dimension as the necessary ground for trusting that other, for risking themselves in relation to him. And all, feeling loved and respected in return, had been able to act in a new way, to reach beyond the narrow confines of the self they had been until that moment. The pattern was this: These situated persons are jolted out of their complacency by an event (another person) who demands their trust. Thrown back on themselves in a reflective "openness" moment, they confront conflicting directives coming from themselves and from the situation. Somewhat aware of the value horizon from which this other person emerges, they appraise the situation as well as they can, and come to a decision. In doing so, they grow and become a new creation, a new current self.

We turn now to Ellen to trace the pattern of her experience.

Final Interviews with Ellen

Like the others, Ellen is situated in the human condition. Like them, she writes about a moment of being shaken out of her complacent life as exemplary Catholic nurse by an event whose consequences were out of her control. At the "end of her rope," unable to find another person whom she could trust to see her through this particular predicament, she still needed to reach out beyond herself to someone. In our conversations I was struck by how many parallels there were between the attitudes she learned to live in relation to God and the attitudes the others espoused in relation to the trusted other person. Ellen, too, went through a reflective process of appraisal in relation to this Other. She talked about her realization that she could believe Christ's words in the New Testament only when she recognized that he was really sent by God, that his horizon was truly the Trinitarian mystery. She also talked about this trust in Christ's words as the ground of her decision-making process even when she felt most "unrespectable." It was trust in what God loved about her (her true identity) that gave her the courage to act, to "go ahead and have the baby" in spite of the obviously adverse consequences for her social self. In doing so, in acting in this new way, she also became new.

As she told me about her crisis, she emphasized how central keeping up appearances (the social self) had been for her all her life. She had never realized how deeply motivated she was to make a "supergood" impression on others until she saw how frantic she became at the thought that this reputation she had built up might suddenly disappear. She was surprised at how tenaciously she clung to this idealized image of herself, and how painful it felt to risk letting it go. She admitted that perhaps she had even tried to "fool God" by not accepting the reality of her ordinariness, her weakness, her need of him. When we discussed the human tendency toward self-sufficiency and isolated functioning, she recognized the form her own pride system took. She saw how she had been "into willful independence and control."

Having identified her underlying conflict as one involving nonacceptance of limits and a determination to plan and even carry out her own salvation, Ellen remembered other times when this orientation had almost paralyzed her. "There is just such a resistance in me to appear in need of any help, so sometimes I'd go for weeks trying to look cool, unable to admit that I couldn't handle everything myself. I guess there were other opportunities to change, but they just passed me by. I was closed and pretty tense a lot of the time, especially when things didn't go smoothly and there was a chance I wouldn't look good." She smiled as she recalled the moment of "letting go" as it happened to her. "Well, I really feel as if I did very little myself. I was just there reading and feeling desperate. There was no one else to turn to. I really had to depend on God. I either believed what it said about seeking first the kingdom of God and all these things would be added, or I didn't. It was as if someone else had to be consulted, as if what I wanted was not the most important issue. Naturally I had learned about Providence and all that, but this was different. This was my real life, and it was out of my hands. I guess it was when I realized that there just wasn't anything clever or efficient that I could do that I was able to relax enough to let God do something. I didn't have to, though. I was still free to go on in my usual style."

Ellen and I talked a little more about her "usual style," which was the human tendency to try to be God, the typical refusal to let God be God. We discussed the human temptation to deny limitations and harden one's heart against a breakthrough from Beyond. She recognized that "probably I was more humble as well as realistic when I accepted myself as I really was in all my disorder and lack of ability to cope. It was the first time I had ever been faced with such an insight into how little I really lived in relation to God. I had just gotten into the habit of planning my life and handling things on my own. And here I was, not able to manage and realizing how far away from God's presence I had drifted. I really did feel guilty, you know. But again, the bad feelings were mostly because I had broken my perfect record as a Catholic." Ellen paused at this point and then continued very slowly. "You know, now that I think of it, my shame at getting caught in such a fleshy sin has been a real help to me since that time. See, before, I had felt sort of above other people, almost above the human condition, you might say. Then when I found out I was just like everybody else, a sinner in a very ordinary type of sinfulness, it somehow made me feel more of a human being, less special, you know?"

Ellen's words reminded me of Merton's joy at recognizing himself as a "member of the human race." I asked what effect, if any, this new way of seeing herself had had on her relations with other people. "Now that you mention it, I think it's made me feel closer to people, not so separated from the average, not perfect people I deal with all the time. I'm not so shocked when people do wrong and make mistakes now, because I know I do it too. Also I realize that it was when I was most imperfect that I felt most loved by God. He loves us all that way I guess, no matter how we appear on the outside. See, now that I know love is the most important thing, I can accept that people are going to be different than me. I can feel closer to people of other races and classes and educational background. Even people of different sexual or religious orientations are a little more trustable for me because first of all they are lovable in God's eyes just like I am myself."

In our last interview, Ellen added to this theme. "After that experience of trusting God, something else changed in me, too. I had always thought that to be God's friend in a special way, you had to be some ideal sort of person, like perfect, you know? But recently I've begun to realize that you don't have to be perfect, because that's impossible anyway. But what you do have to do is to be interested in what he is interested in, to care about what he cares about, to be concerned about what he is concerned about. So you need to get in touch with his thoughts, the "thoughts of his heart," as it says in one of the psalms. You can learn a lot about how God sees things and how he acts in the world from reading Scripture, you know." When I asked her to say more about what happened when she read Scripture, she told me about how she had continued to read the Bible with the intention of learning more about God's trustableness. She gave some examples from both the Old and New Testaments and from the themes brought out in the liturgy for the different seasons of the Church year. What she said sounded right, and I decided to try it myself, keeping in mind the themes that had already emerged from the research.

Part Four

Part Four

TRUST
AND THE
CHRISTIAN MYSTERY

CHAPTER 14

APPROACHING REALITY
WITH TRUST

Changes of Mind and Heart

After reading the first three parts of this book, a friend commented that although I had carefully described every detail of what happened to the six people in my study, I hadn't said much about what had happened to *me*—about how I had changed as a result of all this reflecting on the experience of trust. His remark sent me back first of all to the journal I had kept during the different stages of the research.[1] With some amusement, I rediscovered that my own questions about what it means to trust someone had originated in a personal experience of *dis*trusting someone —a parking lot attendant, to be exact. I realized again how many of my initial thoughts about trusting were related to a parallel interest I had in finding out more about the anxiety that belongs to uncertainty and absence of trusting. From the very beginning, my groping approach to trusting called for reality testing via an empirical method. At the same time, my personal involvement as a distrusting truster inserted me into the very situation I was studying and proved to be more of an asset than a liability. As Ricoeur would say, I was already in "the hermeneutic circle,"[2] ready to be led beyond the first to a second naïveté.[3]

A jolt to my taken-for-granted grasp of what it means to trust came simultaneously with my discovery via the method of qualitative analysis that trusting is not an isolated attitude that can be summoned at will. An "already there" element of reality to which people are or are not present, the initiative for trusting actually comes from beyond the person who trusts—from the trusted reality itself. Ideas about trust received a further shock when, to support the research, I applied for an International Peace grant and learned in the process how many segments of people's lives are affected by our lack of understanding and ability to live trustingly toward one another. As I went over the areas of application for the research— international peace and nuclear disarmament, prejudice and discrimination, cooperatives and credit unions, mental health, marriage and family life, education and psychotherapy, large government and business organizations, source credibility and media communication—my interest in trusting shifted from head to heart. There were so many of us troubled about trusting in so many areas of our lives.

Rereading journal entries that describe the carrying out of the final study recalls especially my conversations with the six men and women who were the "subjects." How can I express what I learned from them? My feelings of disbelief and awe as six absolutely unique styles of trusting were revealed; moments of mutual recognition as one or the other lived experience corresponded exactly to my own, or as someone's spontaneous revelation of personal grace or limitation became the occasion for shared appreciation or the silence of mutual depression. There were tears and laughter both, as well as some really puzzling moments, like the day when the structure of Bill's unique mode of "trusting" refused to fit with the others, threatening the coherence of the whole study. The unfolding of the conditions for authentic trusting in the subjects' lives alerted me to its meaning not only in my own life but also in everything that I read, especially Scripture. The trusting way of being in the world, the very word itself, began to stand out for me, particularly during the liturgical seasons. I found my own Christian faith tradition permeated with this disposition. The Mystery throughout the Old Testament and, especially in the person of Jesus, in the New evokes it often, as will be evident in the following pages.[4]

Another learning moment for me came when I discovered that the categories used in the traditional social and psychological literature about trust between people do not emerge from lived experience.[5] It did not seem to matter much to anyone engaged in the areas of application (international peace and disarmament, for example) whether the phenomenon of mutual trust between nations would be treated in respect to any sort of lived value context or horizon. Having seen from the pilot studies the crucial importance of the truster's context, I found it almost impossible to believe that "the experts" were not taking people's and nation's lived horizons into account in making these life-and-death decisions.

In Chapter 1, I mentioned that "during the course of the original empirical research, conclusions emerged that pointed to a flow of divine life and love lying just beneath the surface of everyday experience."[6] During the years since the completion of the study, my personal interest in the phenomenon of trust shifted gradually from a psychological approach to a more spiritual or "formative" interest in that underlying flow. My experience with groups of people in the Grail movement[7] and at

Duquesne University[8] has uncovered deeper meanings of trust as both a foundational theme in Christian mysticism and a necessary support for the more prophetic or social aspect of life and spirituality. This personal shift might be described as moving from a pattern of seeing reality characterized by privatized empirical perception to one that is more communal and thus formative, that is more open to Gospel revelation and contextualized by a world view expressing a specifically Christian faith. From participating in these groups, I gradually came to a new sense of my own relation with the Mystery, a sense of how I myself need to nourish that Mystery in my own heart and trust there a God who operates from within as energizing source, center, and goal of the whole world—a God who is concerned for this world, with whom we can cooperate and share, and whose divine forming will is at the heart of our universe.

In response to my friend's question about what had changed in me as a result of doing the trust research, I can only point to a story.[9] In the Grail legend, we find the poor knight Parsifal returning to the Grail castle a changed and chastened man. He is moved to ask two questions: "What is your sorrow?" and "Whom does one serve in serving the Grail?" The questions themselves are not answered—it is enough that he has learned to ask them. He has begun to realize the intrinsic connection between a life of committed service to others and the human search for the Mysterious source of life itself. He has begun to see that it is only in trusting surrender of his life to life's source that he can be effective in serving others. Perhaps as a result of my own search, I, too, am now more able to trust that a day of wholeness and healing for all will come.

After Parsifal's forty days of fasting and contemplation, whose metanoia quality has prepared him to ask the right questions, here is how the legend describes the resulting transformation in the environment:

> Then the Fisher King arose radiant and whole, and the Grail shone with a greater light; the knights and ladies who served the Grail sang for joy, and the waste land was delivered from its barrenness. Crops grew in the fields, streams and lakes teemed with fish, cattle and sheep multiplied; for from Parsifal's question, which touched the source of life, all life was born anew.[10]

I am convinced that my own study of the structure of interpersonal trust has helped me see as I never did before how the center of Christian trust, the death and Resurrection of Jesus, *is* the reality of this renewal of the whole of creation symbolized in the Grail story. The study, with all its complexity, helped me see how our human dilemma of finding ourselves always in a state of change and constant becoming[11] is a living sign that we, along with the entire universe, are caught up in a divinely initiated process of transformation with which we can trustingly cooperate or from which we are free to withhold both our assent and our life questions. I moved closer to realizing also that it is only in interaction with others who are responding to God's call to become their deepest selves that the fullness of this new creation can be allowed to emerge. Immersion in the actuation pattern of interpersonal trust has awakened the ears of my ears; now the "eyes of my eyes are opened."[12]

Now, after several years of reflecting on this many-splendored phenomenon called trusting, I am beginning to realize how deeply its mystery permeates the readings from Scripture used in Christian liturgical celebrations. As I heed Ellen's advice and try to learn more about how God sees things and acts in the world, the readings for the Easter Vigil, preceded as they are by forty days of Lent, have taken on new meaning for me. On that night, the account of God's creative plan from Genesis is followed by psalms that echo the themes of new life, of God's initiating promise that extends from the beginning to the end of time: "Behold I make all things new." (Apoc. 21:5) The prayer invokes a dynamic Christ as the Lord who will be present in the New Creation. Then we are invited to partake in the unconditioned trust of Abraham, whose knowledge that God can raise people from the dead is followed by a prophecy of the Resurrection (Ps. 16). God's promise of fidelity to Israel, to the Church, and to all baptized people stands out in the next three readings, where we celebrate and put our trust in a God who moves and acts in history and the cosmos. In the seventh reading from Ezechiel (36: 16–17a, 16–28), we touch again the central meaning of all this for human hearts. God sees our divided hearts, as well as our disunity as people and nations. He initiates again the movement of integration, of gathering together, of bringing home, of cleansing . . . from all idols. Resurrection, transformation, New Creation, consists in our being given a "new heart" and a "new spirit." The catechumens respond with a psalm of longing to encounter the life-giving Lord (Ps. 42); the faithful pray for the joy of forgiveness (Ps. 51), and all ask that we may begin to understand something of this great initiative of love for us so that "the world may see the fallen lifted up, the old made new and all things brought to their perfection through him who is their origin, our Lord Jesus Christ."[13]

A Look at Some Paradigms[14]

On that Paschal night, following Paul's epistle on our liberation (Rom. 6:3–11) and the Gospel account of the Resurrection (Mt. 28: 1–10—Cycle A), the baptismal liturgy sums up the whole context of the Divine Plan for the universe.[15] Christians exist in this new reality like renewed fish in a transformed sea. As children of God in whom the saving work has begun, Christians really do exist in a different environment and are potentially capable of perceiving reality from a unique standpoint of trust in its Crucified and Risen Source. Once again, we touch on the world view of the undivided Church[16] that saw the whole universe as a living field brimming over with created and uncreated energy flowing forth from the heart of the Trinity.[17] We can find something of this Eastern view of the universe also in a Western spiritual classic, de Caussade's little book on abandonment to divine providence. He speaks there of the treasure that is everywhere waiting for us to accept it.[18] To what else could he be referring when he advises us to seek that invisible treasure and accept everything that happens, to abandon ourselves to the "sacrament of the moment" in which we can trust that God's will for us is contained? We hear echoes of Chinese belief in the Tao, the ultimate undefinable reality that underlies and unifies the multiple things and events, the cosmic process that is the foundation for the continuous flow and change we observe in the world around us. To recognize the life-from-death pattern of these changes and go with their flow closely parallels the doctrine of trust in Providence that illumines centuries of Christian wisdom as well.[19]

From the physical sciences also, I was learning that nature is always dynamically dying and rising, forming new constellations as the old ones fall away in patterns of lawful interrelationship that will always remain something of a mystery even for scientists. In 1977, a Belgian chemist, Ilya Prigogine, won the Nobel Prize in chemistry for his discovery of the formation and transformation of energy in natural open systems to which he gave the name "dissipative structures."[20] His explanation of this universal pattern of potential for restructuration that builds up and suddenly regestalts onto a higher level of organization as old forms are discarded in favor of new contributes still another parallel to those we have already considered. Recall the trust event itself as "openness moment"; the conflict that builds up prior to the "letting go" that signals the shift to a new level of being for the people who trust; the risk and creative tension experienced as old familiar ways of prediction and control are discarded in favor of new ways of relating and involvement. Prigogine himself acknowledges a strong resemblance between this "science of becoming" and the world view common to Eastern philosophies and the visions of the mystics. Would he also sense the potential for metanoia or change of heart in the intuitive realization of dynamic to-be-trusted power in the universe common to a group of believing Christians? For that matter, how many individual Christians actually tap into that power and let themselves be transformed by it?

Here is where the beginning and the end of this book come together. We began with the idea that the differentiating or "dissipative" nature of our everyday life calls for a corresponding possibility of integrative reflection.[21] We traced one human experience, that of trust between two people, from its initiation, through its actuation, to its integration on a new level in the life of the person who trusted. We saw that here also there is a moment of breakthrough, an unpredictable moment when the obstacles to trusting precipitate a more or less stressful crisis. In moving beyond this problematic conflict of directives, the entire field-of-relations-with-the-environment that each truster *is*, shifts. This transformative shift in the direction of commitment to new action depends not only on the will or volition of the one who trusts, but also on his or her openness or receptivity to an "otherness" that is already there. Can we not conclude that any individual or group working for both personal and social change or transformation must be open to a new perspective that includes a cosmic framework within which their individual and collective efforts can be integrated and given both meaning and energy? For a Christian group, would this mean a raising of the collective consciousness in the direction of Christ, Lord of the Universe, in the energy of whose love our own attempts to love others are given both their meaning and their transformation power?

Romano Guardini's observation[22] about the very presence of the person who trusts creating a new environment takes on added vibrancy as a new understanding of what trust involves becomes ours. The deepest truth about human beings—about the entire universe, in fact—is their total dependence on the ongoing creative love of God and their potential for being liberated from death into New Creation by the Risen Christ.[23] The heart, symbol of the living, loving *presence* to reality that each person is, serves also as the center of integration for the whole process of formation and transformation that is ours between birth and death. Scripture is filled with references to the human heart. God looks not at appearances, but at the heart (Lk. 16:15); each person speaks from his heart's abundance (Lk. 6:45); those who listen to the word take it to their hearts (Mk. 4:20); out of the heart come all manner of evils (Mk. 7:21); basically what God calls us to throughout life is repeated *change* of heart (Lk. 5:32, Jn. 12:40). The heart of a whole people can be described as sluggish (Mt. 13:5) and far from the very God (Mt. 15:8) whom they are to love with all their hearts (Mt. 22:37); yet whole communities of believers can also change—can become of one heart and mind (Acts 4:32); their hearts can burn within them as they become illumined by the Gospel (Lk. 24:32), and such hearts can be ignited by the fire that Christ comes to cast over all the earth (Lk. 12:49).

Returning to the idea of *presence*,[24] it is possible to imagine the trusting human heart as a fiery core that spreads around it a field of warmth and life and light—that penetrates and ignites ever-widening circles of the environment. The alive, ever-changing cosmic web of interconnected meanings and relations that forms the invisible reality hidden beneath the mechanistic appearances of everyday life becomes permeated and charged with the creative power of God, for whose grace this heart is a channel. Societal systems can begin to move in new directions if hearts that have shifted, have undergone a real metanoia, begin to act like magnetic cores, redirecting scattered energies toward the ever-emergent Kingdom. However, commitment to such a vision of social transformation is not possible apart from a framework that gives this direction a solid mooring in the Mystery, in the "treasure" sought by loving hearts throughout the ages.

A Gradually Shifting World View

Reading connected with the investigation of lived space and the flow of time as situated context of the trust experience[25] made me aware of the startling nature of reality as discovered by both physicists and mystics.[26] It became apparent that ancient spiritual masters' intuitions about the underlying radical pattern labeled "the divine will" are now being confirmed by contemporary scientists, who see all life in our universe as participating in a cosmic web of interconnecting energies to whose source human consciousness has access by means of transcendent aspiration.[27] In this open universe, we live in a field of shifting patterns, a network of relation and connectedness that flows from that one Source, encompassing and carrying everything that is. The person who is able to trust the goodness and mercy of this Divine Source is able to live with greater equanimity and accept life's difficulties with less anxiety than the person whose lived situation does not include a positive view of his or her ultimate context. St. Paul's epistles to the Ephesians, Romans, and Corinthians and the Book of Revelation are particularly helpful in demonstrating how the Holy Spirit binds the elements of the world together in one providential synthesis as Christ's Body, Church, and Bride.[28] Isn't St. Luke pointing to the same providential context when he speaks of the participatory universe of the birds of the air, the lilies of the field, and their anxious human counterparts? (Lk. 12:22–31).

Such a view of the world as a dynamic field of interconnecting forces has been helpful in making me more at ease with the basic structure of life's fabric. Seeing experiences like trust as dynamic patterns whose ever-changing flow reflects movement between complementary poles not only makes sense of the need to take all of these poles into account,[29] but also explains something of the conflict, stress, and paradoxical nature inherent in everyday living. This view gives insight into the possibility for transformative shifts and changes not only in human hearts but among societies and nations as well. It indicates the potential for fragmentation of experience as human pride willfully blocks or denies the flow.[30] It speaks not only to the contradictions in human nature as it flows between polarities of gentleness and firmness, yin and yang, female and male, but also to the human need of intuitive seeing, for glimpsing the underlying order visible only to the gaze of attentive hearts.

Today scientists are finding that this realm of underlying order and interconnectedness yields itself more to modes of intuition than to merely rational analysis;[31] that eyes of faith and a more loving method of questioning are needed to unlock the mysteries of the cosmos. Does their discovery in any way connect with the discovery among theologians of the feminine nature of God?[32] Certainly it finds echoes in the notion permeating this study that by the very quality of our *presence* to what is other than the self, we do affect the lived field, the immediate situation that exists "between."[33]

Consideration of our situatedness in time and space brings to mind also the whole of human history. Its comprehension by someone like Eric Voegelin[34] contrasts significantly with the implied view of the six whose lived consciousness so obviously precluded references to an ultimate horizon.[35] A philosopher who looks for order and pattern in human history, Voegelin holds that:

> History is not a stream of human beings and their action in time, but the process of man's participation in a flux of divine presence that has eschatological direction. . . . The process of history, and such order as can be discerned in it, is not a story to be told from the beginning to its happy or unhappy end; it is a mystery in process of revelation.[36]

At the end of his study of the "ecumenic age," he concludes:

> To formulate the problem [of this Mystery that has no end in time] means practically to resolve it. The divine-human In-Between of historically differentiating experience is founded in the consciousness of concrete human beings in concrete bodies on the concrete earth in the concrete universe. . . . There is no "length of time" in which things happen; there is only the reality of things which has a time-dimension. The various strata of reality with their specific time-dimensions, furthermore, are not autonomous entities but form, through the relations of foundations and organization, the hierarchy of being which extends from the inorganic stratum, through the vegetative and animal realms, to the existence of man in his tension toward the divine ground of being. There is a process of the whole of which the In-Between reality with its process of history is no more than a part. . . .[37]

For Voegelin, to face the mystery of concrete historical reality, whether as an individual or as a member of a specific generation or epoch, means to live in a trusting faith that is "the substance of things hoped for and the proof of things unseen" (Heb. 11:1)[38]—that, in other words, necessarily implies consciousness of and reference to an ultimate horizon.

Trust in an ultimate horizon of meaning that encompasses and carries the whole of human history in all its concreteness and complexity is precisely the thrust of our celebration at Christmas of the event of the Incarnation. Itself a part of the whole Mystery of our Redemption, this entrance of God into the world as one of us accomplishes a radical transformation of the history of the world and of each one of us by rendering present the starting point of our divinization.[39] Seen always in the light of the Paschal Mystery, the Incarnation celebrates the victory of the Light of the World over the darkness of sin and death. Connected as it is with the cosmic renewal that takes place at the time of the winter solstice, the feast of Christmas anticipates Easter and "the glory that will be revealed in us [and] . . . the whole created world [that] eagerly awaits the revelation of the sons of God" (Rom. 8: 19–20). The texts of the Christmas liturgy point consistently to Christ's formative presence in history.[40] The texts for the Mass of Christmas Day emphasize the saving power of this child who is indeed a king and whose reign extends to the ends of the earth (Is. 9:6; Is. 52:7–10; Ps. 98) The second reading (Heb. 1:1–6), in presenting this Son through whom God "first created the universe" and who now "sustains all things by his powerful word," finds its climax in the Prologue to the Gospel of St. John, where the New Creation, the central forming event of all history, "lived among us and we saw his glory." Since no one has ever seen this God, source of all life and sustainer of all that is, it is a responsive trust in the enduring love revealed by his only Son that will make him known to us.

Questioning the Ultimate Horizon

On Ash Wednesday, the first of forty days of solemn preparation for the celebration of the central Mystery of Salvation, the liturgy puts this yearly time of conversion and repentance into context with an entrance antiphon taken from the book of Wisdom. In a time of terror before the threat of nuclear annihilation, when humankind has more reason than ever to question the powers that rule the universe, Scripture reminds us that indeed before God, "the whole universe is as a grain from a balance, or a drop of morning dew come down upon the earth." The liturgical text continues:

But you have mercy on all, because you can do all things; and you overlook the sins of men that they may repent. For you love all things that are and loathe nothing that you have made; for what you hated you would not have fashioned . . . you spare all things, because they are yours, O Lord and lover of souls.

(Wis. 11: 23–24,26)

Here we have the ultimate question: Is ours the terror of a universe without God, or is our world still made livable by a to-be-trusted Other who "loves all things that are" and who is, in the words of Julian of Norwich, at the same time faithful "maker, lover, and keeper" of everything that he has made.[41] We are faced here with the challenge to affirm the plan of salvation proposed by the God who "chose us in Christ before the world began" (Eph.1:4); who desires to enlighten everyone regarding this mysterious design that has been hidden for ages (Eph. 3:9); and who yet remains ambiguous, demanding that we walk by faith and not by sight (2 Cor. 5:6). We are given God's Spirit to "help us recognize the gifts that he has given us" (1 Cor. 2:12) and, "without seeing" (1 Peter 1:8), are asked to believe in the "already there" horizon of our life, to make the connection between our newly developing sense of the cosmos and the mystery of God's providential love for it.

The lived world view that sustained the undivided Church and medieval Christendom has disappeared. It is hard to imagine the reaction of the average person on the street today to the Byzantine antiphon for the Vigil of Christmas:

> Rejoice Jerusalem! All you lovers of Sion, share our festivities! On this day the age-old bonds of Adam's condemnation were broken, paradise was opened for us, the serpent was crushed, and woman whom he once deceived, lives now as Mother of the creator. . . . Let all creation dance and thrill with joy, for Christ has come to call it home and save our souls.[42]

Yet it is in the context of this world view of time and of Creation as destined to be "called home" by Christ that the hard questions of our age must be asked and sometimes answered. Again, the horizon of the Christian faith tradition, of the myth that gives meaning to both Creation and New Creation, is evoked. The question that provides a context for asking about and attempting to alleviate the sorrow of fellow human beings continues to be: "Whom does one serve when serving the Grail?"

It was from Donna and, particularly, Ellen that I learned something about the meaning context that can be conveyed by an alive faith community.[43] Ellen's matter-of-fact insertion into the "Catholic thing,"[44] her personal sense of all life as directed toward the "last things" and the ultimate "reign of God," and the way she was intuitively tuned to the deepest synergy of her own heart with the heart of the universe are memorable for me. My experience of the lived worlds of meaning represented by George and Laurie and the young Trappist monk remains with me also.[45] What stands out here is how the lived world of Christian trust differs from the non-Christian, even though both involve a perception of the "more than." One thing is clear: The notion of a crucified God as to-be-trusted Other has no place in the world view of the non-Christian. Nor does the Christian view of the whole of history as moving toward the last days embodied in the Kingdom feasts of the last part of the liturgical year make much sense in traditions that see reincarnation as an answer to the question we ask. I realized all over again how important it is that we ask the right questions in order to understand better what entering into the reign of God (the object of metanoia) really means. How else can one's faith tradition become context for Jesus' words on the third Sunday in ordinary time (Cycle B):

> This is the time of fulfillment. The reign of God is at hand! Reform your lives [undergo a *metanoia*] and believe [trust] in the gospel!
>
> (Mk. 1:14–15)

It was on a day in "ordinary time" that Ellen, at the end of her rope, was reading Scripture. As she describes the incident,[46] we catch a glimpse of momentary relaxation, the stilling of focused consciousness and clutching ego, a reflective pause in which the inspired words were able to reach into her being and touch her heart. The gift of grace, the uncreated energy of love, was able to flow unhampered into a tranquil core, evoking a trusting yes. There was a change in her whole being, a change of heart and a new possibility for decision and action. We are reminded again of the Lenten liturgy with its appeal on Ash Wednesday:

> Yet even now, says the Lord, return to me with your whole
> heart, with fasting and weeping and mourning;
> Rend your hearts, not your garments, and return to the
> Lord your God.
> For gracious and merciful is he, slow to anger, rich in
> kindness . . .
>
> (Joel 2:12–13).

The stress throughout these days is on the return to obedience and interior worship of the heart, on pursuing divinization through charity and union with God, and on receiving from God the gift of a clean heart, a new and steadfast spirit (Ps. 51). The liturgy of these first three days of Lent is indeed characterized by the trusting approach to the Mystery that was lived out by Ellen in the midst of her difficult situation.

CHAPTER 15

OUR ACTUAL SITUATION

Contemporary Views of the Context

The personal significance of belonging to the here-and-now contemporary situation lies in the fact that it is *our* situation—*we* are the persons who see with contemporary eyes and hear with twentieth-century ears, who are part and parcel of the hidden and not-so-hidden pulsations of this particular historical time and culture. Yet even seemingly static cultural and spiritual views of reality are constantly being transformed. Like the universe itself, they are continually subject to the pattern of "dissipative structures" that, in discarding outmoded ways, opens up ever-new and transcending perspectives on what is. Even the apparently stolid and unchanging way of viewing reality of organized Christian religion has been undergoing major shifts in more personal and experiential directions.

Disillusioned with a secularized technological civilization, and utterly incapable of reviving and living out of the vanished world vision of medieval Christendom, an increasing number of contemporary Christians find themselves moving out of former secure satisfaction with religion as simply another "little beyond" and impersonal mediator of the transcendent. Contemporary Christians have been alerted not only by shifts in their own faith tradition but also by the new vision provided by both scientific disciplines and the meditative techniques common to both Eastern and Western "awakening movements."[1] No longer content with dutiful observance of a list of security-assuring do's and dont's, contemporary Christians are fast losing interest in the kind of religion that merely keeps them busy "saying prayers and organizing things." They are seeking more direct experience of the "more than," a personal atunement to the contextualizing Mystery that underlies not only all that appears but their own deepest core as well. The perspective that best expresses our new situation is not the tunnel vision of a merely functional organized belief structure but the intuitive unitary vision that alters experience, not only of the Whole itself, but also of one another as participators in that Whole.

Science tells us that some animals have the capacity for sensing certain aspects of natural reality to which humans are insensitive. The bee, for example, can see parts of the color spectrum such as ultraviolet and infrared that are outside the possibility of human vision.[2] The lived world of the bee contains colors and forms that we, because we don't know they are there, never even look for. However, just as mystics in the ancient tradition were alert to aspects of reality that escaped the notice of most of their contemporaries, so more and more Christians are now awakening to what have been ignored or repressed spiritual realities. Aided by a new orientation to orders of reality behind or beneath everyday routine appearances of matter, time, and immediate situation, we are now more ready and able to perceive anew "that mystery hidden from ages and generations past but now revealed to us . . . the Mystery of Christ in you" (Col. 1:26–27) and in all that is. With the help of spiritual disciplines, and alerted to the invisible yet real mysterious context of our everyday life, we may be in a better position than past generations to become attuned to the larger domain or context of the divine will, to go with that flow, to consciously seek out the infrared or ultraviolet signs of the Spirit that we need to know are "already there" in our world.

Patterns of Human Trusting in Scripture

In Chapter 11, we looked at the historical-cultural pulsations of our time as they set up obstacles to the trusting mode of being. We saw how, in the opinion of many thinkers, "our twentieth-century society offers us a sense of reality or world view that includes at most a limited possibility of trusting other people."[3] There is no doubt that an illumination of contemporary minds and hearts is needed. These descriptions of our isolation from one another, our self-sufficient pragmatic attempts to manage on our own, our prevailing loss of connectedness with a sacred horizon, recall that we are still living typical attitudes belonging to the human situation after the Fall, even though we are not now totally determined by them. Still, if we look at human history from Creation onward,[4] we find that the "natural attitude" prevails from the beginning for most members of the human race. Israel's history, for example, is filled with the desire to somehow establish itself in self-sufficiency, to have its own king. And Saul, the king God finally gave the Israelites, proves to be a typical representation of the natural temptation to manage on one's own. Fearing the people and wanting to manage things in his own way, Saul offers up the forbidden holocaust and is rejected by God. The words of Psalm 40 come to mind:

Happy the man who makes the Lord his trust;

> who turns not to idolatry
> or to those who stray after falsehood . . .
> Sacrifice or oblation you wished not,
> but ears open to obedience you gave me . . .
> To do your will, O my God, is my delight
> and your law is within my heart!
>
> (cf. 1 Sm. 15:22)

In these very beginnings of human relatedness with the Holy Other, we find problems of trusting obedience versus self-will, of the cultural pressure to bring about one's own salvation versus the inner attitude of receptive trust in ways that are not ours. Even into New Testament times, after the passion and death of the obedient Son of God, we find the same problem. Like their ancestors before them, the Apostles are still looking for an earthly king, still wanting to manage things without having to depend on God. "We were hoping that he was the one who would set Israel free" (who would establish the kingdom of Israel as we had planned) (Lk. 24:21), they complain, blind to the presence of the Risen Christ (Lk. 24: 13–35).

The human temptation to trust in self rather than in God seems to dominate the Old Testament, from individuals like Namaan (2 Kgs. 5), who insist on doing things their own way, to collectivities like the entire Israelite nation, who "believed not God nor trusted in his help" (Ps. 78:22). The Church's liturgy, especially during Advent and Lent, presents to contemporary congregations via readings from the book of Isaiah the futility of allying oneself with anything that goes contrary to the Divine Plan. Chapter 30 from this prophet contains symbolic illustrations both of human insistence on managing by ourselves apart from God and of the illusion on which such a life stance is founded. At the moment when Israel places its trust in the Egyptians rather than in Yahweh, Isaiah warns:

> Woe to the rebellious children, says the Lord,
> Who carry out plans that are not mine,
> who weave webs that are not inspired by me. . . .
> [Therefore] because you put your trust in what
> is crooked and devious and depend on it . . .
> . . . [It shall all] crash like a potter's jar
> smashed beyond reason. . . .
> By waiting and by calm you shall be saved,
> in quiet and in trust your strength lies.
> But this you did not wish.

"No," you said,
Upon horses we will flee. . . .
Yet the Lord is waiting to show you favor . . .
He will be gracious when you cry out . . .
On that day . . .
[But] woe to those who go down to Egypt for help,
who depend upon horses:
Who put their trust in chariots . . .
But look not to the Holy One of Israel.
(Is. 30:1, 12,14,15–16,18,19; 31:1)

We are reminded of the opening days of Lent, when true fasting is described as an interior attitude that follows not its own pursuits but rather seeks to know the ways of the Lord and trust in them.[5] "For my thoughts are not your thoughts nor are your ways my ways, says the Lord" (Is. 55:8).

This tendency to place one's trust in one's own ways of thinking and doing is clearly addressed in many of the psalms. The person secure in his or her doxic confidence, who boasts "I shall not be disturbed" (Ps. 10:6), is contrasted with the person who trusts in God's love, and even in distress never loses his or her unshaken confidence in the God who saves. The following verses from the book of Proverbs address in a striking way human reluctance to put aside our own opinion, calculative thinking, and the drive to control what will and will not be:

Trust in the Lord with all your heart,
on your own intelligence rely not;
In all your ways be mindful of him,
and he will make straight your paths. . . .
Entrust your works to the Lord,
and your plans will succeed. . . .
In his mind a man plans his course,
But the Lord directs his steps. . . .
He who plans a thing will be successful;
happy is he who trusts in the Lord!
[Otherwise] sometimes a way seems right to a man
but the end of it leads to death!
(Prov. 3: 5, 6; 16:3,9,20,25)

Again, a familiar verse comes to mind: "Unless the Lord build the house, they labor in vain who build it" (Ps. 127). What do these Old Testament warnings against our tendency to self-sufficiency have to say in terms of the Western Christian emphasis on involvement, on ego-functional immersion in the labor and achievements of the "world of deeds" expressive of the empirical self? How does Scripture respond to questions raised in Chapter 7 regarding the issue of "social reliability" as typifying the response of our post-Renaissance selves in the twentieth-century situation?[6]

In its delighted discovery and celebration of human capacity to manage and control all areas of life, the post-Renaissance period has an in-built tendency to put trust in man rather than in God. Contemporary perception of reality seems to share the one-sided view brought to our attention by both Isaiah and Jeremiah. The former, in the first part of his famous Book of Consolation,[7] reminds us of God's words: "It is I, the Lord; there is no savior but me" (Is. 43:11), and pleads with those who are deaf to listen, with those who are blind to look and see:

> Remember not the events of the past,
> the things of long ago consider not;
> See, I am doing something new!
> Now it springs forth, do you not perceive it?
> (Is. 43: 18–19)

Here we have the central mystery: that it is God and no other who is the Redeemer, the Savior, the To-Be-Trusted for all people. Here is "something new," in the light of which those who perceive it will give up false gods, forsake the idols their own hands have made, and return to the Lord who has redeemed them:

> The idols of the nations are silver and gold,
> the handiwork of men.
> They have mouths but speak not;
> they have eyes but see not;
> they have ears but hear not,
> nor is their breath in their mouths.
> Their makers shall be like them,
> everyone that trusts in them.
> (Ps. 135: 15–18)

> Those go in disgrace who carve images.
> Israel, you are saved by the Lord,
> saved for ever!
> You shall never be put to shame or disgrace
> in future ages.
> (Is. 45:16, 17)

Commenting on the centrality of this revelation of God alone as Redeemer, Eric Voegelin points to the liberation accomplished in the Old Testament by the Holy One of Israel and promised in the New by the obedient Servant of Yahweh whose liberating Redemption will reach to the ends of the earth.[8] He points also to the condemnation of idolatry—the worship, flowing from human pride, of false gods. Babylon fell because of her bondage to false gods, her trust in her own achievement:

> . . . Because you felt secure in your wickedness,
> and said, "No one sees me,"
> Your wisdom and your knowledge led you astray,
> And you said to yourself,
> "I, and no one else."
>
> (Is. 47:10)

Ultimately this kind of idolatrous trust in one's own efforts apart from God is rooted, as Voegelin points out, in the pride of man aping God.

The prophet Jeremiah is vehement indeed in his judgment of those who fail to place their trust in the true God. In his scathing indictment of idolatry and hardness of heart, he writes:

> Cursed is the man who trusts in human beings,
> who seeks his strength in flesh,
> whose heart turns away from the Lord.
> He is like a barren bush in the desert
> that enjoys no change of seasons,
> But stands in a lava waste,
> a salt and empty earth.
>
> (Jer. 17:5–6)

The psalms are also filled with warnings against trusting in human beings to the exclusion of God. Beginning with the warning that everyone who makes idols and trusts in them shall be like them (Ps. 115), we move in the following psalm to an adverse situation where, the Psalmist says, "No man is dependable" (Ps.116). A psalm used frequently in the Paschal liturgy contends that human beings in time of need will find it "better to take refuge in the Lord than to trust in man; better to take refuge in the Lord than to trust in princes" (Ps. 118: 8–9). The Psalmist also gives us advice in the matter of trusting: "Put not your trust in princes, in whom there is no salvation" (Ps.146), for truly happy is the person who puts his or her primary trust in God. Perhaps these holy writers were looking forward to the New Dispensation, in which those are named happy who are poor in spirit, who know and acknowledge their real need of a savior who is at the same time divinely Other.

The Situation "Between"

In Chapter 7, we found that the trust situation is constituted as personally significant not only by its external meaning but by its internal meaningfulness as well. We found, further, that this meaning has its origin in the inner subjectivity of the persons involved. The dimension of response that we call "intimate" yields a knowledge of the other available more to the heart than to the head. An intimate situation is characterized by knowledge of the other's inner life, by an at-homeness with the other that stems from being able to interpret what the other is thinking and to forecast his or her actions and reactions.[9] Such knowledge is usually available only in terms of how much the other person is willing to reveal about himself and the loves and desires of his heart. It was Ellen's conviction that God somehow does reveal his central concerns to people if they are willing to pay attention. She also indicated that her trust in God originated precisely in her desire to understand and cooperate with what she could know from revelation about his will in her particular situation.

A realistic look at the life of Jesus convinces us that during his time on earth, even though he came to tell humankind about God's will of love for the world, he did not find many people with whom he could be intimate. There was, of course, his mother and St. John, Mary, Martha, and Lazarus, and Mary Magdalene. Not many others seem to have really understood what he was about. Why else would he have exclaimed in frustration, "How long have I been with you . . . and you still do not understand," and on the road to Emmaus, "What little sense you have," to the two who were still expecting the establishment of an earthly kingdom. The Apostles certainly tried to share his concerns, but they were not even able to carry out his commands because they had so little trust (Mt.17:19). They missed the meaning of his closeness to the Father: "after I have been with you all this time, you still do not know me" (Jn. 14:9); and even to the first among the Apostles, he was forced to say, "Get out of my sight, you Satan!" (Mk. 8:33). St. Mark picks up particularly on the lack of trusting intimacy between Jesus and the people he worked with, noting, "He could work no miracles there so much did their lack of faith distress him" (Mk. 6:5); their minds were completely closed to the meaning of the events (Mk. 6:52); "what an unbelieving lot you are" (Mk. 9:19); and an exclamation from the sick boy's father: "I do believe. Help my lack of trust" (Mk. 9:24).

One of the problems for all these people—and for us—is that they were unable to forget their preoccupation with themselves long enough to truly share in the central concerns of Jesus. As Paul puts it, "Everyone is busy seeking his own interests rather than those of Christ Jesus" (Phil. 2:21). Yet if we are to be intimate with another, especially if that Other is God, we must be willing to detach ourselves from our selves. In the midst of any human situation, we must be willing to seek God's kingdom, not our own. We must become interested in it and make space in our crowded hearts for its coming. We must grow through prayer in an intense concern for God's plan, in a lively awareness or feeling that he is invisibly present and at work in persons and events, that if we "keep our eyes fixed on Jesus" (Heb. 12:2), he will eventually reunite us and all creation with the Godhead for which we are destined. On the Feast of the Sacred Heart, as well as on the second Sunday in Lent and the fifth Sunday of Easter, we express our trust in the Lord's providential plan:

> For upright is the word of the Lord,
> and all his works are trustworthy,
> He loves justice and right;
> of the kindness of the Lord the earth is full. . . .
> . . . the plan of the Lord stands forever;
> the design of his heart through all generations.
> For in him our hearts rejoice;
> in his holy name we trust.
> (Ps. 33: 4–5, 11–12, 21)

Intimacy with him asks that we be willing to share concern for the designs of that heart, to trust in the love that underlies them and to commit ourselves not just from the outside but from within to service that is beyond both fusion and isolated striving.[10] The heart that trusts the flow at its source can turn even the stress of contemporary situatedness, with all its change and uncertainty, into opportunities for growth.

Faith Community as Context

On the Feast of All Saints, the Church celebrates the deepest truth about the human situation. On that day, we celebrate the universal solidarity that arises from our common rootedness in the uncreated Source of the death and Resurrection of Christ. The Feast of All Saints is a celebration of the entire human family as redeemed—of the "holy men and women of every time and place" mentioned in the opening prayer. In the first reading (Rev. 7:2–4, 9–14), we find again this "huge crowd which no one could count from every nation and race, people and tongue." The psalm verse makes it clear that "such is the race that seeks for him, that seeks the face of the God of Jacob." The second reading from St. John's First Epistle points to the deepest identity of each individual in this enormous crowd when it notes that they are all children of the Father's love, destined for a still-to-be-discovered future as images of God, "like him . . . as he is" (1 Jn. 3:1–3). His compassion for each is is reflected in the reading of the Beatitudes that follows from Matthew's Gospel (Mt. 5:1–12). No longer are we allowed to remain in the illusion of the separated self. Small fields of energy within a multitude of larger fields, we who partake of the same bread find ourselves to be members of the same body (1 Cor. 10:17), sharing in the same sources of energy and life.

In this celebration, which has been part of the lived tradition of the Church in the East since the fourth century and of the West since the ninth, we find preserved the wisdom of the ordinary Christian people whose lives and deaths celebrated the key directives of faith before intellectually defining them. As they gather to break bread together, to *do* in memory of Him, they discover again as a group what it means to be part of the Christian tribe, united by hope and love in time and destined to share eternally at the table "in the joy of your kingdom where Jesus is Lord for ever and ever."[11] This feast, like all the others, finds its binding force in the communal relationship made possible by the unique relatedness of each one present to the uncreated Source of all life and love. The fact of our intersubjectivity,[12] the "already thereness" of our participative union with others, is given force and solidity by this rootedness in Mystery. Generations of Christians have already lived and died in trusting unity with this communal vision. Today their descendants in the faith assemble on feasts like the Vigil of Pentecost and on the Sundays in "ordinary time"[13] to be reminded again of their basic situation as set out by St. Paul in the eighth chapter of his Epistle to the Romans. In commenting on these verses, Adrian Nocent explains:

> The Church does not preach to us a God who is the Creator of the isolated individual, but a God who is also Creator of all other human beings and of the entire universe . . . in the view of the Fathers, God created the whole of mankind as a single totality, and it is this unity, which extends to the uttermost depth of every being, that explains how one man's sin could implicate the whole human race. . . . The Christian cannot, therefore, have the right attitude toward his Creator unless he stands before him with a soul that is open not only to other human beings but to all created things, animate and inanimate, and indeed to the universe in its entirety. For the latter, like man himself, has been redeemed. To put it another way, it is the whole man, and

not just his soul, that God has created and that Christ has redeemed; and the resurrection of the flesh implies in turn the restoration of the universe as a whole. . . .[14]

This sense of participation in all of life should pervade the Christian faith community as the widest and deepest context of all the more immediate life circumstances in which Christians find themselves or to which they are called by the Spirit.[15] A lived sense of connectedness and love, of universal solidarity, must underlie the possibility of real social consciousness, of being able to see ourselves as brothers and sisters to one another in what the Creed calls a "communion of saints."

This lively sense of the self as a field of meaning inextricably bound up and interconnected with other fields of meaning would do away forever with the illusion of the separated self, the self who trusts in a vacuum. It became clear in Chapters 3 and 4 that from the first moment of their existence, the person who trusts and the other who is trusted are already participating in a "common world," not only mediated by family and culture but also, at least for some, embodied in a communal "myth" or faith tradition.[16] In her personal crisis, we found Ellen reaching beyond herself for directives embodied and enfleshed in the world of the Christian Catholic faith tradition. It was more lived participation in than rational knowledge about the community's perception of life's meaning that came to her aid in a moment of appraisal.

Like Ellen, most of us are called at some time in our lives to appraise and say yes to the overarching faith community to which, as adults, we belong not only by birth but by personal choice. We are also asked from time to time to respond to smaller intermediate groups or communities as trustable-for-me,[17] to identify with a collective style that evokes the yes of one's heart. In somewhat the same manner as people were attracted by the style of mutual caring among members of the early Christian communities (see how they love one another), we now find ourselves being drawn toward groups whose "way" appears to be nourished by rootedness in the same ground as our own. Ultimately we are inclined to trust a community of others whose involvement in the social dimension is motivated by the Grail knight's question, "What is your sorrow?", and finds its context in the larger search for the One whom the Grail serves.

CHAPTER 16

TRUST IN SELF, OTHERS, AND THE HOLY OTHER

Who We Really Are

Immediately after celebrating the New Creation at Christmas, the Church has us look again at God's plan of salvation, at the new reality that is now the context of our lives. As the assembled people read together Paul's letter to the Ephesians,[1] there is an implicit demand that in its light we see ourselves differently:

> We were chosen before the creation of the world to become holy and blameless in the Lord's sight; we were predestined in advance to become children for God through Jesus the Christ. It is the Spirit who now makes us discern God's wisdom and conforms us to the image of the Son. We thereby learn how, through the mystery of the incarnation, we enter into the life of the Trinity. From all eternity God has loved us. . . .[2]

If this is a true picture of the nature of reality, and if, as we have already seen, the nature of the context or field coconstitutes the reality of the persons within it, then we are transformed in our very being as partakers in the Trinitarian Mystery. This is who we *really* are, as St. John reminds us:

> See what love the Father has bestowed upon us
> in letting us be called children of God!
> Yet that is what we are . . .
> Dearly beloved
> we are God's children now;
> What we shall be later has not yet come to light.
> We know that when it comes to light
> we shall be like him
> for we shall see him as he is. . . .
>
> (1 Jn. 3:1–2)

Drawn into a cosmic horizon, we must live in a new sense of self as transcending, as capable of relating to Mystery. We understand ourselves now as awakened spirit demanding a larger horizon than appears for secularized consciousness.

At the beginning of Chapter 3 we spoke of the self as context of experience,[3] coproducing situations out of the central mode of presence we bring to them. Now we discover the self as an ever-changing capacity for presence, capable of moving to new levels of being in relation not only to self but also to others and to God. In the light of Revelation, we understand something of the self who trusts as "New Creation" (2 Cor. 5:17); as God's handiwork, created in Christ Jesus to lead the life of good deeds that God prepared for us in advance (Eph. 2:10); as someone in whom the Trinity will come and make their home (Jn. 14:23); as called to know Jesus and, through him, the Father (Jn. 14: 20–21); as indwelt by the Spirit of him who raised Jesus from the dead (Rom. 8:11).[4] Once Jesus broke into human history, the old order passed away. Now all is new, including all those baptized into his body (2 Cor. 5:17). Granted, this image of Christ in us is obscured by the effects of the Fall and by our repeated refusals to allow him to be God in our lives. Nevertheless, our hearts, attuned as they are to the Mysterious patterns of Divine Will in the universe and in daily life, can become, like the eyes of the bee, continually on the lookout for "infrared."

Intuitively our minds, aided by a prayerful consciousness, can awaken to the "already there." In this state, we are more inclined to look for overall directions and synthesize differentiated experiences as they crowd upon us. We live in trusting confidence toward the "something of God" that is in us, and we long for the final revelation of our "new name" (Rev. 2:17), the true identity that is even now forming at the core of our being. Our hearts, capable of being touched by the "myth" and penetrated by the life of faith, are gradually transformed by reflecting on our experiences in the context of God's providential presence. At each appraisal, the heart's sensibility is deepened, even when we find ourselves resisting life's invitations to grow and respond. This striving, struggling, conflicted heart that loves reality can change, can undergo many metanoias, can shift the field of presence that it is. This heart, rooted as it is in Mystery, can appraise and choose, can commit its love to a future. Living out of a chosen as well as given world of meaning, this heart can shift the quality of its intuitive participation in that Mystery, can expand with human consciousness to a wider view offered by a particular faith tradition. It is with the heart that we live in "internal" relationship to others and the Other.[5] It is with the heart that we go beyond appearances in imaginative anticipation of the future kingdom. It is with the intending heart and its desires that we come to understand and share the lived concerns of the Other who is Christ.

The liturgy of Lent is alive with this notion of change of heart, and we find along with many psalms of trust, a psalm that begs for metanoia at the same time that it acknowledges sinfulness and need for mercy:

> Indeed in guilt was I born
> and in sin my mother conceived me;
> Behold you are pleased with sincerity of heart,
> and in my inmost being you teach me wisdom. . . .
> A clean heart create for me, O God,
> and a steadfast spirit renew within me.
> Cast me not out from your presence
> and your holy spirit take not from me.
> Give me back the joy of your salvation,
> and a willing spirit sustain in me. . . .
> My sacrifice, O God, is a contrite spirit;
> a heart contrite and humbled, O God, you will not spurn.
> (Ps. 51:7–8, 12–14, 19)

The awakening, changing heart is also thematic in the liturgy of the Advent season, as we are invited on the Third Sunday to "rejoice" because the Lord is near. His presence, discovered by hearts that have heeded the warning of the First Sunday to wake from sleep and cast aside the dullness of vision that belongs to the natural attitude, constitutes again the "already there" environment that evokes a primordial yes from the trusting heart.[6]

In Chapter 8, we spoke of the new relatedness to one's community that is possible for one who takes the risk of trusting. In the community of the Early Church, there seems to have been a freedom of relating, a sense of being "with," a koinonia that marks the completely new age entered into by the Church after Christ's ascension and the coming of the Spirit. We are not surprised to find that all the readings for Easter week and the Sundays after Easter are taken from the Acts of the Apostles, because it is there that we find documented in detail the community life of the first believers. We find that in this earliest time, people trusted one another to emerge as ambassadors of the Good News. We also find that there were conflicts not only between persons but also with the Gospel revelation itself. Like the first days of any other human community, the beginnings of this one were fraught with unique opportunities for the members to choose and rechoose whether or not they would yield free allegiance to this people of the Way. Neither fusion nor withdrawal seems to have been necessary for those who had truly understood the message of the community's founder. Yet there are always those of us who are anxious, who for one reason or another cannot feel at home enough to risk a spiritual life of freedom and reflective presence even with like-minded others.[7] Our hearts need to be changed and transformed by an ever-deepening realization of the saving message of the Incarnation, so that we can follow St. Paul's advice (Phil. 4:4–7) and truly rejoice, dismissing anxiety from our minds and hearts because of the nearness of the Risen life-giving Lord and the saving context that he brings.

The Paradox of Embodiment

Today the human body is understood as a dynamic system, a field of energy within other fields, a context of patterns locked into the sensory motor system by one's body memory. Adherents of the holistic health movement see the body itself as process. Health is increasingly understood as being dependent on one's state of harmony or disharmony, on one's ability to relax and flow with experience. Many diseases are considered to have originated in a dissonant "body-mind loop," in some tension or denial of reality that affects the whole. Healing takes place when, in love and relaxation, the syndrome is broken from within. Thus healing is seen to be essentially self-healing, deeply connected with states of consciousness, with the body as preconscious intentional "subject,"[8] and with trusting acceptance of all the uniquely specific genetic inheritance, assets, and liabilities that characterize one aspect of what van Kaam designates as the pole of "preformation."[9] This preformative genetic structure corresponds to the "body subject" that Merleau-Ponty detects beneath the consciously knowing subject, the constellation of "givens" that adapts us to the world before we are consciously aware of giving form to our world. It represents the embodiment pointed out by the Psalmist as being ours from our mother's womb:

> Truly you have formed my inmost being;
> you knit me in my mother's womb.
> I give you thanks that I am fearfully, wonderfully made;
> wonderful are your works.
> My soul also you knew full well;
> nor was my frame unknown to you
> When I was made in secret,
> when I was fashioned in the depths of the earth . . .
>
> (Ps. 139: 13–15)

We are asked to trustingly accept this preformative genetic structure as given to us by God, to see in it the developmental presence of God working through us as through the universe.

Here we return to the notion of the early Greek Fathers,[10] that we live in a transforming universe filled with divine energies from which, even prior to conscious awareness, we receive form both macrocosmically and microcosmically.[11] As the universe unfolds, we are meant to be in touch with it through these given genetic influences that continue to form us throughout our lives. As beings held in existence from moment to moment, followers of Christ are asked to surrender to this absolute Mystery on which we depend. Christians are challenged to have confidence in God's permeation of every atom of their bodies.[12] What matters is not so much the quality of our genetic preformation, but rather the quality of our response to it. Paradoxically, the discovery of the various aspects of one's embodied aliveness and temporality[13] can be the occasion for both positive response and negative reaction as the meaning of the embodied self unfolds in relation to the life of the spirit.

To begin with the positive side of this paradox, we see clearly from the Christian faith tradition the central importance that God himself gives to embodiment, to the dipping of spirit into matter, to incarnation. In fact, the whole of Christian faith is based on trust that God did raise the *body* of his Son as a sign of the victory of life over death (Acts. 13: 30–31). The recollections of the first Christians center around their experiences of Christ's glorified body, no longer subject to the limitations of time and space.[14] The body of Jesus was in fact the instrument of salvation, as the Church reminds us in the Office of Passion Sunday as well as on the Feast of the Annunciation:

> . . . on coming into the world, Jesus said:
> Sacrifice and oblation you did not desire,
> but a body you prepared for me;
> Holocausts and sin offerings you took no delight in.
> Then I said "As is written of me in the book
> I have come to do your will, O God."
>
> (Heb. 10: 5–7)

The liturgy of Holy Saturday is filled with psalms expressing trust in God's care for the body of his beloved Son, the body that, after its painful struggle, "abides in confidence" (Ps. 16:9) because just as the Father will not abandon his soul, he will not allow the body of his faithful one "to undergo corruption." Our bodies also, subject to death though they are, are by Christ's victory over death assured of resurrection. In fact, it is faith in Christ's and our own bodily resurrection that constitutes the central Mystery of God's creative activity in regard to human beings; in regard to the interplay of divine energies that guarantees their eternal existence. Chapter 15 of St. Paul's first letter to the community at Corinth explains:

If there is no resurrection of the dead,
Christ himself has not been raised.
And if Christ has not been raised, our preaching is void of content
and your faith is empty too. . . .
If our hopes in Christ are limited to this life only,
we are the most pitiable of men.
But as it is, Christ is now raised from the dead,
the first fruits of those who have fallen asleep. . . .
What is sown in the earth is subject to decay,
what rises is incorruptible.
What is sown is ignoble, what rises is glorious.
Weakness is sown, strength rises up.
A natural body is put down and a spiritual body comes up. . . .
. . . we shall be changed.
This corruptible body must be clothed with incorruptibility,
this mortal body with immortality.

(1 Cor. 15: 13–14, 19–20, 42–44, 52–53.)

At the beginning of this fifteenth chapter, Paul refers to the ancient Gospel tradition about the Risen Christ: that he "died for our sins" (15:3); that he was buried and, in accordance with the Scriptures, rose on the third day (15:4); and that *"he was seen"* by Cephas, by the Twelve, by five hundred brothers at once, by James, by all the Apostles, and finally by Paul himself. We are reminded of Jesus' remark to Phillip regarding the power of his own embodiment to put us in touch with what is beyond: "Phillip, he who sees me has seen the Father" (Jn. 14:8–9). After the ascension of his body, Jesus sent the Spirit to enable his followers to be always and everywhere in contact with that glorified body. Present-day Christians understand the sacraments as ways of being in contact within our space and time with the Risen Lord, whose Divine Presence has energized and changed forever the entire universe.[15] We begin to understand that the present vital/functional "identity,"[16] the current empirical sensible self, is destined for change, for permeation and transformation by the divine energies of the risen life. We can understand why a certain measure not only of trust but also of ordinary doxic confidence in the self-evident givenness of one's world and one's embodiment in it is a necessary condition for the development of a trusting relationship with God.[17]

On the other hand, just before Lent or just after Pentecost,[18] the liturgy presents us with the ways in which mere doxic confidence can lead to a false absolutizing of complacency in the vital dimension with its capacities for enjoyment and functional achievement. The Gospel taken from St. Matthew points to the duty of being improvident, of not putting confidence in earthly treasure, of not worrying about making a living or providing for the needs of the body. In other words, it warns us that too much care for the body can distract us from the true "treasure" (Mt. 6: 19–34) of the spirit. Overconcern for the bodily aspects of life may even block the flow of divine energy and become an obstacle to transcendence. Like the rich man whose story precedes this parable in the Gospel of St. Luke, we are tempted to "grow rich for ourselves" (Lk. 12: 16–21). Like him, we may begin to build larger grain bins to store our many possessions; we may allow ourselves to become fragmented and sedated with pleasure, with power, with popularity and status; we may lose ourselves in partial truths and become embedded in the common sense of immediacy. Immersed in the good things of the world, in a finite horizon of natural satisfaction, we may forget about "seeking first his kingship over us, his way of holiness," and about trusting that all these things will be given us besides (Mt. 6:33). Instead, in the false security of a life devoted to having and achieving, we may find ourselves boasting; "I shall never be disturbed" (Ps. 30). Having piled up friends, knowledge, and works, and relying on personal capacities, skills, and natural energy, we may continue to build on the sand of human resources rather than on the rock of trust in God's love for us (Mt. 7:24–27). Never poor, never in need, having no thought for "what kind of life will be ours tomorrow" (Jas. 4: 14, Lk. 12:20), we may find that the security we have built for ourselves walls us in so thoroughly that we never notice our need of a savior.

We are confronted here with another paradox in the Christian life. On the one hand, overconfidence in oneself and in one's ability to save oneself by amassing the goods of this world is to be avoided. On the other hand, we are encouraged to grow in a trusting attitude toward the God who works not only in world history but also in the details of our own personal developmental history. We need to cultivate a self-confidence rooted in our natural bodily development, in the various maturational periods already achieved or still to come,[19] a self-confidence flowing from the natural basis for fruitful faith, hope, and love that has already been laid in our lives by loving others and the loving Other. The prophet Jeremiah expressed this notion of the staying power inherent in the feeling of having been loved into existence when he said:

Blessed is the man who trusts in the Lord,
whose hope is in the Lord.
He is like a tree planted beside the waters
that stretches out its roots in the stream:
It fears not the heat when it comes,
its leaves stay green;
In the year of drought it shows no distress
but still bears fruit.

(Jer. 17: 7–8)

Here we have the basic predisposition of grateful yes, of trust in what van Kaam calls the Mystery of meaningful formation. This yes to one's self as formed by a loving God forms the basis of a lifelong ability to reach out beyond the self in loving service to others and to the world. It contains the secret of faithful commitment, of "form effectiveness,"[20] and of the ability to face life without being torn apart by anxiety. It is summed up in the rediscovery that even though we all had limited human mothers, our maternal environment has from the beginning been complemented and sustained by the feminine principle in the Godhead, the One whom Julian of Norwich trusts as "God our Mother."[21]

Discovering the Other "for Me"

In exploring the trustworthiness of the other in Chapter 4, we found that the other's trustworthy style is always coconstituted by the person doing the trusting.[22] Somehow a response of trust is awakened in me only by a style of being that corresponds to what I personally consider to be affirmable from my point of view, from where I am. So I have to ask what is the "something" about Jesus Christ, God as visible among human beings, that is trustable for me? To come close to an answer, I have to have a sense of what really appeals to me, of what I deeply want and value out of life, of where my real interest lies. Perhaps I need to retrace the past and see how God has been trustable in my history, how his invisible good intentions toward me have been implicit in our lived relationship. Have I felt that he affirms me just as I am? How has he been for me a Father who knows how to give good gifts to his child (Mt. 7:11)? Can I honestly say that I have allowed him to be Other, to be God and Savior in my life, or have I rather tried to save myself and thus not discovered him as the One who is always faithful?

Scripture is full of descriptions of the style of God as revealed in Jesus Christ. Throughout the Old Testament, Yahweh is constantly reminding his people to look back on all that he had done for them,[23] and the Good Friday liturgy continues this custom of remembering his mercies in the singing of the "Reproaches," in which God reminds us of the style of his love throughout all generations. Kindness, faithfulness, and merciful love characterize the self-revelation of Yahweh in the Old Testament. Significantly, such knowledge of the Other is available only to his people, to those who have lived through events with him, who have had to depend on him in times of crisis and distress. If we turn to the New Testament revelation of God, we find that our access to him and the "fringes" of our knowledge of his meaning for us are often communicated in times of need, of distress, of being compelled to turn to his saving power, to the Beyond in our midst. It is in moments of acknowledging our own sinfulness, our own brokenness, and our desire for "more" that we may first come to know and trust the One who came precisely to call sinners rather than the self-righteous (Mk. 2:17); who welcomes and eats with quite ordinary people (Lk. 15:2) and whose heart is moved with pity for the crowds (Mk. 8:2). The style of the Son reflects the style of the Father. It is these "fringes," caught only in a lived encounter with the other that enable us to sense his trustworthiness—to believe that even if we are unfaithful, he will still remain faithful (2 Tim. 2:13), and to say with Paul:

> I know him in whom I have believed, and I am
> confident that he is able to guard what has
> been entrusted to me until that Day.
> (2 Tim. 1:12)

It becomes clear that trust in Jesus Christ involves also trust in the uncreated eternal Mystery that is the horizon of his life. It is also clear that if we are totally lacking in a sense of this horizon, we may miss it entirely, just as those without the capacity to perceive it will miss "infrared."

How does Jesus describe the value horizon from which he emerges into the world? In St. John's Gospel, we find him referring constantly to the Father who sent him, and appealing for trust in that value horizon: "Whoever puts faith in me believes not so much in me as in him who sent me" (Jn. 12:44); "This is the work of God: have faith in the One whom he sent" (Jn. 6:29); and "Whoever has seen me has seen the Father (Jn. 14:9). St. John's Gospel, used extensively in the liturgy of Lent and the weekdays of the Easter season, contains many such appeals for trust in the loving Father who sent his Son "and has given everything over to him" (Jn. 3:25). This Father, who has been seen and known only by the Son (Jn. 6:46), has set his seal on this Son (Jn. 1:31–34) and gives us the bread of eternal life through him (Jn. 6:32). He challenges us, without offering us socially reliable proofs, to believe the unbelievable, to trust absolutely in the person of this Son (Jn. 6:69). Never departing from his adherence to this horizon of the Divine Will (Jn. 6:38), Jesus points throughout his public life to the necessity of attentiveness to this invisible horizon if his own mission is to succeed, saying, "No one can come to me unless the Father who sent me draws him" (Jn. 6:44). The chapters of St. John's Gospel containing Christ's final attempt to familiarize his followers with the eternal Mystery that gives meaning and value to his own life and death evoke a response, not primarily of trust or belief, but of love.24

Again we return to the Good Friday liturgy to witness in action Christ's own love and trust of his Father. Psalm 31, with its reference to the suffering and triumph of the Servant of the Lord in the 53rd chapter of the book of Isaiah, is put on the lips of Christ on the cross:

> In you O Lord I take refuge;
> let me never be put to shame,
> in your justice rescue me. . . .
> Into your hands I commend my spirit;
> you will redeem me, O Lord, O faithful God. . . .
> But my trust is in you, O Lord;
> I say, "You are my God."
>
> (Ps. 31:2, 6, 15)

On Passion Sunday, glimpses of the trust between Father and Son shine through as Christ prays, "My Father, if this cannot pass me by without my drinking it, your will be done" (Mt. 26:42), and as someone in the crowd recalls that during his earthly life, "He [Christ] relied on God" (Mt. 27:43). St. Matthew also notes that Christ was praying Psalm 21, which contains the words:

> My God, my God, why have you forsaken me? . . .
> In you our Fathers trusted;
> They trusted and you delivered them.
> To you they cried and they escaped;
> In you they trusted, and they were not put to shame. . . .
> You have been my guide since I was first formed,
> my security at my mother's breast.
> To you I was committed at birth,
> from my mother's womb you are my God. . . .

and ends on a note of certainty in final victory as the Passover that is the source of new life is accomplished.

Who, then, is this God in whose providential care we are to trust? Certainly some of the richest descriptions of this mysterious Other are found in the book of Psalms, especially the ones used in the liturgy of Lent and Holy Week. Echoing other parts of the Bible, where God is described as "a merciful and gracious God, slow to anger and rich in kindness and fidelity" (Ex. 34:6), they praise the greatness and goodness of God:

> The Lord is gracious and merciful,
> slow to anger and of great kindness.
> The Lord is good to all
> and compassionate toward all his works.
> The Lord is faithful in all his words
> and holy in all his works;
> The Lord lifts up all who are falling
> and raises up all who are bowed down.
> The eyes of all look hopefully to you,
> and you give them their food in due season;
> You open your hand
> and satisfy the desire of every living thing.
> (Ps. 145: 8–9, 13–16)

If this is a true description of the horizon of the to-be-trusted Christ, then perhaps it is not so impossible that I begin shifting the axis of my existence, breaking the bonds of my self-sufficient isolation in order to "seek first his kingship," and let him have more control of my life. Following his way of holiness rather than my own calls indeed for an inner conversion of heart and detachment from much that I have heretofore considered to be authentic "riches." In setting aside my own self-containment, I am invited to trust that all these things will be given me besides by this God who in Christ addresses me personally on the deepest level of my being.

It is precisely this abandonment of one's own way in response to the Holy Other, this interior obedience of the heart to the initiative of Another, that constitutes the essence of human trust in God. Yet this trust, like trust of human others, is uniquely structured and nuanced according to the lived predispositions and temperament, the vital/functional capacities, the qualities of transcendent and pneumatic openness of heart that each individual brings to a trusting encounter with the living God. Trust in God, like the search for God, will be different for each person, not only according to the variety of lived attitudes, but also according to the life situation, maturational stage, stratum of society, intellectual level, and embodied sensibility they represent. The trusted Other will emerge in a unique way "for me," just as we see him doing for a wide variety of persons in the Gospels. The common denominator of them all seems to be that no matter what the state of heart with which we meet him, God always manages to be "greater than our heart" (1 Jn. 3:20). It has been suggested that the way of love described in the thirteenth chapter of Corinthians is a description not only of the love we could have for one another, but, more accurately, of the love God already does have for us.

The Kingdom Seeks Us

Although we can agree that we are each the context of our trusting experience of others and of the Holy Other, the Gospel revelation of how this encounter between God and human beings takes place emphasizes a reversal uncovered in the original research.[25] We do not institute a relationship of trust with God. The initiative is always his. Just as the world gives itself to us in events before we have planned or predicted them,[26] so, too, the unpredictable Mystery that is God's presence as created and uncreated overflow of the life of Father, Son, and Spirit communicates itself first as an initiative from what is other than the self. The Advent themes of conversion of heart, of watchfulness and waiting upon, relate directly to this view of God as the One who comes now in the events and eucharist of daily life, in the past at the center of history, and in fulfillment of the eternal design at the end of time. We are asked to wake from sleep and to undergo a radical change that will prepare the way for his advent into our lives and into the darkness of our world. Called to a renewed appraisal of our actions in the light of the Mystery being revealed more fully each year, we are asked to be on the lookout for the presence of God "in his energies"[27] in each event; to be on the watch for the flow of initiatives originating in the Mystery of the To-Be-Trusted One.

Realization of the fact that salvation is God's free gift to us, totally unmerited and outside the realm of human functioning and organization, can come as a great relief:

> . . . when the kindness of God our savior appeared, he saved us; not because of any righteous deeds we had done, but because of his mercy. He saved us through the baptism of new birth and renewal by the Holy Spirit. This Spirit he lavished on us through Jesus Christ our Savior, that we might be justified by his grace and become heirs, in hope, of eternal life. You can depend on this to be true.
>
> (Titus 3:4–8)

These words from the Mass at Dawn on Christmas reveal the way it is between us and the persons of the Trinity. The initiative is theirs. Our part is not even to merit salvation, but rather to live in openness toward this loving mercy, trusting this all "to be true"; trusting, as St. John records it, that God so loved the world, he gave his only Son so that we might have eternal life (Jn. 3:16). Evidently the message is a hard one for human beings to receive. The first epistle of St. John, Paul's letter to the Ephesians, all of Scripture, in fact, are filled with references to the loving initiatives of the Divine Wisdom of God that guides creation with power and love.[28] We are encouraged to get in touch with this energy, to trust this invisible power "already there" beneath the visible surface of our life. No matter how unworthy we are, God's love never falters:

> You were dead because of your sins and offenses,
> as you gave allegiance to the present age. . . .
> But God is rich in mercy; because of his great love
> for us he brought us to life with Christ
> when we were dead in sin. By this favor you were saved. . . .
> This is not your own doing, it is God's gift;
> neither is it a reward for anything you have accomplished,
> so let no one pride himself on it.
>
> (Eph. 2:1–2, 4–5, 8–9)

But pride ourselves we do, and with too much control and functional organization, we attempt to plan our lives and even our own holiness. As we have already noticed, when someone is in a functional demanding mood, the other cannot emerge as to-be-trusted. Perhaps this is why the priest and Levite missed God's initiative lying on the Jerusalem-Jericho road (Lk. 10:25–37). It wasn't that they were of bad will. In fact, chances are they were both full of wonderful plans for doing good to others. But the unexpected takes time, and probably they both had full appointment books!

The question still remains: Why do we find it so difficult to trust this God who loves us first and whose creative energy is constantly at work in the world, relieving our anxiety about "all these things"? Returning to the readings of the Easter Vigil, we find the divinized universe, as it overflows with grace and life, compared to an ocean flowing to and fro, surrounding seekers on all sides. An appeal is made for us to forsake our habitual ways, our obsessively inflexible thoughts, and turn to the Lord, undergo a metanoia:

> For my thoughts are not your thoughts
> nor are your ways my ways, says the Lord.

> As high as the heavens are above the earth
> so high are my ways above your ways
> and my thoughts above your thoughts.
>
> (Is. 55:8–9)

We have only to open our hearts and minds, to call upon him while he is near, to trust this mysterious presence in our lives. Yet the research has shown that it is precisely because of this mystery, this otherness, this unfamiliarity, that we hesitate to trust. Without an intuitive leap of the heart in the direction of ambiguity; without an abandoning of self-centered security measures, without some risk, we find it impossible to grow in relationship with the God who was trusted by Jesus. Even at the close of the *"Te Deum,"* one of the Church's most magnificent hymns of praise to the Holy Other, we find a wonderfully human note, a plea in the face of ambiguity:

> You are God: we praise you;
> You are the Lord; we acclaim you;
> You are the eternal Father:
> All creation worships you.
> To you all angels, all the powers of heaven,
> Cherubim and Seraphim, sing in endless praise:
>> Holy, holy, holy, Lord, God of power and might,
>> heaven and earth are full of your glory.
> The glorious company of apostles praise you.
> The noble fellowship of prophets praise you.
> The white-robed army of martyrs praise you.
> Throughout the world the holy Church acclaims you:
>> Father, of majesty unbounded,
>> your true and only Son, worthy of all worship,
>> and the Holy Spirit, advocate and guide.
> You, Christ, are the king of glory,
> the eternal Son of the Father.
> When you became man to set us free
> you did not spurn the Virgin's womb.
> You overcame the sting of death,
> and opened the kingdom of heaven to all believers.
> You are seated at God's right hand in glory.
> We believe that you will come, and be our judge.
> Come then, Lord, and help your people,
> bought with the price of your own blood,
> and bring us with your saints
> to glory everlasting.

V. Save your people, Lord, and bless your inheritance.

R. Govern and uphold them now and always.

V. Day by day we bless you:

R. We praise your name forever,

V. Keep us today, Lord, from all sin.

R. Have mercy on us, Lord, have mercy.

V. Lord, show us your love and mercy;

R. For we put our trust in you.

V. In you, Lord, is our hope:

R. Let us not be disappointed.

CHAPTER 17

TRUST THAT RISKS COMMITMENT

The Invitation Hidden in Events

Chapter 5, on "Events as Openness Moments," began by recalling the fact that the world gives itself to us in an ongoing stream or flow of life experiences. A revelatory realization—the world *gives itself to us!* Complete reversal of the taken-for-granted assumption that we ourselves are somehow the source of all that happens. The initiative for what happens is with the world. This is the way things *are*. Here was a discovery that regestalted former assumptions and attitudes, that prompted a paradigm shift of major proportions. My presence to reality altered as this new realization gradually helped me to let go of old ways, of closed attitudes, of isolated perceptions, and at least a few familiar illusions of control. A new way of understanding reality opened out. Aided by Prigogine's theory of dissipative structures,[1] I could more easily recognize the providential pattern embedded in events, especially stress-accompanied events; I could tune in to their potential for restructuring fields of energy, for forcing sudden new solutions, and for reordering, for better or for worse, the whole of one's situated human existence.

Understanding this power hidden in not-too-promising life situations changes our way of looking at life's flow. Events, by breaking in on us the way they do, are in themselves a process that changes and forms us. Crisis moments especially can be compared to the more or less stressful incidents of energy buildup and depletion described in Prigogine's theory. At such moments, the entire system is open for new connections with hitherto untapped transformative energy sources. Significant life events, especially those that involve some sort of conflict, can be seen in the same way, not simply as meaningless accidents, but as invitations to growth, to new life, to reconnection with still deeper levels of reality. A serendipity of disasters[2] that circumvents the usual anxious reactions and attempts at regaining autonomous control can emerge. Even when the inner meaning of a distasteful experience tends to evoke isolating security measures and closure, one senses at the same time an alternative possibility. This unexpected and unwanted person, event, or thing may hold within it the germ of new unfolding, the chance for restructuration of presence, the thrust of a new current self.[3] Closing oneself off from life events, on the other hand, may be akin to becoming the branch separated from the vine—cut off from the true sources of its energy, it can "do nothing" (Jn. 15:5).

The key to this alternative way of looking at the stream of one's life lies mainly in the possibility that one has of being able to trust the source of one's world and its initiatives, of being able to let oneself go in confident surrender to an overall loving will behind unexpected interventions of "otherness" in one's life. One parable in particular contains the steps that allow such a moment to be transformative:

> The reign of God is like a buried treasure which a man found in a field. He hid it again, and rejoicing at his find went and sold all he had and bought that field. (Mt. 13:44)

First of all, these few lines seem typical of the way in which the hidden invitations of God enter our lives. We are busy going about our affairs and something happens. The world gives itself to us; our plow hits something buried in the ground. We may stop what we are doing to have a look. But usually we are so busy and preoccupied that we resist interruption. We may with minor inconvenience pass right over the lump. We are late already for the next self-scheduled event. However, if the lump is big enough to disrupt the furrow we happen to be plowing, or even to break the plow, it may capture our attention. In other words, the personal significance of an event evokes our interest, and like the subjects of the trust study, we are drawn out of ourselves by what is "other." The second step in the process consists in a reversal of the former self, who changes perspective because a conflicting directive is offered by the attraction of the treasure; the finder rejoices in this new alternative and trusts that it is real. This shift in presence to reality fosters a third step, the risk of new action. Everything is sold in order to buy the field. This person's entire being has been altered. He or she will never return to that former self again. For those who trust, apparently ordinary and sometimes distressing events and setbacks offer the same treasure of new life as the lump hidden in the ground held for the farmer. "The reign of God is already in your midst" (Lk. 17:21). It needs only to be recognized as "treasure" streaming from a trusted source.

In the Old Testament, we find individuals confronted with, and sometimes overwhelmed by, adverse events. The suffering Job undergoes a series of stressful jolts and, tempted to return to doxic confidence in the visible, utters the classic response of one who trusts the invisible meaning of events: "Slay me though he might, I will wait for [trust] him" (Job 13–15). At the end of his humiliations, Job realizes the way things really are and answers the Lord from the depths of his changed perspective:

> I know that you can do all things,
> and that no purpose of yours can be hindered.
> I have dealt with great things that I do not understand;
> things too wonderful for me, which I cannot know
> I have heard of you by word of mouth,
> but now my eyes have seen you.
> Therefore I disown what I have said,
> and repent in dust and ashes.
>
> (Job 42: 2–6)

Here is a man who has truly undergone a conversion to the reality of the Sacred Other in whom human beings can place their trust. His words are echoed in the unwavering trust of the mother of the seven Maccabees, who encouraged each of her seven sons to die "putting all their trust in the Lord" (2 Mac. 7:40); and in the trust of Macabeus, who encouraged his soldiers thus:

> They [the enemy] trust in weapons and acts of
> daring . . . but we trust in almighty God, who can
> by a mere nod destroy not only those who attack
> us, but the whole world.
>
> (2. Mac. 8:18).

Believing with the Psalmist that "the Lord is close to the brokenhearted" (Ps. 34:19), loving acceptance of God's Providence and trusting acknowledgment of limitations characterize the attitudes of people close to him in both the Old Testament and the New.[4]

The Gospels give examples of more or less stressful "openness moments" that, owing to a similar shift toward a trusting perspective, contain material for transcendence. Such events bring about new and life-releasing action in the persons who live them. These men and women seem to have been able to look first, not at their own reactions and emotions, but at the event itself in openness to its meaning and particular message for them. They were able to sense the larger context of certain situations, to recognize them as the Father's will. They were able to listen and wait upon the answer to their own anguished questions about why they were being asked to live this particular reality. The pattern is especially clear in Jesus' Gethsemane event, when the crisis of trust in God his Father reached its peak. The conflict of directives he experienced then surged up from all aspects of his life. Inwardly, he was filled with fear; outwardly, his distress is obvious (Lk. 22:44). Possibly he was tempted to deny and rationalize, as would any thirty-three-year-old man condemned to death with his whole life still before him. He has been a success, accomplishing much good in a short time. He is aware of the love of his Father, and at the same time, as counterpoint, of the violence massed against him on all sides. In throwing himself unreservedly on the Father's love rather than trusting in his own power, he shifts his perspective to total risk (Lk. 22:42). The next day the shift must have been evident: he goes to his death in such a manner that the centurion exclaims, "Clearly this man was the Son of God" (Mk. 15:39).

Another much less traumatic but nonetheless marginal situation is described as having happened on the road to Emmaus, where the unpredictable "otherness" of God's mysterious plan meets and conflicts with the Messianic expectations of the disciples (Lk. 24: 13–35). The two needed an entire catechesis on the meaning of historical events before any transformation of hearts slow to believe could occur (Jn. 24:25,32). Again, we find that what each person brings to the moment constitutes it as both marginal and open to being restructured. Another person whose growth in faith is connected with situations where his inadequate trust was put to the test and found wanting is St. Peter. For example, when Jesus walked toward them on the lake, Peter, in his insecurity and fear, demanded proof (Mt. 14:28). Only later was he fully able to let go of these tendencies so typical of him. And even then, real trust was only possible for pragmatic Peter when love had cast out fear and he, along with the rest of the young Church, "enjoyed the increased consolation of the Holy Spirit" (Acts 9, 10, 11). Like Ellen and most beings "of little faith" (Mt. 8:26), during an "openness moment" Peter tended to bolster his wavering security by giving a merely functional response, reacting to situations out of his ideal rather than his real self and trying to cope with ambiguity and unpredictability by agitated attempts at mastering the situation on his own, independent of its hidden source.

Insights into Lack of Trust

Because they often conceal directives that conflict with the usual self-enhancing perspective one has of oneself, providential "openness" situations contain a hidden power to elicit responses and unleash growth energy. By their very nature, these somewhat marginal experiences awaken a prereflective initial reaction of resistance to the disclosure of one's woundedness, disordered self-love, innate narcissism, and pride. The temptation to deny these glimpses of one's current self in favor of the ideal self one professes to be is strong. However, as in Ellen's case, a turning point often occurs. A humbling insight into the basic tendencies that motivate one's actions, a revelation in and through the event of some aspect of one's pride form, of one's vital/functional ambitions, of one's self-seeking or unique "search for glory," can come to the fore. Instead of hardening of the heart, such an incident can foster real growth in self-knowledge, followed by repentance for sin and an honest acceptance of one's brokenness and limitation. A breakthrough of this nature in one's routine self-complacency can lead, as it did for both Ellen and Peter, to a real transformation of the heart and a new consciousness of self as a quite ordinary but nonetheless lovable member of the community of believers.[5]

Groups and communities as well as individuals can live through and learn from similar "crises of transcendence."[6] A breakdown of collective exaltation can happen, especially in moments of failure or of acceptance of inevitable and sometimes painful change and ambiguity. For groups, too, the raw material for growth and development is most often to be found in the unplanned situations offered by life itself. These gifted situations, fraught as they are with conflict and differentiation, can often succeed in breaking open the collective pride form, leaving the entire group vulnerable and in need of a savior who tends to bestow his saving mercy on sinners rather than on those who believe themselves to be just. Human pride rebels against such insights. Peter's remark about the high cost of giving up familiar ways and comfortable directives, "We have put aside everything to follow you!" (Mk. 10:28), reminds us of Ellen's reluctance to detach herself from her old way of life in order to be free enough to welcome new directives from beyond herself, from the Holy Spirit.[7] Eventually, both she and Peter found themselves pushed by events into a state they would never have chosen for themselves, where there were fewer security directives and a much larger risk of dependency in relation to Divine Otherness. Francis Thompson describes the dilemma well:

> For, though I knew His love
> Who followed,
> Yet was I sore adread
> lest, having Him, I must have
> naught beside.[8]

Once again, the pattern appears as conflicting directives are sorted out, a reversal or metanoia takes place, and trust in a saving Other releases energy and prepares the way for new action and dispositions of fruitful trust and love.

Why, then, since our daily lives are filled with events containing hidden treasure, is there not more growth? Why do not more of our experiences of reality result in transformed minds and hearts, in shifts toward the fullness of a new creation? Why do we find it so difficult to trust the initiatives of Otherness in our lives? Why do we avoid new learning and change? Why are we not "open systems" interacting and exchanging freely with our environment? Why do we fearfully insist on trying to control the flow of events, clinging to little securities and the illusion of certainty that comes with a scientific world view based on facts and common sense? Why do we, like Bilbo Baggins, the hobbit hero of the prologue to Tolkien's *Lord of the Rings*,[9] always need to find out "the risks, out-of-pocket expenses, time required and remunerations" before setting out on the adventure of life? Do we not need to cast aside our anxiety and learn to trust more in our intuition that the universe is really a divine dance into which we can be drawn by life itself as it comes to meet us? As Marcel noted, we are free to resist, to say no, to systematically withhold ourselves from this incomparably living reality.[10] In a variety of ways, we are able to prevent the transformation, the transfiguration of our whole outlook, so that we miss not only the hints of the invisible Kingdom of God, but also the treasure of

> Orcs, and talking trees, and leagues of grass, and galloping riders, and glittering caves, and white towers and golden halls, and battles, and tall ships sailing . . .[11]

that we might encounter on our way to it.

Perhaps like members of the Baggins side of Bilbo's family, who "never had any adventures or did anything unexpected,"[12] we narrow our lives and thus our possibility of relating to what is Other because we lack the capacity for transcendent imagination. To live in the realm of faith, one needs an expanding mind and heart that do not attempt to restrict the wild richness of the Holy Other to the confines of focused consciousness or merely human willing.[13] Not only is the experience of human trusting permeated with ambiguity; the experience of the Divine is also, for "no one has ever seen God" (1 Jn. 4:12), and our knowing is always permeated with nonknowing, our faith with doubt, our seeing with blindness. What holds us back from trusting God is that we cannot even imagine the heart of Christianity, the utterly gratuitous love of God that comes to us in Christ. We tend, instead, to settle into the mediocrity of doxic confidence in our familiar narrow ways of self-sufficiency and ignorance. Busily making ourselves safe in his eyes, we hide like pharisees behind human prudence and observance of the law, instead of selling all we have and making Christ our security. Lost in anxious substitutions for God,[14] we gradually reduce our ability to respond to transcendent directives. The overarching Mystery of His way becomes lost in the confusion of ours.

At this point, we understand the admonition of Christ that greets us at the beginning of Lent:

> Whoever wishes to be my follower must deny his very self, take up his cross each day, and follow my steps. Whoever would save his life will lose it, and whoever loses his life for my sake will save it. (Lk. 9:23–24)[15]

He is telling us that if we really wish to follow him into life abundant, we must cease relying on the "social self,"[16] the temporary or current self with its apparent roles and identity, and follow his ways or steps instead. As the psalm that precedes this Gospel message points out, the person who lives surrounded by a divine view of the world (i.e., who "meditates on his law day and night") will be

> . . . like a tree
> planted near running water
> That yields its fruit in due season,
> and whose leaves never fade.
>   (Ps. 1:3)

There is an echo here of the Eastern tradition that regards the merely social self as illusion when compared to the true self that lives from participation in the flow of divine energy and never-fading eternal truth.

We have touched already on some of the many shapes taken by the pride form in our lives. We have seen how it blocks the flow of energy,[17] inclining us toward absolutized security directives and exaggerated striving.[18] We have seen how the typical twentieth-century person tends to get caught in the closure of his or her own compulsive security system.[19] We have learned to recognize our own unwillingness to accept unexpected invitations, like the one that appears in the liturgy on the Second Sunday of Lent to

> Go forth from the land of your kinsfolk and from your father's house to a land that I will show you. (Gen. 12:1)[20]

Abraham did undertake the journey into darkness, leaving all that he was familiar with in trust that God would show him a new land. This apophatic leap in being continues to be made by all the generations after Abraham who put themselves in God's hands, who continue to believe, often in spite of appearances, that his plan for them is ultimately one of love. The busyness and overexertion of the ideal self, its tendency to strive for external perfection and to become "anxious and upset over many things" (Lk. 10:41), may be signs of lack of faith and trust in the power of this providential care.[21]

Ellen, caught as she was in societal appraisals and in danger of reducing past saving knowledge of Christ to the level of her own pragmatic ability to solve her problem, was saved from her merely natural presence to reality, not only by the "bone knowledge" of faith, hope, and love implanted in childhood, but also by the recognition of Christ's loving providential presence and forgiveness in her life "now."[22] In a sense, ego-functional despair led to a certain purgation of merely natural effort and opened the way for illumination regarding the uniqueness of her relationship with God. In the security of that trust, she was able to let go of concern about herself, and in so doing, she came into contact with other human beings and the universe she shared with them. Like individuals, communities and groups also need to keep in touch with their own wider horizon of meaning, the particular myth that puts them in contact with God. Then their collective body, in its openness to illumination by the Mystery, will avoid being a merely social presence to the world and its people; their social concern will be grounded not only in the question of the nature of the world's sorrow, but also in the wider horizon of love that their concern is ultimately meant to serve.

Shifting to New Freedom

Here is the way a contemporary woman describes the nature of the shift towards trusting:

> It means renouncing myself as my own base, my own center, my own end. It means so casting myself on another, so making that other my *raison d'être* that it is, in truth, a death to the ego. The whole of the spiritual journey can be seen in terms of trust, growing in trust until one has lost oneself in God. But we are mistaken if we think we can do this for ourselves. Not only can we not do it, we cannot even dream of what is meant by it, what it is like. True, we grasp the words: trust, giving, no confidence in self, poverty, humility . . . but they are words to us, though we think we really do grasp the concepts. What we are talking about is so much part of our fabric that we cannot stand out of it and look on. It is our way of being to be our own center, and we do not realize it until God begins to shift us. It is only one in whom God has worked profoundly who can see the difference. The rest have no yardstick.[23]

Significantly, this writer speaks in terms of "God beginning to shift us." It is his initiative, not ours, that brings about a profound change in the being of the person who trusts, that brings about the metanoia, the New Creation, the transformed relationship between God and the person open to his initiatives. And who are the ones who are most open? They are, as they have always been, the humble ones, the people not caught up in self-satisfaction or self-complacency, the people who throughout Scripture, from Cain (Gen. 4:13) to the persistent widow (Lk. 18:1–8), have known they needed grace, have suspected they were not among the spiritually successful, have acknowledged their wretchedness and help-lessness, and have "cried out to the Lord, the God of our Fathers" (Deut. 26:7). At the beginning of Lent,[24] the first reading reminds us that the liberation of the people of Israel begins, not as a result of their own efforts, but with a cry for help to a God who responds with the Exodus. The theme of trust in this God continues in the psalm verses that follow:

> You who dwell in the shelter of the Most High
> who abide in the shadow of the Almighty,
> Say to the Lord, "My refuge and my fortress,
> my God, in whom I trust. . . ."
> Because he clings to me, I will deliver him;
> I will set him on high because he acknowledges my name.
> He shall call upon me, and I will answer him;
> I will be with him in distress;
> I will deliver him and glorify him;
> with length of days I will gratify him
> and I will show him my salvation.
>
> (Ps. 91: 1–2, 14–16)

The second reading, from Paul's Epistle to the Romans, also contains a cry of trust: we are urged to confess with our lips and believe in our hearts that God's initiative was the energy that raised Christ from the dead. Then, in the Gospel, we have Christ himself who, though tempted for forty days in the desert, continues to trust in and worship the one true God.

Thus the turning point, the moment of conversion to new freedom, consists of recognition at one and the same time of both our brokenness and our giftedness. We are directed to let go of the old self, with its self-enhancing illusions of righteousness and control, and invited to become even more deeply present to the Mystery of Divine Love as it appears in the midst of daily life. Scriptural descriptions of this "letting go" recall the security, relaxed familiarity, and at-homeness with others and the world that in Chapter 6 characterized the "doxic confidence" belonging to the trusting body.[25] That chapter described the life of enjoyment, of being happy in the world that nourishes, of having a natural confidence in the goodness of one's own bodily being, of the leisurely attitude that allows one to be receptive and open to the to-be-trusted goodness already there in the surrounding world. A prerequisite for "letting go" on the natural level seems to be a certain stilling of focused consciousness, a certain relaxation of tension and aggressive, willful *doing.*[26] In an atmosphere of positive relaxation, with little or no reliance on self-sufficient patterns of behavior, the heart can be touched by the Spirit and tied-up energy can be released.

What do we find in Scripture? In the book of Exodus, at the crucial crossing of the Red Sea, when the people were in a panic, pursued by the enemy, they cried out in terror and turned on Moses, who said to them, "The Lord himself will fight for you; you have only to [relax] keep still" (Ex. 14:14). When the people finally saw the power of God in action, they trusted in both God and Moses, not because of what they themselves had accomplished, but because they realized finally the strength of divine initiative. Psalm 46 also sings out the theme of trusting that if we only let go of our own petty achievements, we will see reality as it is. We will "be still and know that he is God,"[27] who is already there in our hearts. Throughout the Advent liturgy also, Isaiah draws attention to the fact that for those who allow God to be God, every event can be a source of new energy:

> They that hope in the Lord will renew their strength,
> they will soar with eagle's wings;
> they will run and not grow weary,
> walk and not grow faint. (Isaiah 40:31)[28]
> For I am the Lord your God,
> who grasps your right hand;
> It is I who say to you, "Fear not,
> I will help you." . . .
> your redeemer is the Holy One of Israel.
> (Is. 41: 13–14)[29]

On the Third Sunday of Advent, we are directed to rejoice and let go of all our anxiety because this God who loves continues to come to save all those whose hearts are not hardened, who are able to be still and avoid overpreoccupation with efforts to save themselves.

Obviously this shift to trusting so prominent in Scripture points in the direction of vulnerability, of defenselessness and risk, of being "poor."

In the final interviews with Ellen,[30] we traced some of the steps that led to her discovery of the To-Be-Trusted Other. From the breakup of her unique "pride system" emerged a shift away from self-preoccupation toward an interest in the Other. She found herself sharing the concerns of the Holy Other, wanting to get in touch with the plan of the Lord, the "design of his heart" (Ps. 33:11), not only for her own small existence, but also as this plan affects other people who are also loved by God. An even more profound shift is reflected in Ellen's new attitude toward the other members of the human race, from whom she had been somewhat estranged by her former conviction that she was above the ordinary. Perhaps instead of speaking again of the theory of dissipative structures, we can detect here the pattern of the Paschal Mystery itself. Ellen moved from a certain stage of Christian maturity wherein she trusted herself (life), through a losing of some of the illusions about herself that were the natural accompaniment of that maturing (death), to a new realization of the importance of lives other than her own and a desire to center her heart's love more on Christ than on herself (resurrection). In more universal terms:

> . . . the Christian's life is a continuous building and a fragmenting and a coming apart in order to come together again less centered on self and more centered on Jesus Christ. Christian life as a process towards holiness is, in its dialectical movement, a participation in the life, in the cross and in the resurrection of Jesus.[31]

Like Peter who had to learn through the defenselessness of old age to trust another to tie him fast and carry him off against his will (Jn. 21:18), like the two disciples on the road to Emmaus who had to relax their focus on achieving a political success in order to perceive and trust the unexpected new way in which the Lord would "set Israel free" (Lk. 24:21), both Frances[32] and Ellen had to give up their cherished privacy in order to enter into a more intimate relation with others. A new way of living was only possible through a process of dying to the old.

The Heart's Orientation toward the Future

All Scripture attests to the fact that the breakthroughs of God's initiatives in history, his divine interventions, are always so "new" and unexpected, so unlike our more unimaginative human ways, that they are usually unnoticed except by a very few. Absorbed in Type A behavior, distracted by preoccupation with "little beyonds" of land, oxen, and new marriage (sometimes translatable as ego-enhancing possessions, workaholism, and vital pleasures), most people do not even notice, much less respond to, invitations to the banquet hidden in the events of daily life (Mt. 22 1–10; Lk. 14:16–24). Embedded in the now, we find it almost impossible to trust the Risen Christ, who breaks into our present from the ultimate future Kingdom where he lives and reigns with God the Father in the unity of the Spirit. Perhaps a few, more aware than others of what they may be missing, are willing to try stilling focused consciousness and cleansing the doors of perception in order to recognize "something new" as it springs forth.[33]

Both liturgy and Scripture can help here as they present us repeatedly with the reality of Christ as the goal of all history, holding all things together and drawing all things to himself.[34] It is the love of Christ's heart that invites our trust as it pours out the basic energy that unites people and moves the world forward into a future eagerly "awaited by the whole created world" (Rom. 8:19). It is not surprising that so many of the psalms used in our liturgies reflect this movement toward the future. Lent and Easter, in particular, are filled with reminders of the Church's need, as future-directed community of love, for ever-renewed outpourings of this mysterious cosmic energy.[35] As we discovered in the research, it is only in hearts surrendered to this oriented flow of the Divine Will in the universe that a shift to new action becomes possible. It is those with hearts softened by the suffering of marginalization and a sense of their own unimportance like poor people, tax collectors, and prostitutes who, according to Jesus, are trusting enough to abandon themselves to this flow, and thus be first in entering the Kingdom of God (Mt. 21:31–32). These "poor in spirit" have already accepted the failure of their ideal selves, have already let go of false notions of their own importance. There is little to prevent their hearts from being touched by new directives streaming forth into this world from the realm of the New Creation.[36] We are frequently reminded to "harden not our hearts," for any day "we may hear his voice" in the events of our daily life.

Unlike "willpower Christians," whose exertions leave little room for outside influences, people who find themselves trusting do so usually because their heart's freedom is of the type that can be described as "receptive volition."[37] Involved in the world in a new way because of their trusting yes to the mysterious presence of the Risen Christ in their midst, such people are more open to receive energizing directives in the way of unexpected happenings, new tasks and responsibilities, and the daily deaths to self that belong to Christian existence. Trusting in the meaningful dynamic presence of God everywhere in the universe, such people are more likely to be motivated by inner dispositions of faith, hope, and charity toward fellow human beings. Their love for the world, their sense of compassion, and their desire for social justice will be more easily evoked by the sufferings of others, with whom they see themselves invisibly connected by the creative love of Christ as well as by the web of global interdependence.

The heart that "hears his voice" is not the sentimental, pitying heart that distances itself from its neighbor in sympathetic benevolence. It is, rather, the heart that responds with spiritual understanding[38] to the designs of Christ's heart as they unfold uniquely in the person's immediate and even global situation.

> "Heart" in the Bible does not, as in our Western tradition, mean the affections, sensibility as opposed to reason. It is rather man's liberty, the centre in which are taken the fundamental decisions; in particular the choices between knowledge and ignorance, light and darkness, understanding and what the prophets call stupidity, foolishness. In the "heart" the strife unfolds that will decide man's destiny, his very essence: according to the essence he has chosen, man will be judged. For man chooses himself as he wills to be and this is the justification of justice upon him. The matter of judgement is this intimate *orientation* of the heart and not the degrees of accomplishment that man may appraise.[39]

As the Gospel for the Feast of All Saints sets forth the spirit of loving compassion that characterizes the life of the Kingdom in time,[40] so the Gospel of the last Sunday in ordinary time[41] gives us a vivid picture of how the response of hearts to the commandment of love will be judged. The heart that is open and receptive, that chooses to abide with the Source of life, is also a heart able and willing to respond, to involve itself in the concerns of a heart larger than itself.[42]

Bearing fruit in loving service to others, this heart lives by the words, "As often as you did it for one of my least brothers or sisters, you did it for me" (Mt. 25:40). Its inner orientation is marked by a trusting yes to the "me" whose presence binds all men and women together in a network of invisible interrelatedness. Its service to the wider community marks it as recognizing the profoundly incarnational nature of Christian spirituality. A sense of the importance of social transformation, of the necessity of pursuing the works of justice, is particularly noticeable at the beginning of Lent. On the Friday and Saturday following Ash Wednesday, we find Isaiah's description of the interior attitudes that accompany true fasting. In place of "carrying out our own pursuits" (Is. 58:3), the Lord tells us:

> This, rather, is the fasting that I wish:
> releasing those bound unjustly,
> untying the thongs of the yoke;

setting free the oppressed,
breaking every yoke;
Sharing your bread with the hungry,
sheltering the oppressed and the homeless;
Clothing the naked when you see them,
and not turning your back on your own.
(Is. 58: 6–7)

Significantly, the theme of the first Monday in Lent is love of neighbor. The acclamation that the leader reads to the assembled people before he proclaims the verses from the twenty-fifth chapter of the Gospel according to St. Matthew is from the familiar invitatory psalm prayed each day in the liturgy of the Hours:

Oh, that today you would hear his voice:
Harden not your hearts. . . .
(Ps. 95:7)

This lived sense of the solidarity of the Church with the whole human family, this practicality of love that must move from mere words and sentiments to action, shines through the liturgical readings after the great feasts of Easter[43] and Christmas:[44]

I ask you, how can God's love survive in a man
who has enough of this world's goods
yet closes his heart to his brother
when he sees him in need?
Little children,
let us love in deed and in truth
and not merely talk about it.
(1 Jn. 3: 17–18)

Love in practice is also the theme of Vatican II's Pastoral Constitution on the Church in the Modern World, whose preface begins thus:

The joy and hope, the grief and anguish of the people of our time, especially of those who are poor or afflicted in any way, are the joy and hope, the grief and anguish of the followers of Christ as well. Nothing that is genuinely human fails to find an echo in their hearts. For theirs is a community composed of men and women who, united in Christ and guided by the Holy Spirit, press onwards towards the kingdom of the Father and are bearers of the message of salvation intended for all. That is why Christians cherish a feeling of deep solidarity with the human race and its history.[45]

True spirituality can never consist of a gnostic escape from the world. As we noted in the opening pages of this book, the sea around us keeps changing, bringing both inner and outer transformation.[46] Our trust must lie in the forces of integration we are discovering both in ourselves and in the universe, of which our many worlds are a part. Our orientation must be forward:

> . . . away from fear towards trust . . . away from despair towards hope . . . away from untruthfulness, prejudice, hatred, oppression, injustice and the structures that support these . . . towards truth, love, freedom, justice and the structures that reinforce these.[47]

Trust as Basis of Commitment

For me, one of the most enlightening results of the research was the realization that it is often when things look most uncertain, when ambiguity and seeming chaos are everywhere, when structures "dissipate" and you literally must "make the road while walking,"[48] that the trusting self or communal group can be guided in the best direction. While I am clinging to my own plans, resisting the unfamiliar, treading the accustomed path and reasoning out every step of the way, I may also tend to resist the new, the unaccustomed, the transformative. However, in risky situations where trust is involved:

> God's plans, disguised as they are, reveal themselves to us through our intuition rather than through our reason. They disclose themselves in various ways: by chance, or by what seems to be a compulsive thrust which allows no choice of action, by a sudden impulse, by some supernatural rapture, or very often by something which attracts or repels us. . . .[49]

The author of these lines, Jean-Pierre de Caussade, wrote an entire book about what he called the "essence of spirituality" (p. 73), which, as a result of this research, I have come to recognize as the trusting attitude. Here are some additional quotes from this small Christian classic:

> What God arranges for us to experience at each moment is the best and holiest thing that could happen to us. . . . (p. 27)

> The present moment is always overflowing with immeasurable riches. . . . (p. 41)

> The whole of history is nothing but the story of God's activity. . . . (p. 44)

> His love wishes to unite itself with us through all that the world contains, all that he has created, ordained and allowed. That is his supreme purpose, and to accomplish it he uses both the best and the worst of his creatures, the most unpleasant and the most delightful of happenings. . . . (p. 48)

> This tremendous activity of God, which never varies from the beginning to the end of time, pours itself through every moment and gives itself in all its vastness and power to every clear-hearted soul which adores and loves it and abandons itself without reserve to it. . . . (p. 53)

What this seventeenth-century writer has to say about trust and abandoning oneself to the activity of God that moves through everything (p. 54) bears an amazing similarity to what contemporary biologists[50] and physicists[51] are finding out about the "divine milieu"[52] of energy that surrounds and penetrates our everyday activities. Assuring us that all is in the hand of the To-Be-Trusted Other, de Caussade continues:

> God's action penetrates every atom of your body, into the very marrow of your bones. The blood flowing through your veins moves only by his will. The state of your health, whether you are weak or strong, lively or languid, your life and death all spring from his will, and all your bodily conditions are the workings of grace. Every feeling, every thought you have, no matter how they arise, all come from God's invisible hand. There is no created being who can tell you what his action will achieve within you, but continuing experience will teach you. Uninterruptedly your life will flow through this unfathomed abyss where you have nothing to do but love and cherish what each moment brings, considering it as the best possible thing for you and having perfect confidence in God's activities, which cannot do anything but good. (p. 55)

In Chapter 14, I pointed out that commitment to the new vision of social transformation is not possible without a base that moors it solidly in a contemporary view of both human history and its underlying Mystery. At the end of Chapter 16, I concluded that a person's lifelong ability to reach out in loving service to others and to the world, the secret of faithful commitment, is also based on a trusting yes to oneself as sustained in existence by this same loving Other.

Energized by trust in the Mystery, acknowledging and acknowledged by the One we serve, it becomes more possible to ask the world Parsifal's question: "What is your sorrow?" and to live the answers that sometimes take us beyond the boundaries of our own limited strength and love. The performatory quality of trusting in the commitment to action becomes available, as human initiative and effort, every day work and fidelity are integrated into building the world toward its final transformation.

Failure to root one's commitment to the world in this meaningfulness can lead to an erosion of social presence or "burnout."[53] Because the needs of the world are so diverse and overwhelming, vital/functional ambitions to "save everyone" can lure people of the utmost goodwill into unrealistic commitment, even overcommitment, of themselves, with little regard for their own limits and those of the situation. Lacking any deep trust in the fundamental meaning of everything that is, and discouraged by encountered negativity and the failure to bring about very much apparent change, after a time their natural enthusiasm dies, and their hearts lose track of whatever original loving interest might have been there in the first place. Disappointed and out of touch with themselves and the others they wanted to serve, these people cannot sustain their commitment. Could it be that "burnout" is rooted in mistrust of what de Caussade calls the ongoing "achievement of God," which he compares to the "front of a lovely tapestry" (p. 104)? As workers involved in the weaving of it, we are familiar with the back, with all its knots and hanging threads. From our time-bound vantage point, we cannot see the symmetry and beauty of the design as it is being created. In our ignorance of the whole, we become discouraged. Unless we continue to move toward the freedom of detachment, the salt of our compassion will gradually lose its savor and our actions will founder on the negative appraisals of a basically anxious, distrustful society.

Contrast this with the optimistic prayer that the liturgy puts before us on Easter Sunday:

> God our Father, by raising Christ your Son
> you conquered the power of death
> and you opened for us the way to eternal life.
> Let our celebration today
> raise us up and renew our lives
> by the Spirit that is within us.

This mystery of the Spirit within us is the principal source of our commitment to action, to renewal of life, and to the Kingdom of justice and peace that lies ahead. If we have risen with Christ, we can now, with confidence, seek the things that lie not so much "above" as before us, in the future where "the joy of the resurrection renews the whole world."[54] The Old Testament is filled with people who, trusting in the promise, risked the shift to a new way of being: Abraham, Sarah, Daniel, Esther, David, Judith, Jeremiah, and Hannah, to name a few. Each one of these persons was able, because of his or her trust, to act in a new way. They were people who took literally the Psalmist's advice:

> Take delight in the Lord,
> and he will grant your heart's request.
> Commit to the Lord your way
> trust him and he will act.
> (Ps. 37:4–5)[55]

In the New Testament, Jesus speaks often of the new action possible for those who trust in him:

> Believe me, if you trust and do not falter, not only will you do what I did to the fig tree, but if you say to this mountain, 'Be lifted up and thrown into the sea,' even that will happen. (Mt. 21:21)

Paul implores the Ephesians to lay aside their former way of life and acquire a new way of thinking (Eph. 4:23). He also tells the Galatians that they are justified through their trusting faith (Gal.3), and testifies to his own personal trust, in the midst of hardships, in him in whom he has believed (2 Tim. 1:12).

Living like Paul in the midst of the minor, and sometimes major, hardships life offers, we realize that trusting Divine Otherness is no guarantee that whatever we do, everything will turn out well. It is instead a trust that in spite of what happens, God's calls embody wisdom and goodness when we allow ourselves to be led by them. Our part is to be willing to let go of self-willed security, of worn-out customs and ideas; and to risk entering upon the ever-new adventure that is our life, accepting all as gift. Our hearts will then be exercising true response-ability, detecting concrete love and growth possibilities in all kinds of unlikely situations that at first glance do not seem to offer much. Throughout life we will be thus called until the inevitable and final invitation comes to leave this life, to die. How can death with all its ambiguity and fear of the unknown, be perceived as to-be-trusted call, as gift?

Death is the final dissipative structure that separates us decisively from all we have clung to for security in this life. It can also be perceived as a liberation from everything that might have been preventing us from being "who we really are,"[56] from being "like him," from "seeing him as he is" (1 Jn. 3:2). Death can be the most free and personally "whole" event of an entire life, an opportunity for new decision and action, for uttering an ultimate yes to the One who till this moment has been veiled from us by all the ambiguities of the human condition.[57] Death asks for a final "letting go," for a decisive shift from distrustful isolation to trustful intimacy; from the ignorance of mere doxic confidence to immense gratitude for the goodness and kindness we now perceive to have "followed us all the days of our life" (Ps. 23:6); from futile striving to escape human limits to humble rejoicing at sharing a common destiny with so many brothers and sisters. As for each one of us, birth gave access to a new world of light, colors, meaning, the world of being with others and of love, so, too, for each one, death is destined to be the entrance into a new life-filled relation to the energized universe of the fully radiant Christ. Present struggles to orient our lives in the direction of a trusting yes take on new meaning when perceived as readying our hearts for an eternity with others and the Other whose loving invitations in this life we have gradually, sometimes painfully, but nevertheless wholeheartedly learned to trust.

NOTES

Chapter 1
Evoking Trust in the Process

1. *Formative* and *deformative* here refer to the releasing or blocking of the true self or soul whose most profound direction, meaning, and incarnation lie in its disclosure as form or image of God. For further reference to this foundational characteristic of human life, see notes 4, 5, and 20 of this chapter; Chapter 2, note 10; Chapter 8, notes 9 and 10; Chapter 12, note 6; and Chapter 13, note 1. For a popular presentation of some elements of the "constantly shifting flow," see, for example, Alvin Toffler's *The Third Wave* (New York: Bantam, 1980), with its bibliography on change in the arts and sciences, business and economics, marriage and family, definitions of work, play, love, and success.

2. Core Form or Heart, *Studies in Formative Spirituality* 1 (1980): 144. Core Form of Life, *Studies in Formative Spirituality* 1 (1980): 139. Throughout this book, an attempt will be made to correlate the original findings with constructs from Adrian van Kaam's "Provisional Glossary of the Terminology of the Science of Foundational Formation," which is published tri-annually in *Studies in Formative Spirituality* (Institute of Formative Spirituality, Duquesne University). Hereafter this journal will be referred to simply as *Studies.*

3. See Johannes B. Metz, *Faith in History and Society* (New York: Seabury, 1980), for a fuller treatment of human responsibility to be "subject" rather than "object" of historical processes.

4. According to Adrian van Kaam, founder of the science of foundational human formation, one of the basic presuppositions we can hold about human beings is their striving to both give to and receive form from the people, things, and events that make up their lives. He describes it as the "unconscious process of gradual realization of a characteristic form each living being, event or thing is tending toward in accordance with its nature and conditions." *Studies* 1 (1980): 137. For further elaboration of the science itself, see Adrian van Kaam, *Formative Spirituality* (New York: Crossroad, 1982).

5. In *The Dynamics of Spiritual Self-Direction,* Part I (Denville, N.J.: Dimension Books, 1976), van Kaam states that his spiritual self theory is based on the assumption that the core of the person's existence is his or her spirit. This incarnated spirit makes persons capable of discovering themselves as endowed with a unique destiny to which they are called to direct their lives. This transcendent direction that emerges over a lifetime, in dialogue with vital and personal experiences as they reveal and unfold themselves within the concrete life situations with which a person must cope, forms the basis of what we mean by "self-direction." It is, in other words, a discovery of one's transcendent destiny through paying attention to the lived experience of one's emerging self.

6. See Carolyn Gratton, "Foundational Formative Direction in Common," in *Studies in Religion* (Montreal: Corporation for Studies in Religion, 1982), for a description of the assumptions and underlying dynamics as well as the originating outline of the process of

direction-in-common embodied in this book. See also Adrian van Kaam, *Dynamics of Spiritual Self-Direction*, Part Two, for a description of direction-in-common.

7. It is thus the dis-integrating nature of life itself that forces us to become reflective, to look again or reflect (from the Latin *reflectare*, to bend back) on our experience in order to once again find its wholeness (Latin *integer*, whole).

8. See Adrian van Kaam, *Religion and Personality* (Denville, N.J.: Dimension Books, 1980), p. 3, for description of differentiation and integration as modes of presence.

9. See Malcom Knowles, *Self-Directed Learning: A Guide for Learners and Teachers* (New York: Association Press, 1975), which the author describes as a resource that both teachers and learners can use to develop their competence as self-directed inquirers. On p. 19, Knowles defines "andragogy" as the art and science of helping adults to learn.

10. Joseph Pieper, *About Love* (Chicago: Franciscan Herald Press, 1974), p. 31.

11. See Thomas Kuhn, *The Structure of Scientific Revolutions* (Chicago: University of Chicago Press, 1970), for a description of the trusting attitude on the part of scientists toward the scientific community's paradigms as revealed in its textbooks, lectures, and laboratory exercises.

12. The idea of change of heart, of interior conversion or metanoia, holds an important place in biblical revelation. Under the heading "Repentance/Conversion," Xavier Léon Dufour, in his *Dictionary of Biblical Theology* (New York: Seabury, 1973), pp. 486–491, comments on the meaning of change of heart in the biblical texts.

13. Romano Guardini, *The World and the Person* (Chicago: Regnery, 1965), p. 194.

14. See Hans Kung, *Does God Exist? An Answer for Today* (New York: Doubleday, 1980), particularly the sections on "The Challenge of Atheism" and "Nihilism—Consequence of Atheism."

15. The results of this phenomenological study, "A Theoretical-Empirical Study of the Lived Experience of Interpersonal Trust," 75–21, 499, c. Mary Carolyn Gratton, 1975, are available from Xerox University Microfilms, Ann Arbor, Michigan 48106.

16. For an introduction to this new paradigm, see Amadeo Giorgi, *Psychology as a Human Science* (New York: Harper and Row, 1970). See "An Application of Phenomenological Method in Psychology," *Duquesne Studies in Phenomenological Psychology*, Vol II (Pittsburgh: Duquesne University Press, 1975), pp. 87–103, for a description of the qualitative approach and method. My study of trust, by employing a method of qualitative analysis of descriptive protocols of experience, was able to remain faithful to the phenomenon of trust as it is lived, to give primacy to the life-world, to use a descriptive approach, and to express the situation from the viewpoint of the subject or self. The insistence on a description of a *situation* in which trust was experienced implied that a structural approach would be forthcoming, and the use of in-depth interviews assured the biographical emphasis. This method of qualitative analysis should not be considered paradigmatic for all phenomenologically based research, but as merely *one* attempt to begin exploring an alternative to traditional quantitative methods. For further implications, see A. Giorgi, "Convergence and Divergence of Qualitative and Quantitative methods in Psychology," *Psychology as a Human Science*, pp. 72–79.

17. Max Scheler, "Versuche einer Philosophie des Lebens," *Vom Umsturz der Werte* (Bern: Francke, 1955), p. 325.

18. Cf. Kuhn, *Structure of Scientific Revolutions*, and Kung, *Does God Exist?*, pp. 106–115. See also Chapter 14, note 14, of this book.

19. The science of foundational human formation has been developed by Adrian van Kaam, C.S.Sp., Ph.D., and his colleagues and students at the Institute of Formative Spirituality, Duquesne University, Pittsburgh, Pa., over the past twenty years. The aim is to foster foundational formation. The science concerns itself with the person as a whole, and thus makes use of comparative religion, theology, philosophy, medicine, biophysics, psychology, education, the arts, anthropology, and sociology, which are dialectically integrated in the service of foundational formation theory and the practice of its art and discipline.

20. For further insight into the meaning of basic originality, see *Studies in Formative Spirituality* 1 (1980), in its entirety.

21. Quoted in Aelred Squire, *Asking the Fathers* (New York: Paulist, 1973), pp. 70–71. (The original author of these words is St. Augustine.)

22. Lk. 12:34.

23. A helpful introduction to the thinking of the Greek fathers regarding uncreated energy can be found in George Maloney's Père Marquette Theology Lecture, *A Theology of Uncreated Energies* (Milwaukee, Wis.: Marquette University Press, 1978).

24. Any other formative experience or situation would have been equally appropriate to this process of guided reflection. However, since I was familiar with the topic of trust and convinced that we can learn dispositions of heart that are important for life in relation to God from examining this particular human experience, most people in the groups agreed to write a description of trusting rather than of some other, more immediately appealing experience.

25. Although the five persons differ from one another in their concrete uniqueness as well as in regard to sex, religion, political preference, life choice, and circumstances, they represent only one segment of the population; namely, white, middle-class, educated persons between twenty-five and forty-five years of age. A sixth person, Frances, whose description of trusting someone will be introduced in Chapter 10, was not interviewed in depth because her protocol belongs to one of several pilot studies conducted prior to the actual research. Thus her remarks do not appear in the initial chapters.

26. Since Ellen's description contained more than passing references to her personal life of Christian faith, it was not included in the original empirical study. However, the data have been validated sufficiently for its inclusion in this book, to which it adds an important dimension.

27. "The science of foundational human formation is an open, systematic, intersubjectively validated structure of rational propositions about the foundations of the empirical formation of human life and the transempirical presuppositions underlying its foundational knowledge and practice." (Adrian van Kaam, unpublished glossary, Fall 1981).

28. For a description of just such a parallel, see Fritjof Capra, *The Tao of Physics* (New York: Bantam, 1977).

29. Ibid., p. 295.

Chapter 2
A Preliminary Look at Trust Situations

1. I have attempted to summarize what for me were some fascinating conversations on tape with each person. Direct quotes are surrounded by quotation marks, as are written quotations from the four initial descriptions contained in Chapter 1.

2. The discovery, in the middle of my research, of this contradictory data, came as a shock. I was even tempted to drop Bill from the research project until I realized that the structure of what he called trusting could provide an illuminating contrast to what were emerging as the other two levels of this complex phenomenon. Ultimately, one of the central discoveries turned out to be the fact that we tend to use the word *trust* rather indiscriminately to designate any one of three distinct human modes that are labeled *doxic confidence, social reliability,* and *interpersonal trust* in this book. See the section in Chapter 4 titled "The Other's Value Horizon" for more on this distinction.

3. In Chapters 2, 7, 11, 12, and 13 we will return to this attitude of needing to be in control that so pervades our lives and becomes one of the major obstacles to trusting.

4. See Alvin Toffler's two volumes, *Future Shock* (New York: Random House, 1970) and *The Third Wave.*

5. A description of life lived in the "natural attitude" is given by Alfred Schutz, *Collected Papers* (The Hague: Nijhoff, 1967). It is a pragmatic attitude that assumes the world could not be otherwise than as it appears to us in the our daily lives. "To it the world is from the outset not the private world of the single individual but an intersubjective world common to all of us, in which we have not a theoretical but an eminently practical interest. The world of everyday life is the scene and also the object of our actions and interactions. We have

to dominate it and we have to change it in order to realize the purposes which we pursue within it among our fellowmen. We work and operate not only within but upon the world. . . . Thus, it may be correctly said that a pragmatic motive governs our natural attitude toward the (intersubjective) world of daily life."

6. For an analysis of the all-encompassing social character of man arising from the underlying ground of human coexistence, see Remy Kwant, *Phenomenology of Social Existence* (Pittsburgh: Duquesne University Press, 1965).

7. Several authors who describe the sphere of intersubjectivity are: Gabriel Marcel, *The Mystery of Being*, Vol. I (Chicago: Regnery, 1964); William Luijpen, *Existential Phenomenology* (Pittsburgh: Duquesne University Press, 1969); Peter L. Berger and Thomas Luckman, *Invitation to Sociology* (New York: Doubleday, 1963); and Martin Plattel, *Social Philosophy* (Pittsburgh: Duquesne University Press, 1965).

8. Plattel, *Social Philosophy*, p. 30.

9. Trinitarian Formation Event, *Studies* 2 (1981): 512. See Chapter 14, section on "Questioning the Ultimate Horizon," and Chapter 15, "Our Actual Situation," for fuller articulation of the human life situation as open to an ultimate meaning horizon.

10. Van Kaam sees the soul as the preempirical, primal forming principle of life in all its dimensions and articulations. *Studies* 1 (1980): 139–141.

11. In a diagram of the formation field entitled "The Formation-Polarity Diagram," van Kaam situates the five poles among which the foundational human and Christian formation process unfolds itself in a constant dialogical tension and mutually formative interaction. They are, the poles of *preformation* (foundational formation of body and soul by eternal Trinitarian formation event), *intraformation* (formation of and by inner dialogue among life forms, dimensions, and articulations), *interformation* (formation of and by significant persons and communities), *outer formation* (immediate formation of and by life situation and mediate formation of and by world situation mediated by life situation). See *Studies* 2 (1981): 140.

Chapter 3
The Persons Who Trusted

1. See the chapter titled "Temporality" in Maurice Merleau-Ponty's *Phenomenology of Perception* (New York: Humanities Press, 1962), where the author states that the terms *retentions* and *protentions* were used first by Husserl to capture the intentionalities that run from my perceptual field itself and anchor me to the environment. This perceptual field (which is the subject) is described as drawing along a wake of retentions from the past, while biting into the future with its protentions. Merleau-Ponty quotes Heidegger, who also speaks of man as temporality that temporalizes itself as future-which-lapses-into-the-past-by-coming-into-the-present (p. 420). He is saying that the essential structures of subjectivity correspond to the essential structures of temporality that are the thrust toward the future, the retentions of the past, and the awareness of the present.

2. For more on "preformation," see Chapter 2, note 11, as well as *Studies* 1 (1980): 137–138, where van Kaam further describes preformation as being the infraorganismic and vital substratum of the fully human life form, its bodily cells, tissues, organs, and systems that is the base for the emergence of an original structuring of vital impulses, needs, and strivings of varying intensity.

3. Merleau-Ponty, "Temporality," in his *Phenomenology of Perception*, pp. 410–433.

4. "Foundational Human Life Form," *Studies* 1 (1980): 291.

5. Cf. "Foundational Christian Life Form," *Studies* 1 (1980): 291.

6. See the section in Chapter 16 titled "Who We Really Are" for a fuller articulation of the person as dynamic tending and aspiration toward abundant life in the Mystery.

7. Cf. previously cited quotation from St. Augustine in Chapter 1, p. 1–13.

8. Donna had evidently been inspired by Malcolm Muggeridge's book, *Something Beautiful for God* (New York: Collins, 1971), about the work of Mother Teresa of Calcutta and her Sisters of Charity.

9. "Universal Initial and Ongoing Formation," *Studies* 1 (1980): 140. Van Kaam points

to the initial outpouring of God's love outside the Trinity in an initial act of creation and the loving continuation of this creation in ongoing formation of the universe by his created and uncreated transforming energies.

10. Ignorance of the true transcendent nature of formation, an ignorance common to people since the Fall, *Studies* 1 (1980): 458.

11. The following paragraph is based on Chapter 2 of André Louf's *Teach Us to Pray* (London: Darton, Longman & Todd, 1974).

12. Cf. Chapter 1, note 12.

13. "Transcendence Crisis," *Studies* 1 (1980): 149. Van Kaam points to the basic insecurity of the heart or integrative center when it undergoes periods of change and consequent uncertainty regarding the appropriate directives for a new current life form. See Chapter 5, "Events as Openness Moments," and also in Chapter 17 the section on "The Invitation Hidden in Events," for a fuller articulation of transcendence crises.

14. See, for example, Louis John Cameli, *Stories of Paradise: The Study of Classical and Modern Autobiographies of Faith* (New York: Paulist, 1978).

15. On the Empirical Life Form, see *Studies* 1 (1980): 144–145.

Chapter 4
The To-Be-Trusted Others

1. "Formative Social Consciousness," *Studies* 2 (1981): 296.

2. For further articulation of the meaning of "participative," see Marcel, *The Mystery of Being*, and the more contemporary view set forth by Fritjof Capra in *The Tao of Physics* (New York: Bantam, 1977).

3. Contemporary historians of religion, literary critics, and social scientists use the word *myth* not to suggest fantasy or legend, but to describe a symbolic story that demonstrates the inner meaning of the universe and human life. Thus does Rosemary Haughton in *The Catholic Thing* (Springfield, Ill.: Templegate, 1979) point to the "unknown factors" in Catholicity revealed by its myths.

4. "Deformative Consequences (of Individualism) for Social Life Directives," *Studies* 2 (1981): 500. Van Kaam points out that the refusal of the social dimension of our conscience, an asocial ideal of autonomous personality fulfillment, or isolated self-actualization can take the place of personality fulfillment, actualization, and salvation by the mystery of divine formation as forming our lives (also) in and through the restrictive limitations and painful demands of an always imperfect society and imperfect permanent or temporary communities into which we are providentially inserted.

5. Karl Rahner in *Foundations of Christian Faith* (New York: Seabury, 1978) points to man as the "Event of God's Free and Forgiving Self Communication."

6. "Social Structures of the Core Form of Life," *Studies* 2 (1981): 301. The enduring core form or human heart is meant to be social through and through.

7. In view of the study's findings about the gratuitous nature of the interpersonal trust experience, Bill's view of trust as something that can be built should have raised questions from the very beginning. It is possible to uncover facilitating conditions for the emergence of trust, but the study points to its essential "giftedness."

8. See Gabriel Marcel, *Being and Having* (New York: Harper and Row, 1965); and Erich Fromm, *To Have or to Be* (New York: Harper and Row, 1976).

9. *Horizon* can here be equated with the limits of the person's world of meaning, and can open possibilities that the figure itself of an encountered phenomenon does not contain. For further reference, see Herbert Spiegelberg, *The Phenomenological Movement* (The Hague: Nijhoff, 1969), p. 718.

Chapter 5
Events as Openness Moments

1. Cameli, in *Stories of Paradise*, p. 62, points to what he calls a triad of sequential moments belonging to the movement of the faith relationship as a developing reality. He names these moments *openness, actuation,* and *integration,* and comments that actuation is the moment when "something happens."

2. Cf. Chapter 3, note 13.

3. See Part Three for cultural, developmental, and other deformative dispositions that increase anxiety and prevent the flow from actuation to integration.

4. "Resonance," *Studies* 1 (1980): 150.

5. See Carolyn Gratton, *Guidelines for Spiritual Direction,* pp. 60–65, for a description of these negatively tinged experiences that accompany moments or periods in life of not being able to function adequately, of feeling split within oneself, of being shocked out of embeddedness in the taken-for-granted world of pragmatic meanings. Further references to the ego and its necessary moments of powerlessness or desperation can be found in the chapter on "The Nature of the Ego and Its Termination" in Meher Baba, *Discourses* Vol. 3 (San Francisco: Sufism Reoriented Inc., 1976).

6. See Adrian van Kaam, "Transcendence Therapy," in Raymond J. Corsini, ed., *Handbook of Innovative Psychotherapies* (New York: Wiley, 1981), pp. 855–872, for a description of a therapeutic method of dealing with transcendence crises. See also van Kaam's *The Transcendent Self* for the crises belonging to the middle years and suggestions for their creative transcendence.

7. For guidelines on the integration of psychotherapeutic counseling techniques and traditional spiritual direction, see Gratton, *Guidelines for Spiritual Direction.*

8. Martin Heidegger, *Being and Time* (New York: Harper and Row, 1962), pp. 296–297.

9. For further elucidation of this point, see Ernest Becker, *The Denial of Death* (New York: The Free Press, 1973), and also the final paragraphs of this book.

10. See Charles J. Sabatino, "The Paradox of Death," *Studies in Formative Spirituality,* May 1981, 2 (2), pp. 217–229.

11. This notion of being "poor," of existing in poverty of spirit, is thematic in Jean Vanier's *Be Not Afraid* (Toronto: Griffin House, 1975). He says, "When we become conscious of our own poverty, our lack of fidelity, our fears; when we become conscious that we need our liberation, then Jesus will reveal Himself to us as the quiet and gentle Healer, drawing us from the world of darkness to a world of light, from a world of death to a world of life" (p. 47).

12. In checking back over the more than one hundred descriptions of the experience of trusting collected in preparation for this study, I did not find one where there was not at least some shift or change in attitude on the part of the person trusting, even when the trust was later discovered to be unfounded. However, it became clear that if the person's presence to the other, his reflective awareness, perception, interpersonal relatedness, body feeling, sense of risk and vulnerability, possibility for acting, volition and acceptance of creative tension, did not undergo some modification, he was not describing an experience of *interpersonal* trust. Persons who had never trusted anyone or who had confined their relations of confidence in others to the level of functional reliability, either declined to write descriptions at all, or wrote descriptions that lacked most or all of the shifts described in Chapter 6.

13. Part Two of this book consists of reflections on the embodied shift, the lived situations, the personal transformation, the other person, and the renewed involvement in one's world resulting from the experience of trusting. The orientation of Part Two is basically phenomenological, featuring theorists like Merleau-Ponty, Husserl, Heidegger, Schutz, James, Kwant, Marcel, and Ricoeur.

Chapter 6
Facilitating Freedom to Trust

1. It is understood that trusting is only one aspect of the larger ongoing complexity of the experiential flow of each person. Thus the "before trusting" experience is never merely one of absence of trust, but usually includes a complexity of reflective and prereflective awareness and experience. Also the experience of interpersonal trust itself may be only one aspect of the person's total lived experience, even at the moment of its emergence into the flow of his or her life.

2. Indries Shah, *The Sufis* (New York: Doubleday, 1964), p. 356.

3. In speaking of restructurings of experience, Merleau-Ponty says that "each 'formation' [*mise en forme*] appears to us (on the contrary) to be an event in the world of ideas, the institution of a new dialectic, the growing of a new region of phenomena, and the establishment of a new constitutive layer which eliminates the preceding one as isolated moment, but conserves and integrates it." *The Structure of Behavior* (Boston: Beacon Press, 1967), p. 208.

4. Cf. Chapter 3, where the person who trusts is seen from the point of view of his or her "temporality."

5. "Structure of Current and Apparent Life Forms," *Studies* 1 (1980): 146.

6. See Merleau-Ponty, *Phenomenology of Perception*, p. 430. This notion of presence points to a kind of openness onto reality of the person, an openness that is loving or nonloving, trustful or mistrustful. It also points to the Divine as presence, as loving, answering Other.

7. See Chapter 3, note 2, as well as Chapter 12, "Developmental Aspects of Trusting."

8. Theorists other than Merleau-Ponty have discovered the body as core of all lived experience, which orders and systematizes all things with reference to itself as focus of action and interest. For example, William James is quoted by James M. Edie in the *Review of Metaphysics* 23 (1970): 515, as having written in *Essays in Radical Empiricism*, "The world experienced (otherwise called the 'field of consciousness') comes at all times with our body as its center of vision, center of action, center of interest. Where the body is, is here; when the body is, is now; what the body touched is this; all other things are there and then and that. These words of emphasized position imply a systematization of things with reference to a focus of action and interest which lies in the body; and the systematization is now so instinctive (was it ever not so?) that no developed or active experience exists for us at all except in that ordered form. So far as 'thoughts' and 'feelings' can be active, their activity terminates in the activity of the body, and only through first arousing its activities can they begin to change those of the rest of the world. The body is the storm center, the origin of co-ordinates, the constant place of stress in all that experience-train. Everything circles around it and is felt from its point of view; the 'I' then, is primarily a noun of position, just like 'this' and 'here.' " Somewhere, Merleau-Ponty refers to this situated bodily openness to reality as the body's "collusion" with the world, and William Luijpen describes its mysterious way of knowing or being able as its "pact" with the world, which preexists the more personal reflective modes of knowing and deciding to, yet is never superseded by them.

9. Sources for this meaning of doxic confidence are: (1) Edmund Husserl, *The Crisis of European Science and Transcendental Phenomenology* (Evanston, Ill.: Northwestern University Press, 1970), p. 65. Husserl differentiates between *doxa* (vague and relative everyday knowledge) and *episteme* (rational knowledge); between being thought to be unquestioned and obvious through *doxa*, and true being, which is everywhere an ideal goal, the task of *episteme* or "reason." He sees the life-world, in its everyday givenness, in the obvious appearance of things, as the foundation or taken-for-granted ground of all human life and science. (2) Alfred Schutz, *Collected Papers;* (3) Hans Linschoten, *On the Way Toward a Phenomenological Psychology* (Pittsburgh: Duquesne University Press, 1968), p. 214. The certainty that reality is such is what we have chosen to call *doxa*. William James characterized *doxa* as a feeling that tells us: This *is*, these things are *real* (Linschoten, p. 203). Husserl speaks of the doxic certainty that belongs to experience, that "it is so," and in *Erfahrung und Urteil*, he defined the most basic doxa (ur-doxa) more closely as world consciousness, and the universal

foundation of confidence in the "self-evident" pregiven world that is presupposed in all action. Even all doubting and questioning is done within that ur-doxic whole that I take for granted as there (Linschoten, p. 205). This is where William James got his conviction that doxic confidence is the *feeling* of confidence in the self-evident reality of the life-world, and why Linschoten concludes that "doxic confidence is the way we participate in the life-world through the body, and experience this participation."

10. Cf. Chapter 2, note 5.

11. For fuller description of this notion of *chiasm,* see "Working Notes" in Maurice Merleau-Ponty, *The Visible and the Invisible* (Evanston, Ill.: Northwestern University Press, 1968), pp. 214–275.

12. In the chapter on "The Thing and the Natural World" in *Phenomenology of Perception,* we find Merleau-Ponty's theory of the systems "lighting-thing lighted" and "touching-thing touched," which seems to be extended in his analysis in *The Visible and the Invisible* of "seer-seen." Within this circular system, the seen always involves a response of the seer, the appropriate response, a welcome for the atmospheric existence of the seen, which is never merely "given." The participation of the seen in its context, in its inner and outer horizons, refers to the invisible flesh that sustains the visible and lets it be seen, enveloping it in just the way that is required for it to reveal itself in a certain intending or constituting movement. This analysis points to a preestablished harmony between the seer and the seen that is prior to the act of seeing itself. It may point also to what could be called the preact dimension of interpersonal trust—a dimension that is not yet trust, but which underlies it and is a necessary condition for it.

13. Cf. note 8 above.

14. Emmanuel Levinas, *Totality and Infinity* (Pittsburgh: Duquesne University Press, 1969), pp. 110 seq.

15. Merleau-Ponty, *The Structure of Behavior,* Chapter III, "The Physical Order; the Vital Order; the Human Order," pp. 129–184.

16. "Pneumatic Dimension of the Life Form," *Studies* 2 (1981): 522.

17. See entire issue of *Humanitas* 8 (1972): on "The Leisurely Attitude" for detailed description of the kind of relaxation that is meant here.

18. This is not to suggest that the body in interpersonal trust is a "projectless" entity, not directed to any task at all in the world. However, at the moment of trusting, the other projects were not in the forefront of focused consciousness.

19. David Steindl-Rast, "Work and Leisure," summarized in *Humanitas* 8 (1972): 395–396.

20. See, for example, Herbert J. Freudenberger, *Burn-Out: How to Beat the High Cost of Success* (New York: Bantam Books, 1981); or Meyer Friedman and Ray H. Rosenman, *Type A Behavior and Your Heart* (New York: Knopf, 1974); or Edmund Jacobson, *You Must Relax* (New York: McGraw-Hill, 1934), and *Anxiety and Tension Control* (Philadelphia: Lippincott, 1964). See also Herbert Benson, *The Relaxation Response* (New York: Morrow, 1975).

21. See Remy C. Kwant, *Phenomenology of Social Existence* (Pittsburgh: Duquesne University Press, 1965). In Chapter 2, "The All-Encompassing Social Character of Man," Kwant claims that our relationship to our fellow man permeates our entire human existence (p. 67), and in Chapter 3 he contends that the social dimension of our existence gives rise to what might be termed a second body or "nature" (p. 127), even though each one is free to take up this social facticity in an individual way (p. 137).

22. Friedman and Rosenman, *Type A Behavior,* p. 4.

23. Ibid. See also pp. 82–88 for a description of the characteristics of Types A & B.

24. From personal notes of weekend course on "Physiology, Psychology, and Spirituality" given February 7–9, 1980, at Duquesne University by George Freemesser, M.D.

25. See "Dimensions of Consciousness," *Studies* 1 (1980): 149; Adrian van Kaam, *In Search of Spiritual Identity* (Denville, N.J.: Dimension Books, 1975); Robert E. Ornstein, *The Psychology of Consciousness* (San Francisco: Walter Freeman, 1972); Aron Gurwitsch, *The Field of Consciousness* (Pittsburgh: Duquesne University Press, 1964); Patricia Carrington, *Freedom in Meditation* (New York: Doubleday, 1978). For further references on consciousness and its alteration, see Chapter 8, note 3.

26. For further reflection on the stress factors involved in various social and interpersonal situations, see Chapter 7, "Looking Again at the Trust Situations."

Chapter 7
Looking Again at the Trust Situations

1. I am referring here to the methodology of Alfred Schutz, who criticizes Weber for confusing the points of view of the actor and the anonymous observer in the interpretation of subjective meaning. He implies that we have certain "typifications" that we count on in our understanding of a subject in a "business" situation, in discussing teaching with a colleague, in a typical marriage proposal situation. But how does the observer (or researcher) know when the moment of interpersonal trust in that situation begins? And how does he understand the meaning of the phenomenon for the subject? Schutz contends that he does not unless, either in the description of the situation, or, more likely, by means of face-to-face interviews, he actually participates in a direct social relationship with the subject. See the chapter on Max Weber's methodological concepts in Alfred Schutz, *The Phenomenology of the Social World* (Evanston, Ill.: Northwestern University Press, 1967).

2. Cf. Chapter 3, note 1.

3. "The human person is not closed upon himself like a stone. We are a restless, spontaneous movement towards transcendence. We experience ourselves as incomplete, unfinished, longing to be . . . called to repeated resurrection." Van Kaam, *The Transcendent Self,* pp. 166–167.

4. See Maurice Merleau-Ponty, *Phenomenology of Perception,* especially the chapters on "The Body"; and also Alfred Schutz, *Collected Papers,* I, p. 178, where he notes that "My own body is for me the center of orientation in the spatio-temporal order of the world. It alone is given to me as being 'Here' whereas the Other's body is given to me as being 'There.' . . . What was pointed out for the perspectives of the 'Here' and 'There' has to be worked out (although not immediately referring to the body) . . . by an analysis of the time-bound perspective of 'Now' and 'Then.' . . ."

5. See Eugene Minkowski, *Lived Time* (Evanston, Ill.: Northwestern University Press, 1970).

6. Edmund Husserl, *The Crisis of European Sciences and Transcendental Phenomenology* (Evanston, Ill.: Northwestern University Press, 1970), pp. 168–169: ". . . perception itself, as the 'flowing-static' present, is constituted only through the fact that the static 'now' (as a deeper intentional analysis shows) has a horizon with two differently structured sides, known in intentional language as a continuum of retentions and protentions."

7. You could say that in place of Husserl's commonsense idealization of "I-can-do-it-again," referring to a typical constellation or structure of experience that is anticipated, it is possible to transpose this typical constellation of experience into the past, into the person's recognition that "I-have-done-it (that typical familiar structure I call trusting) before." Schutz might say that the subjects called on their "stock of knowledge at hand" to help them recognize and identify a segment of the flow they could call "trusting." Schutz, *Collected Papers,* II, 285–286.

8. Schutz, *Phenomenology of the Social World,* p. 13.

9. Schutz's meaning of the intersubjective world is confined to the horizon of the taken-for-granted world of everyday life, in which "vivid presence," "communication," and "face-to-face" relation take place. See Schutz, *Collected Papers,* I, 207–222, for above references; see also *Collected Papers,* II, 23–36, for his analysis of the "face-to-face situation," the "Thou-orientation," and the "We-relation." Naturally I would also agree that trust that is truly interpersonal in the sense of inter*subjective* can endure temporary separation between the persons involved.

10. See Chapter 8, note 28, and Chapter 10, note 19, for more on the basic human need for fusion with others.

11. Huston Smith, *The Religions of Man* (New York: Harper and Row, 1965), p. 24. Referring to the Hindu trust in the self that underlies man's ego life, Smith reveals the need

for a lively sense of this self that underlies the phenomenal (ego) personality, and shows how easy it is for people to lose their centering in their true self ("in eternity") when they lapse into the ego modes of pragmatic competition and anxiety for "the outcome of their deeds" (p. 47). Later in the section of the book on Taoism, Smith refers to the renunciation of ego modes of one who knows the nature of the basic life force (Tao), and who "knows that it will sustain him if he will only stop his thrashing and flailing and trust it to buoy him and carry him gently forward" (p. 206). It would seem from this that trust is in some way connected with the renunciation of ego modes in the sense of the empirical ego.

12. In *Young Man Luther* (New York: Norton, 1958), p. 193, Erik Erikson sees that "the Renaissance is the ego revolution *par excellence.* It was a large-scale restoration of the ego's executive functions. . . . The Renaissance gave man a vacation from his negating conscience, thus freeing the ego to gather strength for manifold activity."

13. See Chapter 11 for a review of some of the particular obstacles to trusting that exist in Western culture and society.

14. Chapter 13 is an attempt to further describe this approach of simultaneous resistance and attempts to cope.

15. In speaking of the objective context of meaning that surrounds the experience of contemporaries (as contrasted with the more subjective context of the experience of con-sociates or fellowmen), Schutz remarks that "my knowledge of the world of contemporaries is typical knowledge of typical processes." He calls this relating by means of typifications a "They-orientation," implying a relation to another who is not a "Thou" or subject—but rather almost an anonymous object. "The synthesis of the interpretation by which I know any contemporaries as ideal types does not apprehend the unique self of a human being in his vivid present." Schutz, *Collected Papers,* II, 44.

16. Schutz, *Collected Papers,* II, 28. Schutz also points out that the other appears in differ-ent perspectives and that the subject may be either tuned attentively to the other's experi-ence (e.g., his conscious processes and subjective motivations), or may be only remotely interested in these, concentrating instead on overt acts.

17. Ibid., p. 70. "Thus the social world . . . is arranged around the self as center in various degrees of intimacy and anonymity. Here am I and next to me are 'alter egos' of whom, as Kipling says, I know 'their naked souls.' Then come those with whom I share time and space and whom I know more or less intimately . . . of whom I have an indirect knowledge. . . ."

18. Ibid., p. 113. Also the chapters on "Foundations of a Theory of Intersubjective Understanding" and "The Structure of the Social World: the Realm of Directly Ex-perienced Social Reality, The Realm of Contemporaries and the Realm of Predecessors" in *The Phenomenology of the Social World* (pp. 97–214) have many references to the "intimate" aspect of an interpersonal situation as opposed to the degrees of anonymity that are also possible between two interrelated persons.

19. See Aelred Squire, Chapter 8, "Soul-keepers," in *Summer in the Seed* (New York: Paulist Press, 1980), for an account of the intimacy of friendship, especially as regards "the open sharing of all one's secrets and plans" (p. 151).

20. On p. 202 of *The Phenomenology of the Social World,* Schutz remarks that "as social relationships in the face-to-face situation are based on the pure Thou-orientation, so social relationships between contemporaries are based on the pure They-orientation. . . . In the face-to-face situation the partners look into each other and are mutually sensitive to each other's responses. This is not the case in relationships between contemporaries. Here each partner has to be content with the probability that the other, to whom he is oriented by means of an anonymous type, will respond with the same kind of orientation. And so an element of doubt enters into every such relationship." For example, because of its necessary anonymity, a relationship between oneself and the token seller in the subway or the person who repairs the sidewalks is usually characterized by the latter typology.

21. Karen Horney, *Neurosis and Human Growth* (New York: Norton, 1950), pp. 8 seq.; and *The Neurotic Personality of Our Time* (New York: Norton, 1937), pp. 41 seq.

22. See Samuel Greenberg, *Neurosis Is a Painful Style of Living* (New York: New American Library, 1977), for a popular treatment of Horney's theory.

23. Maurice Natanson, *Literature, Philosophy and the Social Sciences* (The Hague: Nijhoff, 1962), p. 36. "To live in the natural attitude then, is to live 'believingly' in the world, to have the massive content of experience unfold not only as part of the world but as inevitably given within a tacitly accepted frame of reality. . . . Moreover, along with what Husserl calls this 'doxic' belief in the existence of the world, there is an unsophisticated commitment to its intersubjective character."

24. Martin Plattel, *Social Philosophy*, p. 91. Maurice Natanson in *The Journeying Self* (Reading, Mass.: Addison-Wesley, 1970), p. 8, adds, "Ordinarily, we believe in the reality and validity of our world, its history, and its likely future. For practical purposes, we trust in the machinery of commerce and the efficiency of societal procedures. . . . Ordinary, matter-of-course believing in the reality of the world, then, is not only an aspect of public life; it is a fundamental presupposition of mundanity, a philosophical ground for the organization and character of our experience of the world."

25. See Merleau-Ponty, *The Structure of Behavior*, pp. 129–184, on the difference between being embedded in certain "vital structures" and being able to transcend them. There will be no attempt in this book to deal with the embeddedness in vital structures that gives rise to the deep mistrust clinically labeled "paranoia."

26. For further reference to "perceptual faith," see Merleau-Ponty, *The Visible and the Invisible*, especially Chapter 1, pp. 3–4.

27. See Chapter 2, section on "Personal Significance of the Situation."

28. See Michael Gelvan, *A Commentary on Heidegger's Being and Time* (New York: Harper and Row, 1970), pp. 196–200, for commentary on Section 69 of Heidegger's *Being and Time* (New York: Harper and Row, 1962), in which the shift from unquestioning praxis to reflection is somewhat·similar to this break in the taken-for-granted relationship with the other.

29. Internal marginal situations where trust is disrupted seem to be the ones where trust also emerges. Of the over one hundred descriptions I received prior to this research, I could not find one that described trust as emerging from a totally tensionless situation. They all described at least some degree of personally significant problematics that appeared as obstacles to the smooth flow of a trusting response. Some, it is true, were much less marginal than others, and certainly not all were externally risky. But there was always a certain degree of internal marginality that made it necessary for the person to "trust" rather than simply take the situation for granted. See in this regard Chapter 5, note 5, on "ego desperation."

30. See, for example, Bernard Bro, *The Little Way* (London: Darton, Longman & Todd, 1979), for a description of the humble trust of Thérèse of Lisieux.

31. See Jean-Pierre de Caussade, *The Sacrament of the Present Moment* (London: Collins, 1981), translation by Kitty Muggeridge of his *L'Abandon à La Providence Divine* (Desclée de Brouwer, 1966). See also Chapter 17, section on "Trust as Basis of Commitment."

Chapter 8
A New Level of Being for People Who Trust

1. Jan Ehrenwald, *Psychotherapy: Myth and Method* (New York: Grune and Stratton, 1966), p. 203.

2. Ibid. Ehrenwald notes that the levels of human consciousness range "from Western man's standard, technological mode of experience, to the satori of Zen masters; from dreaming to wakefulness; from the normal to the paranormal; from the sacred to the profane; from primary process functioning to the artist's creative self-expression and the therapist's regression in the service of treatment; from compulsive rigidity to the schizophrenic's headlong plunge into darkness and insanity and, hopefully, to his emergence to sanity again." Cf. "Four Dimensions of Human Consciousness," in *Studies* 1 (1980): 149.

3. Transformation of consciousness is a popular term with many meanings. According to Charles Tart, *Altered States of Consciousness* (New York: Wiley, 1969), a transformed or "altered state of consciousness" takes place when an individual clearly feels a "qualitative

shift" in his pattern of mental functioning. Other psychologists like Robert Ornstein, *The Psychology of Consciousness* (San Francisco: Freeman, 1972), Claudio Naranjo, *On the Psychology of Meditation* (New York: Viking Press, 1971), and Lawrence LeShan, *Alternate Realities* (New York: Evans, 1976), have explored the nature of consciousness and its transformation. This limited bibliography is merely an introduction to a vast field that is opening up in terms of spirituality as well. See, for example, William Johnston's *The Mirror Mind* (San Francisco: Harper and Row, 1981).

4. See Alfred Schutz, *Collected Papers*, I, Chapter "On Multiple Realities."

5. Merleau-Ponty, *Phenomenology of Perception*, p. 163, commenting on this awareness says, "In any case, in psychological treatment of any kind, the coming of awareness would remain purely cognitive, the patient would not accept the meaning of his disturbances as revealed to him without the personal relationship formed with the doctor, or without the confidence and friendship felt towards him, and the change of existence resulting from this friendship. Neither symptom nor cure is worked out at the level of objective or positing consciousness, but below that level." See also Chapter 6 and pp. 346–365 for description of the anonymous level of bodily perception, the prepersonal consciousness that is beneath the level of decision, thought, and self-consciousness.

6. William James, *The Varieties of Religious Experience*, p. 298. One can compare "normal waking consciousness" with Schutz's "natural attitude of everyday life."

7. In his "Action and Disposition Chart," *Studies* 1 (1981): 134, van Kaam points to what he calls Empirical Life Form Sources, both transcendent and incarnational. He differentiates formative transcendent mind and will (chief sources of the appraisal and decision-making process) from formative transcendent functional mind and will (chief sources of incarnating the decisions resulting from completed appraisal).

8. Marcel, *The Mystery of Being* II, p. 209. See also Gratton, *Guidelines for Spiritual Direction*, chapters 5 and 6, for descriptions of the human spirit's capacity for being reflectively present to the "more" of human existence.

9. Van Kaam sees the central dynamic of human formation to be the innate, transcendent aspiration after a final, ideal life form, and the central dynamic of Christian formation to be the infused pneumatic inspiration of and subsequent enlightened and graced aspiration after one's final, ideal life form in Christ. *Studies* 1 (1980): 293.

10. "Formative" refers to whatever in life is capable of disclosing and embodying form. The word itself connotes direction, meaning, incarnation, or embodiment in life. A provisional glossary of the terminology of the science of foundational formative spirituality can be found in Volumes 1, 2, and 3 of *Studies in Formative Spirituality*, 1980–1982. The principles of formative spirituality can also be found in van Kaam, *The Transcendent Self*, pp. 149–163.

11. Kung, *Does God Exist?*, p. 437. The paragraph that follows reflects the contents of pp. 437–453 of this book.

12. It is interesting to note that trust is hardly ever given directly as an observable action, but is present in actions (like chatting with a friend, discussing a litigation with one's lawyer, making a decision, or responding to a proposal of marriage) through the awakening of *spirit*, the interior change in reflective consciousness that is brought about in the person who trusts. In other words, trust usually has more to do with inner change in the person than with external changes in his world.

13. Merleau-Ponty, *Phenomenology of Perception*, p. 456.

14. Marcel, *The Mystery of Being*, II, 19.

15. Ibid., I, 221. In the following pages, Marcel points out that relationships between things are external or "beside" each other, while relationships between people are internal or "with" one another (p. 222). Van Kaam speaks of the character of the formative movements or affects of the heart as marked by a specified, unique, yet global moving "toward," "away from," "against" or "with," the last signaling love, acceptance, union with, or benediction of the other. *Studies* 1 (1980): 145.

16. Marcel, in *The Mystery of Being*, I, 224, contends that from the moment of birth, each man is involved in the intersubjective nexus through his family. He is never at his deepest level a totally separated ego, but from the beginning is figure on the ground of others-in-the-world. See also "Spiritual Formation and Family Life," *Studies* 2 (1981), particularly the

bibliographic section on family systems as interformative, and also Capra, *Tao of Physics,* regarding the unity of all things.

17. Marcel, *The Mystery of Being,* I, 142.

18. Martin Heidegger, *Discourse on Thinking: A Translation of Gelassenheit* (New York: Harper and Row, 1966), p. 55. See also p. 46 where he says, "Calculative thinking never stops, never collects itself. Calculative thinking is not meditative thinking, not thinking which contemplates the meaning which reigns in everything that is. . . ."

19. Marion Milner, *A Life of One's Own* (Harmondsworth, Middlesex, England: Penguin Books, 1957).

20. See this chapter, note 28, and Chapter 10, note 19, on the concept of universal fusion.

21. Merleau-Ponty, *Phenomenology of Perception,* p. 360. The extreme of living in this withdrawn way, as if cut off from one's bodily reality, is labeled "schizophrenic" by pathologists. R. D. Laing has described this solipsistic isolation as "living out of one's mind."

22. In a forthcoming article to be published in *Duquesne Studies in Phenomenological Psychology* IV (September 1983) I will look more closely at trust and the therapeutic relationship. The implications of trust as context for emancipation from anxiety are many and involve more areas than can be dealt with here.

23. Andras Angyal, *Neurosis and Treatment: A Holistic Theory* (New York: Viking, 1973), p. 100.

24. Ernest Schachtel, *Metamorphosis: On the Development of Affect, Perception, Attention, and Memory* (New York: Basic Books, 1959), pp. 44–55.

25. Horney, *Neurosis and Human Growth,* p. 18 seq.

26. Erich Fromm, *Escape from Freedom* (New York: Holt, Rinehart, 1941).

27. Erhenwald, *Psychotherapy,* p. 77.

28. Louis B. Fierman, ed., *Effective Psychotherapy: The Contribution of Hellmuth Kaiser* (New York: The Free Press, 1965). Briefly, Kaiser posits a "universal conflict" (the client's refusal to confront his basic aloneness), a "universal symptom" (the client's preference for duplicity rather than straightforwardness in communication), and a "delusion of fusion" (the client's desire for oral incorporation of the therapist) as key concepts in psychotherapy.

29. *Risk:* the possibility of suffering harm or loss; danger. A factor, element, or course involving uncertain danger; hazard. *The American Heritage Dictionary of the English Language* (New York: Houghton, Mifflin, 1969).

30. One yoga teacher describes the sensation of total relaxation of muscular tension subsequent to the "relaxation posture" as being like that of a sponge, completely open and undefended against whatever may invade it from the outside. Once a person has experienced this letting go of the muscle tension involved in defending oneself from the world, he or she recognizes that one's vulnerability begins with the body.

31. Robert J. Ringer, *Looking Out for No. 1* (New York: Fawcett, 1977), and *Winning Through Intimidation* (New York: Funk & Wagnall, 1974); Michael Korda, *Power: How to Get it, How to Use it* (New York: Ballentine, 1976) and *Success!* (New York: Ballantine, 1977); Sidney J. Harris, *Winners and Losers* (Niles, Ill.: Argus Communications, 1973), are examples of this genre.

32. In our present situation there are many powerless persons. I speak here not only of those who are poor and hungry or socially disenfranchised, but also of persons from affluent middle-class suburbs, as well as from ghettos and urban slums, who, because of their sex or race or historical circumstances, are very much within their rights to struggle to become more independent and self-sufficient. Such persons cannot be accused of merely feeling threatened in the area of personal myth.

33. Erikson, *Young Man Luther,* p. 111.

34. See William James, *The Varieties of Religious Experience,* p. 56, for a description of the attitudes of dependence and surrender; see also William Johnston, *The Stillpoint,* p. 127, where he points to the "elements of risk" involved in the Christian's desire to find an ultimate object of dependence.

Chapter 9
Appraising the Other as To-Be-Trusted

1. Merleau-Ponty, *Phenomenology of Perception*, p. 321.
2. William James, *Talks to Teachers* (New York: Dover Publications, 1962), p. 8.
3. Since the "other" is also always subject or person in a situation of interpersonal trust, all that has been said about the person who trusts applies equally to the other who is trusted, and is implicit in what follows.
4. Merleau-Ponty, *The Visible and the Invisible*, p. 248. For further reference to Merleau-Ponty's notion of the "flesh" and related notions of "chiasm," "intertwining," "wild being," etc., see Chapter IV of *The Visible and the Invisible*, which is an ontological interpretation of the perceptual dimension of reality that was first exposed in the *Phenomenology of Perception*. In this attempt to penetrate beneath the subject/object distinction to the "flesh" of the world, Merleau-Ponty tries to uncover the invisible premeaning that is latent *within* sensible, visible appearances.
5. See *Studies in Formative Spirituality* 1 (1980): 464–475, for glossary entries on the process of reflective appraisal.
6. "The Four Stages of Provisional Formation Appraisal," *Studies* 1 (1980): 469.
7. Directives are messages or instructions that give direction or guidance. Van Kaam sees that they may be formative or deformative, and may function as security directives coforming our lives. *Studies* 2 (1981): 2, p. 534.
8. Edmund Husserl, "The Clarification of the Transcendental Problem of the Related Function of Psychology," in *The Crisis of European Sciences and Transcendental Phenomenology*, refers in Section 45 to the "sense of the same" as he begins his analysis of the object of experience in the life-world. He sees it always as a structured relationship of data plus context that fulfills the sense of "the same" (e.g., a type or style identifiable as "trustworthy") in spite of the fact that the "manners of its sensible exhibition" are different. In terms of interpersonal trust, we might add that each appearance of the other who is to be trusted, whether it correlates with a different sense for the subject (seeing, hearing, etc.) or presents a different aspect to his view (loving, accepting, seriously concerned, etc.), points back or refers in some way to aspects of the whole (other person) that do not appear but that the subject can anticipate as being part of the same type of whole (structured) that he recognizes from past experiences as trustable-for-him. Husserl speaks thus of a whole that refers to an invisible system of possible stylistic fulfillments, which, in turn, refer to a margin or field.
9. Lack of space prevents further elaboration of the external similarities and internal differences between the two life-styles.
10. "Worlds" are prominent in the thinking of William James (see especially *Principles of Psychology*, Vol. II, Chapter XXI on "The Perception of Reality") and Alfred Schutz (see especially *Collected Papers*, Vol. I, the chapter "On Multiple Realities," pp. 207–259). This notion is also a key one in the writing of Husserl, Heidegger, and Merleau-Ponty.
11. Manfred Frings, *Max Scheler* (Pittsburgh: Duquesne University Press, 1965).
12. Pierre Thevanz, *What Is Phenomenology? And Other Essays* (Chicago: Quadrangle Books, 1962).
13. Simon Tugwell, *Prayer: Living with God* (Springfield, Ill.: Templegate, 1975), pp. 53–55.

Chapter 10
New Possibilities for Involvement

1. For an explanation of executive willing, see the section in this chapter titled "The Kind of Willing That Was Involved."
2. For more on creative tension, see the section in this chapter titled "Creative Tension in the Face of Uncertainty."
3. "Function of Formative Mind in Final Appraisal," *Studies* 1 (1980): 470. As mentioned

in Chapter 9, notes 5 and 6, reflective appraisal as a process is fully worked out in this issue of *Studies.*

4. *The Jerusalem Bible* (New York: Doubleday, 1966) translates Rom. 8:28: "We know that by turning everything to their good, God co-operates with all those who love him."

5. See Schutz, *The Phenomenology of the Social World,* section on "The Concept of Action," pp. 57–63, and *Collected Papers,* section on "The Manifestations of Man's Spontaneous Life in the Outer World and Some of its Forms," I, 209–212. Mediated by the body with its protentional and retentional threads, the meaning of any action originates in the internal time consciousness (the future orientation) of the one who acts.

6. The following analysis of interpersonal trust as a "performatory" utterance or gesture is from an article on H. H. Price's distinction between "belief in" and "belief that" as applied to the basic trust involved in belief in a friend. See Edward Mooney, "Commitment and Belief," *Man and World* 3 (1970): 116–121. For more on commitment, see John C. Haughey, *Should Anyone Say Forever?* (New York: Doubleday, 1977).

7. Mooney, "Commitment and Belief," p. 120.

8. For an article dealing with the "future" dimension of trust, see Thomas Mermall, "Spain's Philosopher of Hope," *Thought* 45 (1970): 103–120.

9. The notion of "receptive volition" is found in the address "Philosophy of Will and Action" given by Paul Ricoeur to the Second Lexington Conference on Pure and Applied Phenomenology, and reprinted in E. W. Straus, ed., *Phenomenology of Will and Action* (Pittsburgh: Duquesne University Press, 1967), pp. 7–33. In that address, Ricoeur's notion of volition as including a nonvolitional element is somewhat similar to Leslie Farber's distinction between the two realms of willing (primary and secondary) in Leslie H. Farber, *The Ways of the Will* (New York: Basic Books, 1966), and to van Kaam's idea of will as "self-orientation" and will as "executive" in his *On Being Yourself* (Denville, N.J.: Dimension Books, 1972). See also Paul Ricoeur, *Freedom and Nature: The Voluntary and the Involuntary* (Evanston, Ill.: Northwestern University Press, 1966); and Adrian van Kaam, *Religion and Personality,* pp. 91–119.

10. Ricoeur, "Philosophy of Will and Action," p. 24. "We have only underlined the active dimension of volition under the aspect of 'taking a stand'; but the 'taking of a stand' is itself correlative with an aspect of passivity, or better, of receptivity, which is expressed precisely in the relation of choice to its motives . . . there is a point of passivity or of receptivity at the heart of volition by which will renders itself sensitive to anything which can incline it without necessitating it, which can provide it with an impulsion and a legitimization."

11. From Straus, *Phenomenology of Will and Action,* pp. 56–57.

12. Farber, *The Ways of the Will,* p. 7.

13. Merleau-Ponty, *Phenomenology of Perception,* p. 169.

14. Frederick S. Perls, *Gestalt Therapy Verbatim* (Lafayette, Cal.: Real People Press, 1969), pp. 46–47.

15. For further thought on this concept of the creative imagination in its relation to hope, see William Lynch, *Images of Hope: Imagination as Healer of the Hopeless* (New York: New American Library, 1965).

16. In *The Ways of the Will,* Farber comments that the problem of the will lies in our recurring temptation to apply the will of the second realm to those portions of life that will not comply, but will rather become distorted under such coercion. Thus, when will of the second realm (mere functional reliability or social trust) seeks in its utilitarian way to capture the style of interpersonal trust, we get a false situation and much anxiety, because interpersonal trust cannot be willed. In Chapter 13 we take up again the conflictual nature of the human will when it is dominated by the pride form. In his discussion of appraisal (*Studies* 1 [1980]) van Kaam points out that the quasi-foundational pride form obscures and weakens both mind and will, thus setting up obstacles, especially in vital fulfillment and functional exertion strivings, to the aspiration after transcendent and pneumatic fulfillment proper to the person.

17. Typification, according to Schutz, is that form of abstraction that leads to more or less standardized, more or less vague conceptualizations of the world (and/or the other person) based on an unquestioned stock of knowledge derived from previous experiences

of objects of this type. Typification tends to overlook what is individually unique about the experience of another as subject. See Schutz, *Collected Papers,* I, 7, 59, 283, 323, and II, 37 seq.

18. See William Luijpen, *Existential Phenomenology,* pp. 304 seq., for a discussion of "Phenomenology of Indifference."

19. We are reminded again of Hellmuth Kaiser's remarks about the universality of attempts at living in fusion: "Man is subject to a basic need that conceptually transcends and cannot be reduced to libido or aggression . . . it is a need for contact with another person . . . [which] may be conceptualized as the universal wish or fantasy of fusion . . . the attempt to create in real life by behavior and communication the illusion of fusion." In Fierman, *Effective Psychotherapy,* pp. 208–209.

20. See Merleau-Ponty, "Other People and the Human World," *Phenomenology of Perception,* pp. 346–365, for the possibility of solipsistic withdrawal "into the core of our thinking nature."

21. Several possible subjects for the empirical study who found themselves unable to write descriptions of trusting explained that they had never trusted anyone "because I am such a bastard myself," "because nobody could trust me." This type of "realism" also reflects the generalized attitude of contemporary Westerners who, in their often justified skepticism, refuse to take a chance on being taken in or duped by others. Or perhaps they are "realistically" aware of human fallibility to the extent that, like Ellen, they simply cannot risk trusting anyone.

22. Emmanuel Mounier, *The Character of Man* (New York: Harper, 1956), p. 165.

23. On the other hand, since every situation carries several possibilities of action (both positive and negative) within it, the decision *never* to trust may open up diverse realms of distrust, fear, closure, rigidity, withdrawal, prejudice, etc. The need for balanced appraisal becomes evident here as the disposition that accompanies our freedom to say no.

24. Cf. Chapter 5, note 1; the triad of sequential moments belonging to the movement of the faith relationship. In a situation where trust is lacking, the pattern is blocked—there is neither actuation nor integration.

Chapter 11
Cultural Obstacles to Trusting

1. "Historical Formation Potential," *Studies* 1 (1980): 147. This gloss speaks of the potency and tendency of all human life to be formed by and give form to the pulsations of movements, feelings, and ideas that pulsate in one's period of history.

2. "Formation Ignorance," *Studies* 1 (1980): 458, is seen as ignorance of the true transcendent nature of formation, an ignorance common to people since the Fall.

3. Since the Fall, van Kaam contends, all human beings are touched by the autarchic pride form, with its shared illusions of autonomous fulfillment and self-exertion that give rise to certain exalted social rites, standards, and ideals. Their existence presupposes, maintains, and deepens society's shared ignorance of the true nature of formation. See "Societal Exaltation," *Studies* 1 (1980): 459.

4. Martin Buber, "Hope for This Hour," in *Pointing the Way* (New York: Harper and Row, 1963).

5. Erich Fromm, *Escape from Freedom* (New York: Avon Library, 1965), and *The Sane Society* (New York: Rinehart, 1955), for example. See also Fromm's description of the "receptive orientation" (pp. 206–207 in Theodore Millon, ed., *Theories of Psychopathology* [Philadelphia: Saunders, 1967]) as a caricature of the "trusting" person whose source of good is totally outside himself.

6. John H. Schaar, *Escape from Authority: The Perspectives of Erich Fromm* (New York: Basic Books, 1961). The analysis of Fromm's thinking that follows is based on Schaar's book and was also influenced by Hannah Arendt's *The Human Condition* (New York: Doubleday, 1959), especially her concept of "world-alienation."

7. See Karen Horney, *The Neurotic Personality of Our Time.*

8. Kenneth Keniston, *The Uncommitted: Alienated Youth in American Society* (New York: Harcourt, Brace and World, 1965).

9. R. D. Laing, *The Politics of Experience* (New York: Pantheon Books, 1967), is among these critics. In his attempt to deal with the ambiguities of sanity and madness, Laing uncovers the irrationalities of society, the Procrustean bed that often requires man to devastate his experience in order to fit "normally" into it. Trust in such a society is actually madness, according to Laing. See also Philip Slater, *The Pursuit of Loneliness: American Culture at the Breaking Point* (Boston: Beacon Press, 1970); and Fritz Pappenheim, *The Alienation of Modern Man: An Interpretation Based on Marx and Tonnies* (New York: Modern Reader Paperback, 1959). The latter is one of many books devoted to the theme of contemporary society as alienated and thus constituting an obstacle to trusting relations between persons. Other critics include Eric and Mary Josephson, Eds., *Man Alone: Alienation in Modern Society* (New York: Dell Publishing, 1962); William C. Bier, Ed., *Alienation: The Plight of Modern Man?* (New York: Fordham University Press, 1972); Richard Schacht, *Alienation* (New York: Doubleday, 1970); and Frank Johnson, *Alienation: Concept, Term and Meanings* (New York: Seminar Press, 1973).

10. Charles P. Loomis and Zona K. Loomis, "Social and Interpersonal Trust—Its Loss by Disjunction," *Humanitas* 9 (1973): 317–331. The Loomises base this article partly on an article by Paul Bohannan entitled "Our Two-Story Culture" that appeared in *Saturday Review*, September 2, 1972.

11. George W. Morgan, *The Human Predicament: Dissolution and Wholeness* (New York: Delta, 1968), p. 250 seq.

12. For further insight into this underlying intersubjective, interformative reality, see the already cited works of Maurice Merleau-Ponty, Alfred Schutz, Gabriel Marcel, and Martin Plattel; in addition, see Remy Kwant, *Encounter* (Pittsburgh: Duquesne University Press, 1960); and William Sadler, *Existence and Love* (New York: Scribner's, 1969).

13. See Paulo Freire, *Pedagogy of the Oppressed* (New York: Herder and Herder, 1970).

14. Burkhart Holzner, "Sociological Reflections on Trust," *Humanitas* 9 (1973): 333–345. In his article, Holzner also refers to Alfred Schutz, "Multiple Realities," *Philosophy and Phenomenological Research* 5: 533–576; to Kurt H. Wolff, "Sociology, Phenomenology, Surrender-and-Catch," *Synthese*, Vol. v (Dordecht-Holland: D. Reidel, 1972); and to the analysis of trust as a mechanism for the reduction of social complexity in Niklas Luhmann, *Vertraunen* (Stuttgart: Ferdinand Enke, 1968).

15. William James in *The Principles of Psychology*, Vol. I (New York: Dover, 1950), p. 329.

16. Many of the points in this section were made by Theodore Rozak in the early 1970s in his book *Where the Wasteland Ends: Politics and Transcendence in Post-Industrial Society* (New York: Doubleday, 1972), and are now being reemphasized in the 1980s by writers such as Marilyn Ferguson, *The Aquarian Conspiracy* (Los Angeles: Tarcher, 1980).

17. Peter Berger, *The Sacred Canopy: Elements of a Sociological Theory of Religion* (New York: Doubleday, 1967), pp. 107–108.

18. Peter Berger, *A Rumor of Angels: Modern Society and the Rediscovery of the Supernatural* (New York: Doubleday, 1969), p. 65 seq. See also Berger's *The Heretical Imperative: Contemporary Possibilities of Religious Affirmation* (New York: Doubleday Anchor, 1980).

19. Robert Ornstein, *The Psychology of Consciousness* (San Francisco: Freeman, 1972). See especially his chapters on "Toward a Complete Psychology" and "Two Sides of the Brain." See also Ernest Schachtel's chapter on the two basic perceptual modes—autocentricity and allocentricity—in *Metamorphosis* (New York: Basic Books, 1959); and Ferguson, *The Aquarian Conspiracy.*

20. The following paragraphs on racism and prejudice reflect the thinking of T. W. Adorno and others in *The Authoritarian Personality* (New York: Harper & Row, 1950).

21. Ibid., p. 406.

22. See Gordon W. Allport, *The Nature of Prejudice* (New York: Doubleday, 1954), Chapters 25 and 27. In *The Psychological Development of the Child* (Englewood Cliffs, N.J.: Prentice-Hall, 1963), pp. 96–97, Paul Mussen notes that mothers of prejudiced, intolerant children are inclined to be highly critical, rigid, authoritarian, and controlling in their disciplinary practice. Characteristically, a prejudiced child lacks confidence in himself, is distrustful,

uneasy, and insecure in social relationships; feels discontented about his current status; and is hostile and bitter in his view of the world.

23. Ian Suttie, *The Origins of Love and Hate* (London: Kegan Paul, 1935). See also Irenaus Eibl-Eibensfeldt, *Love and Hate: The Natural History of Behavior Patterns* (New York: Schocken, 1974).

24. The amount of literature being produced in relation to all these fields makes it difficult to give specific recommendations. However, readers are encouraged to approach this literature with both the obstacles to and the facilitating conditions for interpersonal trust in mind.

25. Four of the many volumes published featuring the "laboratory approach" are: Leland P. Bradford, Jack R. Gibb, and Kenneth D. Benne, *T-Group Theory and Laboratory Method; Innovation and Re-Education* (New York: Wiley, 1964); Arthur Burton, ed., *Encounter; Theory and Practice in Encounter Groups* (San Francisco: Jossey-Bass, 1969); Robert T. Golembiewski and Arthur Blumberg, eds., *Sensitivity Training and the Laboratory Approach* (Itasca, Ill.: F. E. Peacock, 1970); and Jack R. Gibb, *Trust: A New View of Personal and Organizational Development* (Los Angeles: Guild of Tutors Press, 1978). A fifth leading exponent of the Human Potential Movement, William Schutz, in his book *Joy: Expanding Human Awareness* (New York: Grove Press, 1967), claims that through techniques of group thinking, talking, touching, hugging, and acting out life situations, it is possible to transform suspicion into trust, hostility into love, dullness into awareness—and then achieve a fuller enjoyment of one's human potential.

26. See Gibb, *Trust,* for a description of how persons must learn, amid the prevailing defensive climate in most cultures, to create for themselves in their dyadic and group relationships defensive-reductive climates that will reduce their own fears and distrust.

27. See Sigmund Koch, "The Image of Man in Encounter Groups," *The American Scholar* 42 (1973): 636–652.

28. See Schutz, *Joy,* pp. 181–186.

29. Koch, "The Image of Man in Encounter Groups," pp. 649–651.

30. Ibid.

31. See references to "trust" in Carl Rogers, *Freedom to Learn* (Columbus, Ohio: Charles Merrill, 1969), and *Carl Rogers on Encounter Groups* (New York: Harper and Row, 1970).

32. For example, Karlfried Graf von Dürckheim, *Hara: The Vital Centre of Man* (New York: Fernhill House, 1962); Edmund Jacobson, *You Must Relax* (New York: McGraw-Hill, 1934); *Anxiety and Tension Control* (Philadelphia: Lippincott, 1964); Alan Schoonmaker, *Anxiety and the Executive* (New York: American Management Association, 1969); and Meyer Friedman and Ray H. Rosenman, *Type A Behavior and Your Heart.* Interestingly enough, Friedman and Rosenman's description of the Type B behavior pattern has many constituents in common with my description of the lived experience of interpersonal trust.

33. Ashley Montagu, *Touching: The Human Significance of the Skin* (New York: Columbia University Press, 1971). There is also an increasing amount of literature on the use and abuse of drugs and alcohol in contemporary efforts to relax tension and "make it through the day."

34. William Sadler, "Play: A Basic Human Structure Involving Love and Freedom," *Review of Existential Psychology and Psychiatry* 6 (1966): 237–245.

35. Cf. Chapter 7, note 29, for the "internal marginality" that seems to be common to most trust situations.

36. Karl Jaspers, *Philosophy,* Vol. II (Chicago: University of Chicago Press, 1970), p. 178.

37. Herbert J. Freudenberger, Jerry Edelwich and Archie Brodsky, *Burn-Out: Stages of Disillusionment in the Helping Professions* (New York: Human Science Press, 1980); and John Howard et al., *Rusting Out, Burning Out, Bowing Out* (Toronto: Financial Post Books, 1978).

38. "Foundational Social Orientation," *Studies* 3 (1982): 123. One of the foundationals inherent in human life is the basic potential orientation toward social presence, toward presence to other people. This presence we are to others transforms our life of inspiration, aspiration, ambitions, impulses, and historical-cultural pulsations, and is nourished by our trust in the meaningfulness of the underlying Divine Mystery.

39. Peter Berger, *The Sacred Canopy* (New York: Doubleday, 1967), pp. 43–44. Berger also

speaks in this book, and in its companion, *A Rumor of Angels,* p. 7, about the marginal situation of twentieth-century Western man (called "secularization of consciousness"), which has succeeded in banishing the supernatural as a meaningful horizon of his everyday life. Maurice Natanson also speaks to the practice of negating the possibility of one's own death by seeking refuge in the typified reality of the commonsense world (*The Journeying Self* [Reading, Mass.: Addison-Wesley, 1970]). See also Ernest Becker, *The Denial of Death.* Becker begins his book by noting that "the fear of death is indeed a universal in the human condition" (p. ix).

40. See also the issue on "Death and Dying," *Humanitas* 10 (1974):; and Elizabeth Kübler-Ross, *On Death and Dying* (New York: Macmillan, 1969). For a specifically religious context, see "Trustful Dying; Death and the Sacred," in Robert Ochs, *The Death in Every Now* (New York: Sheed and Ward, 1969), in which the author points to the horizon of ultimate meaning in which the dying person trusts when he says, "Dying in darkness and powerlessness can be done only if one hopes for a meaning from elsewhere. This meaning from *elsewhere* must be a *meaning* from elsewhere. One agrees *to* it because one agrees *with* it" (p. 93). See also Becker, *The Denial of Death,* Chapter 5, regarding death and its breakthrough potential; and the first paragraphs of this book.

Chapter 12
Developmental Aspects of Trusting

1. See Adrian van Kaam, *The Transcendent Self,* chapter on "The Middle Years," pp. 17–38.

2. Cf. Chapter 3, section on "Present Identity or Social Self."

3. The following theory regarding the coformation of personal identity by the culture and its transcendence by the emergence of the original or real self is taken from various writings of Adrian van Kaam, particularly *On Being Yourself* and *Living Creatively,* and from various glossaries published in *Studies in Formative Spirituality.*

4. For further information on this point, see *Taking Sexism Out of Education,* H.E.W. Publication No. 77–01017 (Washington, D.C.: U.S. Government Printing Office, 1978); and Barbara Spring, *Non-Sexist Education for Young Children* (New York: Citation Press, 1975).

5. In his psychological commentary on *The Tibetan Book of the Great Liberation,* C. G. Jung says that because of his attentiveness to the grasp of his ego on the world, Western man is in danger of losing his deepest humanity, his real or whole self. Jung addressed one of his works to this dilemma of contemporary Western consciousness: *Modern Man in Search of a Soul* (which can be translated as modern man in search of his real self behind and below the phenomenal ego level of the psyche). In much of his work, Jung points to Western man's concentration on the isolated instrumental ego that merely functions and is not permeated by a deeper spiritual dimension that would root it in the nonalienating realms of man's transconscious as well as subconscious existence. In *The Stillpoint,* by William Johnston (New York: Harper and Row, 1970), p. 50, Jung is quoted as seeing the value of Zen meditation as a "breakthrough by a consciousness limited to the ego-form, into the non-ego-like self." All this, continues Johnston, "is linked with Jung's distinction between the empirical ego and the Self. The former, the empirical ego, is that 'I' which we know and experience in everyday life but which is, to some extent, illusory. That is to say, most of us build up an image of an ego that we want to exist, an ego constructed by our vanity and desire to be something, while our real self (some notion of which is grasped by those around us who see objectively) is quite different. And this empirical ego must be destroyed if we are to find the true self." Here it is important to note that the ego that must be destroyed is not the embodied structure that is man's means of appearing and functioning in the world, but rather its empirical aspect that belongs to the world of merely utilitarian control and domination.

This distinction between the empirical ego and the true or real self is to be found in a different way in Stephen Strasser's analysis, *The Soul in Metaphysical and Empirical Philosophy* (Pittsburgh: Duquesne University Press, 1957). See also chapters in van Kaam's *The Tran-*

scendent Self on the dynamic of formative death and resurrection of the transcendent self, and the positive and negative phases of formative transcendence.

6. "Foundational Christian Life Form," *Studies* 1 (1980): 139. "The pre-empirical unique form or image of Christ in the soul tending to manifest itself to the appraising Christian and to incarnate itself into his unfolding core form and provisional current, latent and manifest forms of Christian living."

7. What follows elucidates the organic and vital infra or preformative influences suggested by van Kaam in *Studies* 1 (1980): 137–138; and as seen by Helen Witmer and Ruth Kotinsky, eds., *Personality in the Making: The Fact-Finding Report of the Mid-Century White House Conference on Children and Youth* (New York: Harper and Row, 1952), p. 8; and L. Joseph Stone and Joseph Church, *Childhood and Adolescence* (New York: Random House, 1968), pp. 107–116. See these and other more recent developmental texts for descriptions of the infant's growth in trust of world through early encounters.

8. Ibid., p. 107.

9. Erik Erikson, *Insight and Responsibility* (New York: Norton, 1964), p. 181.

10. These expressions represent, in order, the thinking of Therese C. Benedek, *Psychosexual Functions in Women: Primary Unit of Mother-Child* (New York: Ronald Press, 1952); Andras Angyal, *Neurosis and Treatment: A Holistic Theory* (New York: Wiley, 1965); Ernest C. Schachtel, *Metamorphosis* (New York: Basic Books, 1959); Abraham Maslow, *Toward a Psychology of Being* (Princeton, N.J.: Van Nostrand, 1962).

11. See Ashley Montagu, *Touching;* see also Harry Guntrip, *Personality Structure and Human Interaction* (New York: International Universities Press, 1961); and *Schizoid Phenomena: Object Relations and the Self* (London: Hogarth Press and the Institute of Psychoanalysis, 1968).

12. In *Studies* 1 (1980): 477–479, van Kaam points to the severely deformative consequences and deformative reactions and responses manifested in the lives of persons whose parents or significant others were unable or unwilling to manifest genuine faith, hope, and love in vital and functional acts and gestures of response to their needs as infants.

13. To mention a few of these theorists: Rene Spitz, "Anxiety in Infancy: A Study of Its Manifestations in the First Year of Life," *International Journal of Psychoanalysis* 31 (1950): 138–143; John Bowlby, *Attachment and Loss* (London: Hogarth Press, 1969–1973); W. C. Blatz, *Human Security: Some Reflections* (Toronto: University of Toronto Press, 1966); Mary D. Ainsworth and Leonard Ainsworth, *Measuring Security in Personal Adjustment* (Toronto: University of Toronto Press, 1958); Betty Flint, *The Security of Infants* (Toronto: University of Toronto Press, 1959).

14. J. M. van den Berg, *Dubious Maternal Affection* (Pittsburgh: Duquesne University Press, 1972), pp. 48–49. Many others also question the importance of maternal care in infant training and personality adjustment. See, for example, the monograph of the World Health Organization on *Deprivation of Maternal Care* (Geneva: World Health Organization, 1962); and S. Sewell, "Infant Training and the Personality of the Child," *American Journal of Sociology* 58 (1952): 150–159.

15. Sigmund Freud, "Three Essays on the Theory of Sexuality," in Sigmund Freud, *Collected Works,* Vol. 7 (London: Hogarth Press, 1953). See also Freud's *Therapy and Technique* (New York: Collier Books, 1963), p. 112, for his connection of the feeling of trust with sexuality; Erik Erikson, *Childhood and Society* (New York: Norton, 1950), pp. 44–76, pp. 219–222; "Growth and Crises of the Health Personality," in C. Kluckhohn and H. Murray, eds., *Personality in Nature, Society and Culture* (New York: International Universities Press, 1959), pp. 55–61; and Erik Erikson, *Identity, Youth and Crisis* (New York: Norton, 1968), pp. 91–107.

16. Erikson, *Insight and Responsibility,* p. 116.

17. There is much in Erikson's writing, particularly in *Young Man Luther* and *Insight and Responsibility,* that touches on the question of the relationship of basic trust or mistrust to the possibility of religious experience. He says in *Young Man Luther,* p. 255, that it is the ratio or relation of basic trust to basic mistrust established during early infancy that determines much of the individual's capacity for simple faith, and he implies (p. 265) that the original faith that Luther tried to restore goes back to the basic trust of early infancy. In *Identity, Youth and Crisis* (pp. 74–103) he explores the distinction between man's urge for "wholeness" and

its distortion in the urge for totalism or totalitarianism, seeing the former alternative as related to basic trust and the latter as related to basic mistrust. In several places, also, he comments on the sense of basic trust as an ontological source of faith and hope for the person, and in an article on "The Sense of Inner Identity," in R. M. Knight and Cyrus Friedman, eds., *Psychoanalytic Psychiatry and Psychology* (New York: International Universities Press, 1954), p. 353, he sees religion as offering man, by way of ritual, a periodic collective restitution of basic trust, which reopens adults to a continuation of faith and realism. In the article "On Selfhood and the Development of Ego Structures in Infancy," *Psychoanalytic Review* 59 (1972): 389–416, Henry Elkin speaks to this point when he says, "The age-old view that man is a 'child of God' accurately, though figuratively, applies to the psychic state of the six-month-old infant. Whatever distinctive qualities, as determined by heredity, environmental influences, and the absorption of the mother's and others' emotional patterns, he is a fully integrated personal being who, unaware of the mother's existence, lives in total mystical communion with the primordial Other, in whose ultimately merciful love he has acquired a certain abiding, or 'basic trust.'"

18. According to Scripture, the New Creation has already begun in Christ and in human beings who are renewed interiorly by baptism according to the image of their Creator. Xavier Léon-Dufour, *Dictionary of Biblical Theology,* (New York: Seabury, 1973), p. 101.

19. See *Studies* 1 (1980): 475–476.

20. See ibid., pp. 473–474.

21. "Little beyonds" refers to the substitution of safe, controllable worlds of meaning for the unpredictableness of the sacred. The phrase originated with Ernest Becker, *The Denial of Death.* In Chapter 13, "Beyond the Pride Form," we will attempt to describe this and other obstacles to a mature life of trusting.

22. At one point in the research I suggested that each of the five try to imagine themselves as either ten years older or younger, going through the same trusting experience they had described. They agreed that maturational stage does make a difference in one's experience.

23. Lk. 9:23–24. Cf. Chapter 17, note 15.

24. A reminder of the quotation in Chapter 1, note 13, from Romano Guardini, *The World and the Person,* about the very presence of the person who trusts creating a new environment.

25. Carroll Davis, *Room to Grow: A Study of Parent-Child Relationships* (Toronto: University of Toronto Press, 1966).

26. The phrase "undivided Church" refers to the universal revealed tradition held by the great spiritual masters before the division between East and West. See Aelred Squire, *Asking the Fathers.*

Chapter 13
Beyond the Pride Form

1. "The original, created foundational life form (the soul) has been obscured in its clarity and obedience since the Fall. Its dynamic divine formation power has been inhibited and weakened by inherited personal sinfulness. The gift of the foundational Christ form is necessary to disclose the obscured and weakened original divine form of life." *Studies* 1 (1980): 292. "Since the Fall, the counterfeit form of life, the autarchic pride form, tends to dominate formation at least initially." *Studies* 1 (1980): 459.

2. Aelred Squire, *Asking the Fathers.* See also Rom. 3:23: "All men have sinned and are deprived of the glory of God."

3. "The Binding of Formation Powers and Energies," *Studies* 1 (1980): 299.

4. "In the state of fallen formation, the free flow of formation powers and energies is repeatedly lost, especially in the beginning of one's formation history. This loss is due to the continual re-assertion of the exalting, greedy, grasping, clinging, manipulating, absolutizing and fixating counterfeit form of life." *Studies* 1 (1980): 299.

5. The main proximate causes of formation ignorance are: (1) the autarchic pride form;

(2) societal exaltation; (3) escape into functionalism; (4) immersion in vitalism; (5) evasion of interformative responsibility; and (6) demonic seduction.

6. See Karen Horney, *Neurosis and Human Growth,* for an analysis on the ego-functional level of this search for glory and autonomous self-fulfillment, and the "tyranny of shoulds" that accompany it.

7. "Security Directives," *Studies* 2 (1981): 534.

8. Cf. Chapter 6, section on "Letting Go as Needed Element."

9. "Informative Thinking as Contrasted with Formative Thinking," *Studies* 1 (1980): 153.

10. Thomas Merton, *Conjectures of a Guilty Bystander* (New York: Doubleday, 1966), pp. 140–142.

Chapter 14
Approaching Reality with Trust

1. Mary Carolyn Gratton, "A Theoretical-Empirical Study of the Lived Experience of Interpersonal Trust," Appendix E, Chronological Record, pp. 354–370.

2. On p. 362 of this journal I had written, "Precisely because I am in the world of trust/distrust, I can know it in a way that the standpointless observer (if there were such a person) never could." Later on, I came across Paul Ricoeur's *The Symbolism of Evil* (Boston: Beacon Press, 1967) and his explanation of the "hermeneutic circle" in the concluding chapter, pp. 347–357.

3. See ibid., "Conclusion: The Symbol Gives Rise to the Thought."

4. At this point, the reader may want to turn back to Chapter 8, the section on "New Relatedness to the Community." Ellen's experience of being "drawn out of her complacent tunnel vision in the direction of a much wider vision of reality" can happen to the rest of us in various ways and at various times of our lives. It was from Ellen that I learned how to read Scripture in tune with the different seasons of the Church year in order to widen my own vision of the Mystery of the Divine Plan. It is primarily as a result of her experience of discovering what is "already there" to be trusted in the Christian faith tradition that I began tracing this theme in Scripture for myself. Thus Part Four on "Trust and the Christian Mystery" is a direct result not only of my empirical research into trust but also of my friendship with a person who was actually living this trust, as the section on "Final Interviews with Ellen" in Chapter 13 indicates.

5. Another excerpt from the journal kept during the research, Chronological Record, p. 365: "The categories about trust in the traditional scientific literature do not emerge from the experience of trusting. This came out most clearly for me in a discussion with a visiting professor from Germany who is translating a European sociological study on "Trust." He had quite clearly never examined any of his operational concepts in terms of the structures of the actual lived experience of interpersonal trust. What surprised me was that he felt no need to do so, in spite of the fact that sociologists and psychologists as well as government and business leaders, clinicians and media men, husbands and wives, servicemen and customers, blacks and whites, insiders and outsiders, religious leaders, parents and children, doctors and patients, are all struggling at the moment for insights into the lived meaning of "trusting someone."

6. Cf. Chapter 1, p. 6.

7. These groups of adults involved in an international women's movement called the Grail met regularly at the Grail Center, Cornwall-on-Hudson, New York, over a period of two years. They pioneered the use of these questions and this text as a means of self-direction and direction in common and provided the author with many helpful suggestions for a forthcoming workbook to accompany and stimulate reflection on the themes treated in this book.

8. See Chapter 1, note 19, for Duquesne University as the site of the Institute of Formative Spirituality and the place where these questions about trusting were first formulated.

9. See "The Fisher King," a retelling by Ann Himmler of Wolfram von Eschenbach's *Parzival* in *Parabola* 3 (1978): 16–22. This legend of the quest for the Grail is a famous and

powerful symbol of the quest for the source of life itself, of the search for wholeness and healing, of the quest for God. It offers us an image in which the search for God and concern for the sufferings of others are inseparably connected without either being reduced to the other.

10. *Parabola* 3 (1978): 21.

11. See Chapter 1, opening paragraph: "Like the universe itself, we are in a constant state of becoming."

12. E.E. Cummings, "i thank You God for most this amazing day," in *Complete Poems, 1913–1962* (New York: Harcourt, Brace, Jovanovich, 1972), p. 663.

13. Alternate prayer after the seventh reading in the Easter Vigil.

14. A paradigm is an explanatory conceptual model that articulates the fundamental perspective or intuition that founds and unifies a science. See also Chapter 1, note 16.

15. See, for example, Aiden Kavanaugh, *The Shape of Baptism* (New York: Pueblo, 1978); and *The Rite of Christian Initiation of Adults* (Washington, D.C.: U.S. Catholic Conference, 1974).

16. Cf. Chapter 12, note 26.

17. According to George Maloney, *A Theology of Uncreated Energies*, the Byzantine Church and Eastern mystics always thought in terms of created and uncreated energies. They saw the whole universe influenced by them, like one vast interwoven energy field in which the smaller fields of human presence are to be found.

18. Jean-Pierre de Caussade, *Abandonment to Divine Providence* (New York: Doubleday, 1975), p. 25. See also Chapter 17, section on "Trust as Basis of Commitment," for additional material on abandonment to Divine Providence.

19. See Capra, *The Tao of Physics,* for a more complete mystical understanding of the Tao and the parallel patterns to be found in modern physics.

20. For a helpful article on the application of this theory, see Wil Lepkowski, "The Social Thermodynamics of Ilya Prigogine," *Chemical and Engineering News* 57 (April 1979): 30–33.

21. Cf. Chapter 1, section titled "Experience Calls for Integrative Reflection."

22. Cf. Chapter 1, p. 4.

23. See Gustave Martelet, *The Risen Christ and the Eucharistic World* (New York: Seabury, 1976), p. 84.

24. Cf. Chapter 6, section on "The Trusting Body," and especially note 6.

25. Cf. Chapter 2, section on "Space/Time as Basis of Situation," and Chapter 7, "Lived Time and Interpersonal Space."

26. Among those writing about new discoveries on the nature of reality are Fritjof Capra, *The Tao of Physics;* Marilyn Ferguson, *The Aquarian Conspiracy;* Lawrence LeShan, *Alternate Realities* and numerous process theologians.

27. The Christian articulation of this transcendent aspiration toward the final, ideal life form is the pneumatic inspiration and subsequent enlightened and graced aspiration after one's final ideal life form in Christ, the Word made flesh. *Studies* 1 (1980): 293.

28. Christians see the world as flowing out from its source in the Trinity, into a universe bound together in all its elements by the Spirit of God who, according to 1 Cor. 12:27, 28/Rom. 12:5/Eph. 4:12, 5:22–32/Rev. 19:7, 21:2, 9, makes everything into one whole, variously symbolized as Christ's Body, Church, and Bride.

29. See "Formation-Polarity Diagram," *Studies* 2 (1981): 140, which includes the five poles: preformation, intraformation, interformation, immediate and mediate outerformation, around which the chapters of this book are structured. Cf. Chapter 1, p. 13.

30. Cf. Chapter 13 for some of the ways in which the pride form sets up obstacles to the flow of human and divine energy in the universe.

31. Writers like William Johnston, *The Mirror Mind;* Marilyn Ferguson, *The Aquarian Conspiracy;* and Robert Ornstein, *The Psychology of Consciousness* represent some attempts in this direction.

32. See Joan Chamberlain Engelsman, *The Feminine Dimension of the Divine* (Philadelphia: The Westminister Press, 1979), for some of the typical neglected themes now being uncovered again by Western cultures.

33. Cf. Chapter 2, section on "The Quality of the Lived Life Between."

34. Eric Voegelin, *Order and History,* 4 vols. (Baton Rouge: Louisiana State University Press, 1956).

35. Cf. Chapter 2, "Reference to an Ultimate Horizon."

36. Eric Voegelin, *The Ecumenic Age* (Baton Rouge: Louisiana State University Press, 1974), p. 6.

37. Ibid., p. 333.

38. Ibid., p. 329.

39. Adrian Nocent, *The Liturgical Year* Vol. I (Collegeville: Liturgical Press, 1977), p. 182.

40. "The Formation Mystery in Eternity: Time, Fullness of Time and End of Time," *Studies* 2 (1981): 512. In the light of biblical revelation, *eternity* points to the Trinitarian formation mystery before, during, and after time was created. *Time* refers to the transcendent-immanent divine mystery of formation as unfolding in time. The fullness of time signals the transcendent-immanent Mystery of transformation in Christ. The end of time refers to the completion of transformation in Christ in eternity. See also "Forming Presence of the Seminal Word," *Studies* 2 (1981): 513.

41. Julian of Norwich, *Revelations of Divine Love* (New York: Doubleday, 1977), p. 88.

42. Nocent, *The Liturgical Year,* I, 221.

43. Ellen's suggestion (cf. p. 168) that I pay more attention to the themes brought out in the liturgy for the different seasons of the Church year resulted in an interformative shift of my perception of the Mystery of the Divine Plan, a shift to a world view that is still unfolding and giving ever-new meaning to the people, things, and events of my lifetime.

44. Rosemary Haughton, *The Catholic Thing.*

45. Cf. Chapter 9, section titled "The Lived World of the Other."

46. Cf. Chapter 9, p. 117.

Chapter 15
Our Actual Situation

1. More accurately, it is not that the Christian faith tradition itself has changed, but rather, since Vatican II—for Catholics at least—that what van Kaam calls directives from that particular form tradition have shifted. These shifts are most apparent in the areas of liturgy, ecumenism, religious and lay life, and the Church's role in the modern world. See Karl Rahner, *The Church After the Council* (New York: Herder and Herder, 1966), for the new image of the Church and the new challenges to theology posed by this council.

2. I am indebted to Adrian van Kaam for this example, which he originated in lectures at the Institute of Formative Spirituality, Duquesne University, 1980–1982. See Faber Birren, *Color: A Survey in Words and Pictures* (New Hyde Park: University Books, 1963), p. 169.

3. Cf. Chapter 11, "General Absence of Trusting Relations in Society," p. 133.

4. See Eric Voegelin, *Israel and Revelation* (Baton Rouge: University of Louisiana Press, 1956).

5. See readings from Isaiah 58 for the Friday and Saturday following Ash Wednesday.

6. See Chapter 7, section on "Two Responses: Social Reliability and Intimacy."

7. The Book of Consolation begins with Chapter 40, according to *The New American Bible* (New York: P. J. Kenedy, 1970).

8. See the book of Isaiah, Chapter 11.

9. Cf. Chapter 7, p. 88.

10. See Mark Searle, "Serving the Lord with Justice," in Mark Searle, ed., *Liturgy and Social Justice* (Collegeville, Minn.: Liturgical Press, 1980), pp. 13–35. In this essay, Searle points to a certain tension that has always existed between the inner life and social reform, between contemplation and action. He also notes that the liturgy celebrates the justice of God himself, to which each Christian is committed by baptism, and that while not every Christian is necessarily called to be a social activist, no one can safely celebrate the liturgy who is indifferent to the claims of God's justice upon the world and who is not willing to surrender a free heart to God's will for this world.

11. Prayer after Communion on the feast of All Saints.

12. For further reflections on intersubjectivity, cf. Chapter 2, notes 6 and 7, and also *Studies* 3 (1982): 123, where van Kaam speaks of the basic potential orientation toward social presence as one of the foundationals inherent in human life.

13. See especially the Sundays in ordinary time of Cycle A from the Fourteenth through the Eighteenth Sunday, where the second readings are from Romans 8.

14. Nocent, *The Liturgical Year*, II, 7.

15. Hence the need felt by members of these various immediate life circumstances (e.g., members of families, of certain work or professional circles, or interest or political groups) to identify themselves not only with their group but also with its wider context, whatever that may be. See *Studies* 2 (1981): 527–530, for discussion of what van Kaam calls "formation segments" of society.

16. See especially Chapter 4, "Community as Influential 'Other.'"

17. Cf. Chapter 9, "The Other's Trustworthiness."

Chapter 16
Trust in Self, Others, and the Holy Other

1. Second Sunday after Christmas.

2. Adrian Nocent, *The Liturgical Year*, I, 247.

3. Cf. Chapter 3, p. 31.

4. Cf. "Foundational Christian Life Form," *Studies* 1 (1980): 139.

5. Cf. Chapter 9, p. 115.

6. Cf. Chapter 8, p. 98.

7. Cf. Chapter 8, p. 101.

8. Cf. Chapter 6, section on "The Trusting Body."

9. See Chapter 3, note 2; Chapter 12, note 7; Chapter 14, note 29; and this chapter, note 11.

10. See George Maloney, *A Theology of Uncreated Energies*, for the synthesis of St. Gregory Palamas's dynamic view of God's uncreated energies.

11. These paragraphs on preformative influences owe much to the thinking of Adrian van Kaam.

12. Cf. references to de Caussade in Chapter 17, especially p. 224.

13. See Chapter 3, section on "Embodied Aliveness and Temporality."

14. See Xavier Léon-Dufour, *Dictionary of Biblical Theology*, pp. 53–56. "While the evangelists stress the reality of the body of the risen Christ in their accounts of the apparitions (Lk. 24, Jn. 20), they also indicate that it is no longer under the same limitations as before his passion" (p. 55).

15. See Gustave Martelet, *The Risen Christ and the Eucharistic World*.

16. Cf. Chapter 12, section on "The Present Empirical Identity."

17. Cf. Chapter 6, section on "The Body and Doxic Confidence."

18. The position of the liturgy for the Eighth Sunday of the Year in Cycle A, to which this paragraph refers, varies according to the placement of Easter Sunday in that particular year.

19. See Chapter 12, section on "The Future, Anxiety, and Security."

20. According to van Kaam, the principle of the maintenance of form effectiveness or form potency states that in and through the entire formation process, human beings seek to maintain the conviction that they are effective or potent to give proximate form to their lives both productively and receptively. All human formation experiences are expressions of the foundational human striving to maintain and enhance the conviction of form effectiveness—to, in other words, "feel good" about oneself.

21. Julian of Norwich, *Showings* (New York: Paulist Press, 1978), p. 295.

22. Cf. Chapter 4, section on "The Other's Trustworthiness."

23. For example, see Psalm 78, 105, or 136.

24. See the entire Last Discourse of Jesus (Jn. 13–17) and commentary on it by Adrian van Kaam, *The Mystery of Transforming Love* (Denville, N.J.: Dimension Books, 1982).

25. Cf. Chapter 4, section on "Initiative from the Other."

26. Cf. Chapter 5, section on "Dynamics of the Ongoing Life Flow."

27. See George Maloney, *Nesting in the Rock* (Denville, N.J.: Dimension Books, 1977), particularly Chapter 6, "Discovering God in the Event."

28. In the Liturgy of the Hours, the first of the antiphons for the Magnificat, the "O" antiphon for December 17, brings out this theme:

> "O Wisdom, O holy Word of God (Sir. 24:3), you govern all creation with your strong yet tender care (Wis. 8:1). Come and show your people the way of salvation. (Is. 40:3–5).

Chapter 17
Trust That Risks Commitment

1. Cf. Chapter 14, note 20.

2. In commenting on the effects of commitment to this new vision of life's flow, Marilyn Ferguson, *The Aquarian Conspiracy*, p. 224, says, "We become less surprised when surprising things happen. After all, in a creative universe, even an apparent disaster may prove to be serendipity."

3. See "Current Life Form," *Studies* 1 (1980): 139; "Christian Current Form," ibid.; and "Transcendence," ibid., p. 149, for the process of going beyond a current life form in search of a partially or totally new current life form.

4. For example, in the Old Testament, Joseph, who was sold into Egypt by his brothers and later saves them from starvation, remarks on God's Providence even in the face of their wickedness: "But now do not be distressed, and do not reproach yourselves for having sold me here. It was really for the sake of saving lives that God sent me here ahead of you" (Gen. 45:5). In the New Testament, the industrious and reliable servant who lovingly accepted God's Providence with regard to the small matter of two thousand silver pieces entrusted to him was commended for his trusting acceptance of the limited reality that was his (Mt. 25:14–23).

5. Cf. Ellen's experience, pp. 93–94.

6. Cf. Chapter 5, note 6.

7. Cf. Ellen's experience, p. 106.

8. Francis Thompson, *The Hound of Heaven* (Mount Vernon, N.Y.: Peter Pauper Press, n.d.), pp. 6–7.

9. J. R. R. Tolkien, *The Hobbit* (New York: Ballantine Books, 1966), p. 34.

10. Cf. Chapter 3, p. 96.

11. J. R. R. Tolkien, *The Return of the King* (New York: Ballantine, 1975), p. 288.

12. Tolkien, *The Hobbit*, p. 15.

13. Cf. Chapter 10, p. 128, for need of creative imagination in trusting. For more on the imagination and its restrictions, see William Lynch, *Images of Hope and Christ and Apollo* (New York: New American Library, 1960); and "Transcendent Formative Imagination," *Studies* 2 (1981): 126.

14. See Carolyn Gratton, *Guidelines for Spiritual Direction*, pp. 161–167, "Substitutions for God."

15. From the Gospel for the Thursday following Ash Wednesday.

16. Cf. Chapter 3, section titled "Present Identity or Social Self."

17. Cf. Chapter 13, section on "The Conflict That Blocks the Flow."

18. Cf. Chapter 13, p. 160.

19. Cf. Chapter 13, p. 161, Bill's pattern as typical.

20. First reading from Second Sunday, Cycle A.

21. Cf. Chapter 13, section on "The Conflict That Blocks the Flow," particularly pp. 158 and 159.

22. Cf. Chapter 9, p. 117, for the moment when, at the end of her rope, Ellen reads the words from Tugwell, who quotes the prophet Isaiah. See also Susan Muto, *A Practical Guide to Spiritual Reading* (Denville, N.J.: Dimension Books, 1976); *Approaching the Sacred* (Denville,

N.J.: Dimension Books, 1973); *Steps Along the Way* (Denville, N.J.: Dimension Books, 1975); and *The Journey Homeward* (Denville, N.J.: Dimension Books, 1977), for suggestions regarding this type of reading and its relation to daily life.

23. Ruth Burrows, *Guidelines for Mystical Prayer* (Denville, N.J.: Dimension Books, 1980), p. 59.

24. First Sunday of Lent, Cycle C.

25. Cf. Chapter 6, p. 75.

26. Cf. Chapter 6, section on "Stilling the Focused Consciousness."

27. Translation used in *The Liturgy of the Hours* (New York: Catholic Book Publishing Co., 1976), p. 1192.

28. Reading for Wednesday in the Second Week of Advent.

29. Reading for Thursday in the Second Week of Advent.

30. Perhaps the reader should read again the section "Final Interviews with Ellen" in Chapter 13.

31. Robert Faricy, *The Spirituality of Teilhard de Chardin* (Minneapolis, Minn.: Winston Press, 1981), p. 84.

32. Cf. Chapter 10, p. 119, and Chapter 1, note 25.

33. Cf. Chapter 15, p. 187 (Is. 43:19).

34. This theme of the centrality of Christ—which is particularly clear in the pre-Advent "Kingdom" feasts such as All Saints, All Souls, Dedication of St. John Lateran, and Christ the King—is emphasized by St. Paul in the Epistle to the Ephesians.

35. "Trinitarian Formation Event," *Studies* 2 (1981): 512–513. Van Kaam sees the Divine Formation Mystery pouring itself out in time, manifesting itself in the emergence and unfolding of cosmos, world, and humanity, and entering time initially in and through the Divine Word, the *Logos Spermatikos*, the Seminal Word.

36. Cf. Ellen, p. 73, in her acceptance of the failure of her ideal self.

37. Cf. Chapter 10, section on "The Kind of Willing That Was Involved."

38. Claude Tresmontant, *A Study of Hebrew Thought* (New York: Desclee, 1960), p. 133, Chapter 3 on "Spiritual Understanding: Faith."

39. Ibid., p. 119.

40. The Gospel for the Feast of All Saints is the passage from the Sermon on the Mount containing the Beatitudes (Mt. 5:1–12).

41. The Gospel for the Feast of Christ the King, Cycle A, is taken from Mt. 25: 31–46.

42. At this point, we recognize and draw together certain descriptions of intimacy, especially regarding Ellen's desire to know the central concerns of God's heart (p. 88) and get in touch with those concerns through reading Scripture (p. 168), plus Squire's description of friendship as the "open sharing of all one's secrets and plans" (*Asking the Fathers*, p. 151), and the Psalmist's reference to "the plan of the Lord [that] stands forever; the design of his heart through all generations" (Ps. 33:11). Trusting intimacy with God involves the heart's expansion to the wider concerns of "the mystery, the plan he was pleased to decree in Christ" (Eph. 1:9).

43. See Sundays after Easter, where the theme of life in the Christian community is emphasized in readings from the Acts of the Apostles and, in Cycle B, from the First Epistle of St. John.

44. St. John's First Epistle predominates in the readings after the Christmas feast also.

45. Austin Flannery, *Vatican Council II: The Conciliar and Post-Conciliar Documents* (Collegeville, Minnesota: The Liturgical Press, 1975), pp. 903–904.

46. Cf. Chapter 1, p. 1. See also Chapter 5, section on "The Shifts that Signal Growth."

47. Gerald and Patricia Mische, *Toward a Human World Order* (New York: Paulist Press, 1977), pp. 347–348. See also Patricia Mische, "A New Genesis in Religious Communities and World Community," *Sisters Today* 53 (1982): 387–398. The author ends this article thus: "We are in a new age of the world and a new age of the Church. Our building now, our mission now, is to build new systems of greater justice and peace at local and world levels, to develop a global world-view and a global spirituality that will manifest in the world—as Christ manifested in the world—the love and compassion of God for all creation and for all people. Now we are called to build the planet of God."

48. Theme from a Mexican song: "Traveler there is no road, one makes the road walk-ing./Walking one makes the road."

49. De Caussade, *Abandonment to Divine Providence,* p. 105. Page numbers in the text refer to this volume.

50. Lewis Thomas, *The Lives of a Cell* (New York: Viking, 1974).

51. Capra, *The Tao of Physics.*

52. Pierre Teilhard de Chardin, *The Divine Milieu* (New York: Harper, 1960).

53. Cf. Chapter 11, note 37. See also van Kaam's description of the crisis and erosion of social presence in *Studies* 3 (1982): 124–154, for an in-depth treatment of what he calls "social presence erosion" and its consequences and reformation. The explanation given here is much oversimplified and needs to be supplemented by further reading and reflection on this phenomenon of contemporary life.

54. Preface for Easter II.

55. During my exploration of Scripture for the meaning of trust, I came across a transla-tion of Psalm 37 that translated the word "trust" in verse 3 of that psalm as "lie flat on, rest on" the Lord.

56. Cf. Chapter 16, section on "Who We Really Are" as images of God, children of God destined to be transfigured with Christ.

57. I am indebted to Ladislaus Boros, *Pain and Providence* (New York: Seabury, 1966), for these insights into the moment of death as the event par excellence that evokes a response of trust.